Thinking Antagonism

D1615528

Thinking Antagonism

Political Ontology after Laclau

Oliver Marchart

EDINBURGH
University Press

Edinburgh University Press is one of the leading university presses in the UK. We publish academic books and journals in our selected subject areas across the humanities and social sciences, combining cutting-edge scholarship with high editorial and production values to produce academic works of lasting importance. For more information visit our website: edinburghuniversitypress.com

© Oliver Marchart, 2018

Edinburgh University Press Ltd
The Tun – Holyrood Road,
12(2f) Jackson's Entry,
Edinburgh EH8 8PJ

Typeset in 11/13 Adobe Sabon by
IDSUK (DataConnection) Ltd, and
printed and bound in Great Britain.

A CIP record for this book is available from the British Library

ISBN 978 1 4744 1330 5 (hardback)
ISBN 978 1 4744 1332 9 (webready PDF)
ISBN 978 1 4744 1331 2 (paperback)
ISBN 978 1 4744 1333 6 (epub)

The right of Oliver Marchart to be identified as the author of this work has been asserted in accordance with the Copyright, Designs and Patents Act 1988, and the Copyright and Related Rights Regulations 2003 (SI No. 2498).

Contents

Abbreviations

E   Ernesto Laclau, *Emancipation(s)*, London: Verso, 1996.

HSS Ernesto Laclau and Chantal Mouffe, *Hegemony and Socialist Strategy: Towards a Radical Democratic Politics*, London: Verso, 1985.

NR Ernesto Laclau, *New Reflections on the Revolution of Our Time*, London: Verso, 1990.

PR Ernesto Laclau, *On Populist Reason*, London: Verso, 2005.

RFS Ernesto Laclau, *The Rhetorical Foundations of Society*, London: Verso, 2014.

Introduction: What is Antagonism?

Every thinker, as Heidegger used to say, follows the line of a single thought. What he forgot to mention was that no thought belongs to a single thinker. Ideas are not born from the depths of a self-enclosed mind. They always come from somewhere else, from a place 'out there': an intellectual tradition, an academic teacher, a school of thought, a social movement, an academic or non-academic discussion, a reading that turned out decisive, or simply an inspirational moment in a conversation. Intellectual work, rather than being a solitary endeavour, is a collaborative one. If there is originality in intellectual work, it is originality without determinable origin. For this reason, ideas are never the property of an individual. It is impossible to 'own' an idea – which is but an ideological fantasy rooted in the capitalist system of property ownership. Ideas can only be *disowned* – in a movement described in this book as one of self-implication – as they emerge from, and return to, an a-subjective, collective effort that cuts across temporal and geographical barriers. One of these ideas bears the name 'antagonism'.

This concept, which rings the bell of conflictuality but is not equivalent to conventional notions of 'conflict', 'struggle' or 'war', has an extended history. Antagonism is the name that was given to the phenomenon of social negativity in the tradition of German Idealism, Early Romanticism and Marxism. It was carried forward by the Heideggerian Hegelians of the first half of the twentieth century, among them Kojève, Sartre and Lacan. This concept was born from a collective inquiry that reaches back more than two hundred years, but it was in the work of Ernesto Laclau, initially in his path-breaking book *Hegemony and Socialist Strategy* (*HSS*), co-written with Chantal Mouffe, that 'antagonism' found a contemporary systematic treatment. When the book appeared in 1985, it was immediately realised by Slavoj Žižek that this conception constitutes 'the most radical breakthrough in modern social theory' (Žižek 1990: 249).

Laclau, who passed away in April 2014, was one of the major theoretical voices on the Left. Born into a radical-liberal family in Buenos Aires in 1935, Laclau turned to Peronism as a university student. He became a militant of the Socialist Party and the Peronist student movement and later became a member of the leadership of the Socialist Party of the National Left, founded in 1962 by Jorge Ramos, and the editor of the party's weekly *Lucha Obrera*. Laclau was deeply immersed in the political struggles of Argentinian politics of the 1960s. Shortly after having been appointed professor at the Universidad Nacional de Tucumán, he was sacked, together with many other leftist university teachers, by the junta of General Onganía. In 1969 he therefore accepted an invitation to Oxford by Eric Hobsbawm, from where he moved to the Department of Government at the University of Essex in 1973. During his time in Essex, he founded the Centre for Theoretical Studies in the Humanities and Social Sciences and an immensely successful MA and PhD programme in 'Ideology and Discourse Analysis'. For many years, this programme would constitute the gravitational centre of an expanded international network of former students and collaborators known today as the 'Essex School' (Townshend 2003).

Laclau's academic work, which stands in the tradition of Louis Althusser's structural Marxism and Antonio Gramsci's hegemony theory, is influential in many areas of inquiry, from the theory of populism to International Relations, from political discourse analysis to rhetorics, from Cultural Studies and art theory to critical geography.[1] This book is not the place to elaborate on these many areas of influence (I will touch upon Laclau's work in relation to critical geography in Chapter 5, to Birmingham Cultural Studies in Chapter 6 and to populism in Chapter 7). What is rarely seen, however, is that his influential work is organised around a key philosophical problematic that can be identified as *Laclau's question* – as formulated by Laclau himself:

I am not asking myself what are the actually existing antagonisms in society, but something more fundamental: What is an antagonism? What type of relations between social forces does it presuppose? This is a question usually overlooked in the sociological literature, which usually concentrates on actual 'conflicts', 'confrontations' and 'struggles', but which does not pose the question about the ontological nature of these categories. It is, however, on this nature that we must focus if we want to advance on the theoretical front. (Laclau 2014: 102)

My proposal, in this book, on how 'to advance on the theoretical front' will be to not only concentrate, with Laclau, on the question of 'What is *an* antagonism?', i.e. what is a conflictual relation and what are the laws that govern this relation? – but to ask the more fundamental question: What is *antagonism*? My main reason for doing so is that Laclau's notion of antagonism can serve as a cornerstone for a post-foundational *ontology of the political*. Such an ontology – the science, not simply of politics, but of the political nature of social being as such – is implicitly present in Laclau, but not fully elaborated. In the above quote, Laclau employed the term 'antagonism' to indicate the 'ontological nature' of actual conflicts, struggles and confrontations. *Laclau's question* is a question as to the very being of empirical conflicts. But he did not inquire into the ontological nature of antagonism itself. What is antagonism? What is its theoretical status? How to intellectually approach a phenomenon that appears to indicate a constitutive negativity – a paradoxical blockade or incommensurability – at the ground of all social being? What, if anything, can be said about such an oddity? In fact, questions like these were posed – in different guises – by a countless number of philosophers, writers and theorists from Kant via Marx to Laclau. The question of antagonism is the question of modernity. It attests to our modern condition, to a time, that is, when social and intellectual foundations, previously considered unalterable, started to appear fungible, contingent and contestable. It is with the notion of antagonism that the precarious nature of the social bond comes into view as such. And it is via this notion that we should approach the much-discussed 'ontological turn' in contemporary political theory.

Laclau can be of enormous help in our endeavour to revisit and revive the intellectual tradition of 'thinking antagonism'. In the preface to his posthumous book *The Rhetorical Foundations of Society* (*RFS*) he had announced his intention to present his own political ontology at a future stage (*RFS* 1). Tragically, his sudden death means that his ontology will remain a torso. But the elements are there to be reconstructed and integrated into a post-foundational ontology of the political that will be systematic and broad enough to accommodate other sources of post-foundational political thought – including Foucault, Deleuze, Negri or Balibar.[2] However, are we not engaging, it might be asked, in a futile exercise of abstract speculation? Should we not content ourselves with better manageable questions as to the *laws* and *types* of empirical conflict? Is it at all possible to approach the phenomenon of social negativity head-on? Well, it is certainly not possible as long as we adhere to the protocols of mainstream social science or academic philosophy. Antagonism – understood as a name for the intrinsically political nature of social being – is not an empirically given or scientifically determinable object of political reality (in the sense in which 'ontic' conflicts are). It is that which undermines the very positivity of 'positive facts'. For this reason, an ontological notion of antagonism escapes the grasp of positive science. For mainstream social scientists, averse to anything that smacks of thinking, there can be no political ontology; nothing could bring them to think beyond the bounds of their objectivist horizon – which is why Heidegger famously claimed that 'science does not think' (Heidegger 1968: 8). Our inquiry, on the other hand, will be directed at this very instance, antagonism, which does not exist within the world of ordinary objects, but nonetheless insists, by way of radical negation, from outside this world, thus imposing itself on thought. *Thinking antagonism*, hence, is an active response to something that forces itself to be thought: the antagonistic nature of society, encountered both in political struggles and in a myriad of micro-conflicts in our daily life.

In this regard, antagonism *eo ipso* cannot be a matter of scientific inquiry. It can only be a matter of thinking[3] – which is not of the order of philosophy either. Thinking has never fully succumbed to the disciplinary procedures of the academy. The encounter with antagonism – with an ontological condition that can be inferred from our life-world experience of conflict and contingency – may take place everywhere: in daily life as much as in the academy. The practice of thinking antagonism, for this reason, is both 'above' and 'beneath' academic philosophy – in the sense in which Claude Lefort once described his own ambivalent identity (as a political theorist to whom the role of a 'philosopher' was attributed) with the medieval formula: *major et minor se ipso* (Lefort 2000: 239) – a formula that could be applied to Laclau as well. Thinking means to position oneself in an eccentric place that is both above and beneath oneself as a 'philosopher', to involve oneself in a practice that is both more and less than philosophising. It is 'above' (or 'beyond') philosophy because, as Heidegger insisted, by thinking we destruct the realm of occidental metaphysics and, in this regard, have to abandon the traditional academic discipline of philosophy. And it is 'below' the latter because thinking has no particular institutional location and is, as initially mentioned, a collective, if not political, activity.

For this reason, this book is as much concerned with thinking as it is with antagonism. The words in the title constitute the two foci of an ellipse. Equal weight must be given to 'antagonism' and 'thinking'. And yet, it is undeniable that both sides remain intrinsically connected: antagonism is a matter of thinking (there is no other way of approaching antagonism) as much as thinking is a matter of antagonism (it brings conflict to theory and only gets started when touched by the external force of antagonism). Hence, our aim in the course of this investigation must be to compress, as much as possible, the two foci of the ellipse, thereby producing a circle. What motivates this aim is my conviction that the question of 'thinking' and the question of 'antagonism' should be treated on their own terms, but, at the same time, cannot be tackled separately. It will thus be demonstrated that the 'question of being' and the 'question of thinking' – in Heidegger's famous rendering: 'What is called thinking?' – are two questions that cannot be separated and, at the end of our inquiry, should even be fused into a third one – the perennial question of politics: 'What is to be done?'

Obviously, the latter problem – vanishing point of the previous two – cannot be solved by way of concrete political recipes. What 'is to be done' in a given politico-historical conjuncture can only be determined within that conjuncture – it cannot be derived from ontology. To concede this is not to imply that *nothing* could be said about concrete political issues; yet this would require a different project that, with regard to our current post-democratic condition, is outlined in an accompanying volume entitled *Post-Foundational Theories of Democracy: Reclaiming Freedom, Equality, Solidarity* (Marchart forthcoming). So, for our present purpose of ontological reasoning, the question of 'What is to be done?' (to which, in that other project, my reply is: 'Reclaim democracy!') should be rephrased: 'What does it mean to act?', i.e. 'What is the nature of political action?' – a question that, while appertaining to the field of political ontology, simultaneously flags out the exit point where, eventually, we will have to abandon our engagement with ontology and engage with politics. As I hope to demonstrate in the course of this investigation: *thinking the political* and *politicising thought* are but two complementary sides of a single operation: thinking antagonism.

* * *

The ontology of antagonism was discussed, contested and advanced collectively, as many other ideas were, within a group of people affiliated with, or sympathetic to the Essex School mentioned above. Many ideas presented in *Thinking Antagonism* have profited greatly from more than two decades of discussions with close friends and companions in a conversational network that spans around the globe. Ernesto Laclau's unexpected death in 2014 left an enormous gap in this network. It goes without saying that this book is deeply indebted to him and, of course, to Chantal Mouffe. My gratitude extends to all with whom I have had the pleasure of debating the issues touched upon in this book. They are too many to name here, so I restrict myself to at least mentioning some: Aristotelis Agridopoulos, Niels Akerstrom Andersen, Benjamin Arditi, Leonor Arfuch, Sebastián Barros, Paula Biglieri, Paul Bowman, Cornelia Bruell, Luciana Cadahia, Tamara Caraus, Gustavo Castagnola, Philipp Casula, Julia Chryssostalis, Simon Critchley, Lincoln Dahlberg, Daniel de Mendonça, Mark Devenney, Lisa Disch, Torben Bech Dyrberg, Alan Finleyson, Javier

Franzé, Charlotte Fridolfsson, Dilip Gaonkar, Jeremy Gilbert, Jason Glynos, Allan Dreyer Hansen, Eva Herschinger, Andreas Hetzel, David Howarth, Giorgos Katsembekis, Seongcheol Kim, Friederike Landau, Juan Pablo Lichtmajer, Shu-fen Lin, Felicitas Macgilchrist, James Martin, Tomas Marttila, Samuele Mazzolini, Aysem Mert, Jean-Claude Monot, Kate Nash, Martin Nonhoff, Aletta Norval, Martin Oppelt, Vassilios Paipais, Emilia Palonen, David Payne, Jenny Gunnarsson Payne, Luisa Ortiz Pérez, Rado Riha, Drehli Robnik, Nikolai Roskamm, Benjamin Christoph Seyd, Urs Stäheli, Yannis Stavrakakis, Nora Sternfeld, Jelica Sumic-Riha, Rahel Süß, Meghan Sutherland, Paulina Tambakaki, Davide Tarizzo, Mathias Thaler, Lasse Thomassen, Jeremy Valentine, Mathijs van de Sande and Linda Zerilli.

1 'What's Going on with Being?': Laclau and the Return of Political Ontology

Decapitating Hydra: The Ontological Turn

Thinking Antagonism is an exercise in political ontology. It participates in the current 'ontological turn', i.e. 'the ubiquitous return of the question of being in the field of political thought today' (Bosteels 2011: 42).[1] In opposition to the quantitative mainstream of the social sciences, theorists associated with this turn inquire into the fundamental ontological presuppositions that inform political research and theory. The endeavour is not as extravagant as it may appear. Presuppositions about the nature of social being are implied by any kind of research – sometimes openly, but most often silently. Any political interpretation, as William Connolly convincingly argued, invokes a set of ontological assumptions about the very nature of the social bond: 'every interpretation of political events, no matter how deeply it is sunk in a specific historical context or how high the pile of data upon which it sits, contains an ontopolitical dimension' (Connolly 1995: 1). In a more radical sense, which will be at the centre of our investigation, social analysis warrants 'ontopolitical interpretations', not of particular social phenomena, but of the nature of social being in general: of being-qua-being. All 'ontopolitical interpretations' can thus be referred back to a very simple question which, in the language of ordinary life, was framed by Gianni Vattimo as follows: 'what's going on with Being?' (Vattimo 2011: 28).

In daring to pose such a question, today's political ontologies represent a shift away from the hitherto dominant paradigm of epistemology.[2] Some would go as far as denouncing epistemology – the science concerned with the conditions of possibility of true knowledge – as the 'the Hydra', as Charles Taylor once put it, 'whose serpentine heads wreak havoc throughout the intellectual culture of modernity – in science, in criticism, in ethics, in political thinking, almost anywhere you look' (Taylor 1995: vii). According to Taylor, it would be a mistake to think 'that we can get to the bottom of what knowledge is, without drawing on our never-fully-articulable understanding of human life and experience' (vii–viii). In a similar vein, Connolly (1995) criticised mainstream social science for seeking a neutral method which, in actual fact, is not attainable for human, that is, social and historical beings. Taylor and Connolly are in illustrious company. In his Collège de France lecture course published under the title *The Government of Self and Others*, Michel Foucault famously observed that, from Kant's three *Critiques* to today's analytic philosophy, the mainstream of philosophical inquiry proceeds as an analytic of truth: a quest for the conditions of possibility of true knowledge. However, beginning with Kant's engagement with the question of *Aufklärung* and the historical event of the French Revolution a counter-tendency took root:

> This other critical tradition does not pose the question of the conditions of possibility of a true knowledge; it asks the question: What is present reality? What is the present field of our experiences? What is the present field of possible experiences? Here it is not a question of the analytic of truth but involves what could be called an ontology of the present, of present reality, an ontology of modernity, an ontology of ourselves. (Foucault 2011: 20–1)

As presented here, ontology serves as an antidote to the dominant paradigm of epistemology. This turn to the ontological was in fact prepared by Heidegger.[3] For it was Heidegger, more than any other thinker, who initiated a shift from questions regarding being-qua-*understanding* to questions regarding being-qua-*being*.[4] This shift is feasible only if the disembodied position of an outerworldly calculating mind, entirely detached from the affairs under analysis, is abandoned. As soon as we start implicating ourselves in the process of interrogation – by asserting the locatedness of our own vantage point – we abandon our search for the conditions of true knowledge and begin interrogating our own conditions.

The Foucauldian question 'What is present reality?' (Foucault 2011: 20) not only leads to an 'ontology of the present', but also leads, as Foucault adds, to 'an ontology of ourselves' (21). *Sein* and *Dasein*, to speak Heideggerese, stand in a relation of reversibility. 'What's going on with Being?' is just another way of asking: 'What's going on with us?'

Evidently, the wager in political ontology is that *something political* is going on with us. More than that, it will be argued in this book that the social world is based on political grounds. This would imply that we will not get by with an ontology of *politics*, i.e. a regional ontology of political being (about the nature of social actors, institutions, functions, etc.). It is thus imperative to terminologically distinguish between political ontologies that refer to the nature of all things political (for example, the nature of political institutions, organisations, functions, actions or actors) and *ontologies of the political* the scope of which is much broader. In the latter case, 'the political' refers to the nature or constitution of all things social (including, of course, those things that are conventionally labelled as 'political'). If political ontologies, as defined above, are by their nature 'regional ontologies' – they are concerned with phenomena typically classified as political (in a broad or narrow sense of politics) – an ontology of *the political*, however, would be concerned with the being of the social world as such, i.e. the politicality of *all* social being.

The ontology of the political to be proposed in this book places a bet on the political nature of social being-qua-being. This will be not only an intellectual bet, but, more than that, a political one in itself. Our interrogation, therefore, must be conducted in a political mode. Rather than constituting a quest for true knowledge, untainted by the political, ontological questioning becomes a way of implicating ourselves in the field of actuality. It results in an ontology of ourselves as political beings. And, vice versa, any ontology of ourselves, given the reversibility of *Sein* and *Dasein*, may refer us back to an ontological questioning of the political. In this sense, thinking, more than being an 'existential' act, is a political one.[5] What we need to envisage, and what this book is about, is a self-implicated form of thinking *in the ontologico-political register*.

It is precisely because any attempt at thinking the political nature of social being remains implicated in the domain of the political that the typical accusations of epistemologists are so misplaced. There is absolutely no need to succumb to Habermasian-style blackmailing and the infamous charge of 'performative self-contradiction': How can you *know*, a staunch epistemologist might ask, that the nature of all being is political? Are you not operating yourself, when claiming true knowledge about the nature of the social world, as a closet epistemologist? And, by asserting the political nature of all things social, are you not implicating yourself – a social being – in your claim? Hence, are you not making a political rather than a scientific claim? An unapologetic answer in the affirmative should be given to charges of this kind. Of course, political ontology cannot claim exemption from the political. Once it is granted that the latter overlaps with the realm of social being in general, nobody can purport to adopt a trans-political vantage point. Unavoidably, there is always a political dimension to claims of political ontology. But there is nothing to be regretted here. Political ontology, as I said, is not a quest for true knowledge. It is a political endeavour, engaged in politicising the ways in which we envisage the social world in general. This is what I will propose to call *thinking*: implicating oneself in the matter of one's thought. The charge of 'performative contradiction' should thus be redirected against the epistemologists.[6] For Heidegger, as Lee Braver puts it:

> [K]nowing is not basic but 'founded upon Being-in-the-world'. Theorizing can only take place on the basis of years of more practical interactions with equipment and others, making skeptical questions about their reality a kind of performative contradiction. Our immersion in them is a condition for the possibility of questioning their reality; our ability to ask the question contains the answer. (Braver 2012: 130)

For the same reason of self-implication, criticism from the Left regarding an alleged danger of depoliticisation is equally misplaced. As was suspected by Susan Buck-Morss (2013: 57), the move from everyday politics to political ontology is a 'one-way street' never leading back to political practice. While this verdict was delivered *ex cathedra* and with little argumentation, others have engaged in a more thorough examination of political ontologies, criticising their 'social weightlessness' (i.e. an insensitivity towards social suffering) (McNay 2014) or the 'negative aura' conferred upon political processes labelled, by political ontologists, as 'merely positivist, sociologist, empiricist, or ontic' (Bosteels 2011: 68). In most cases, ontologists are confronted with allegations of excessive abstraction at the cost of sociological concretion and political engagement. I do not believe, however, that political ontologies proceed by devaluing ordinary politics or by ignoring forms of social subordination. On the contrary, their aim, in the majority of cases, is to rejuvenate political practice in order to open up spaces for, precisely, challenging patterns of subordination. In this spirit, their attack is not directed against 'ordinary politics' *per se*, but against a post-conflictual politics that seeks to divest 'politics' of anything political. What is more, by redirecting attention to the, ultimately, conflictual nature of social being-qua-being – that is, of *all* things social – an ontology of the political compels us to develop a comprehensive political perspective on the social. Not in the sense of assuming that everything is political in terms of politics, but in the sense that all social affairs are political in terms of being grounded, to greater or lesser degree, by *the political*, that is to say: through instances of conflict, power, subordination, oppression, exclusion and decision as much as, of course, resistance, opposition, confrontation, association or consensus-building. These are all political modalities that structure our social world; and political ontologies, in their variety, tend to highlight one modality or another.[7] The perspectival shift towards political ontology, when radicalised into what I call an ontology of the political, will thus allow to generalise what feminists, in the 1970s, have diagnosed with regard to the personal and the private: that what appears unpolitical on the surface may, in fact, have deeply political roots. Sensitised by such an ontology, social analysis will be prompted to search for modes of the political in the most unexpected places.

Politics and the Political

To claim that our interrogation will be conducted in a political mode is also to say that it must be conducted with a view to *the political* rather than politics in a narrow sense. At stake is not simply, or not only, a form of critique that remains engaged in 'current affairs' of political urgency, but one that, beyond the present moment, dares to reflect upon the political conditions of possibility of social being. The key to any ontology of the political, hence, lies in the differentiation, introduced by numerous authors, between 'ordinary' ontic *politics* and an ontological notion of *the political* (as appertaining to the entire field of the social rather than a particular field or practice). This differentiation does not imply a hierarchy where the political would be an elevated term and political practice is devalued. There is nothing intrinsically bad about a politics in the mode of the 'ordinary'; on the contrary, without politics it would make no sense to speak about the political. But without a notion of the political, as differentiated from politics, political ontology would also be impossible.

Conceptually, the difference between 'politics' and 'the political' (or *la politique* and *le politique*) can be traced back, in the French context, to Paul Ricœur's article of 1956, 'The Political Paradox', and forcefully re-emerged in the 1980s when many philosophers – among them Jean-François Lyotard, Claude Lefort, Alain Badiou, Jacob Rogozinski, Jacques Rancière and Étienne Balibar – were invited by Jean-Luc Nancy and Philippe Lacoue-Labarthe to give lectures at the Centre for Philosophical Research on the Political and discuss what the initiators referred to as the 'retreat of the political' (Lacoue-Labarthe and Nancy 1983). From that historical moment on, what in *Post-Foundational Political Thought*, my previous monograph on the intellectual paradigm of left Heideggerianism (Marchart 2007a), I have called the *political difference* came to be canonised as a basic conceptual differentiation in political thought. As the emergence and genealogy of the political difference, from Schmitt and Arendt to contemporary French thought, was presented there, I will not renarrate the same story. I would still like to emphasise that in the recent ontological turn in political thought the concepts of 'politics' and

13

'the political' are silently modelled upon the later Heidegger's notion of an ontico-ontological difference: the difference between ontic beings and ontological Being. Metaphysics has always been the quest for an ontological instance that could serve as a ground for all 'ordinary' ontic beings – no matter whether this ground was called logos, substance, subject or God – without taking into account what Heidegger called the 'grounding question': the question as to the nature of this difference *as difference*. The task of thinking (*die Sache des Denkens*), for Heidegger, is to pass to this grounding question and engage, not with a new metaphysical ground, but with the never-ending play of differencing between the side of the ontic and the side of the ontological. As we will constantly return to the ontological difference (as well as to the task of thinking), I will postpone its further discussion. But it is important to understand that the political difference was not simply mapped onto the Heideggerian ontological difference. It would be disingenuous to believe that the theoretical innovation of the political difference was motivated by a desire to pretentiously imitate philosophical discourse. Quite the contrary is true: philosophical discourse was effectively politicised. Ontological and political difference converge as soon as the ontological register of being-qua-being is identified with the political and, vice versa, conventional politics is perceived as simply an 'ontic' way of actualising the political. The entire social realm, the realm of being-qua-being, is thus perceived in the light of the political, which in turn has to be differentiated from politics.

Such cross-fading between the ontological and the political registers, which lies at the heart of recent political thought on the Heideggerian Left, does not appear from nowhere. It attests to an *ontopolitical need*.[8] My suspicion is that the political difference – the conceptual differentiation between politics and the political – emerged out of a historical conjuncture where it was increasingly realised that neither can our social world be based on a firm ground or ultimate principle, nor is it entirely without any ground or principle (as we are not living in a vacuum) – rather, it is based on what Judith Butler calls 'contingent foundations' (Butler 1992). These foundations will always be plural, they will only be established temporarily, they can be reversed, and they have to be established against conflicting foundational attempts – which is why it makes sense to describe theories that register the contingent and yet necessary nature of social foundations as *post*-foundational rather than simply anti-foundational. 'Contingency', as the technical term for the fundamental absence of an ultimate foundation, does not imply that societies are able to make do without any foundations, principles or norms. It is only to say that none of these norms can claim to have super-temporal validity or would transcend the world of social relations. Every norm, ground or principle can always be displaced, potentially at least, by conflicting norms, grounds and principles. It is clear that a conventional notion of politics – as, for instance, a functional social system among others – would be too narrow to account for this process of contingent, temporary, conflictual and plural grounding of *all* social relations. This explains why the political difference was introduced. It was felt we would need a broader concept, a concept of *the political*, in order to account for the more, indeed, *fundamental* function of reinstituting a world whose grounds had become fungible.

So, the process of grounding cannot be halted even if it is agreed that all grounds are contingent, contested and temporary. If for Heidegger the ontological never appears as such, if it always recedes and still chiasmatically intertwines with the ontic, this is because the differential play between the ontological (the 'ground') and the ontic (what is grounded) never stops. The ground, for Heidegger, 'grounds as a-byss' (Heidegger 1994: 29). Don't we have to assume an analogous relation between the political and politics? Isn't the political, understood as the grounding or instituting moment of the social, constantly in search of its ontic actualisation via politics? Isn't politics, on the other side, necessarily 'touched' by the political, without ever fully merging with it (because in the latter case a firm ground would be reached – the political would be turned into a metaphysical 'Ground' – and the political difference would dissolve)? I hope that the heuristic value of what at this preliminary stage of the argument must appear as abstract speculation can be convincingly elaborated in the course of our investigation. But it is easy to anticipate a particular line of criticism. Even those inclined to agree on the differential nature of politics and the political may ask what playing around with abstract concepts can tell us about social reality.[9] Later on I will expand on what was said about the intrinsic relation between political ontology and the 'ontology of ourselves' and the perspectival shift it engenders with regard to the ubiquitous conflicts surrounding us in our daily lives. For now I would like to emphasise that no unbridgeable gap exists between apparently abstract thought and more empirically oriented political theory – which will become clear when we now turn to the work of Ernesto Laclau and his conception of antagonism.

The Laclauian Legacy

Antagonism, as a name for 'the political', is not only the cornerstone of Laclau's political ontology (which, as we will see presently, should be extended into an ontology of *the political*), it is also the hidden organising principle behind his ground-breaking theory of populism, his reworking, with Chantal Mouffe, of the intellectual tradition of Marxism, and his rearticulation of the Gramscian concept of hegemony within the framework of discourse theory and rhetoric. By combining the intellectual resources of post-structuralism with other philosophical approaches, such as phenomenology, Laclau opened the way for the development of a post-foundational ontology of the political. Each one of these mutually interconnected dimensions of his work constitutes a significant achievement in its own right. Taken together, they constitute what I would consider Laclau's legacy.

The first dimension is, evidently, his theory of populism. His first book, *Politics and Ideology in Marxist Theory: Capitalism, Fascism, Populism* (Laclau 1977), brought Laclau immediate recognition as the foremost Marxist theorist of populism. Nearly thirty years later, his book *On Populist Reason* (*PR*) came to huge fame in Latin America during the time of neo-populist governments in Venezuela, Argentina, Bolivia and Ecuador. On the scholarly level, the later book grew out of Laclau's dissatisfaction with mainstream sociological perspectives on the phenomenon. These mainstream perspectives are characterised by what one could describe as their 'ochlophobia'.

Populist mobilisation of 'the people' is seen as an irrational or deviant phenomenon, an aberration from the normal functioning of politics. In a bold move, Laclau pushed the theory of populism into the centre of political reasoning. The role usually assigned to populism was inverted and populism turned from an aberrant phenomenon at the margins of the social into the central feature of the political. Populism, Laclau claimed, was now to be considered 'the royal road to understanding something about the ontological constitution of the political as such' (*PR* 67). This is because the antagonistic construction of the political space – the latter's simplification around the core antagonism of 'the people' against those who ignore popular demands (the power bloc, 'the elite', *'la casta'*) – is not only a feature of populist mobilisation. Antagonisation, envisaged as the construction of heteroclite demands into a chain of equivalence vis-à-vis a 'negative outside', is, as we will see, the very condition of all political action. Populism, thus, is not a particular form of politics among other forms. Populism encapsulates political rationality and, as will be shown in the course of our investigation, directs our view both towards the political (in the sense of antagonism) and to a general logic of politics.

This 'logic', for Laclau, comes under the generic name of *hegemony*. And here we encounter the second advance presented by his work. By revisiting the Marxist tradition, Laclau and Mouffe, in their landmark study *Hegemony and Socialist Strategy* of 1985, managed to transform the very presuppositions of the Marxian problematic. Far from simply refuting Marxism, they followed a double strategy. On the one side they aimed at deconstructing the essentialist assumptions of orthodox Marxism: its class reductionism and economic determinism. On the other side they strengthened and brought to new life Antonio Gramsci's category of hegemony, which turned out to be the key tool for undermining the deterministic assumptions of more traditional variants of Marxism (see Gramsci 1971). Hegemony, for Gramsci, is attained as soon as a corporate class, by uniting disparate social forces, has managed to *universalise* its own objectives, thus establishing a new common sense or worldview that transcends the particularity of that corporate class. In such a hegemonic relation the dominating role of a particular social force is naturalised by way of consensus and unforced consent. Translated by Laclau into the lexicon of the ontological difference, this means that an ontic being has assumed an ontological role: 'Certain contents are *invested* with the function of representing the absent fullness of the community' (*RFS* 121). In *Emancipation(s)* (*E*), a collection of Laclau's essays that was published in 1996, hegemony came to denote the general 'logic' of politics: a particular actor takes up the role of incarnating the universality of a given community, a universality that nonetheless remains unachievable.

But Laclau was not satisfied with a theory of politics. The concept of hegemony also came to denote the way in which, in one or the other way, *all* social relations are politically impregnated, if not instituted. With regard to this instituting function of hegemony, our conventional notion of politics would be far too narrow. For this reason, Laclau tends to speak about 'the political' when referring to the way in which the social is instituted and given form by forces struggling to construct a particular hegemonic formation. As the political cannot be derived from any underlying reality – such as, for instance, the economic laws of motion that govern the relations of production – Laclau tends to insist on the 'primacy of the political' with regard to the social. We will return to Laclau's theory of hegemony in more details. May it suffice to mention that an operation similar to the one observed in the case of populism is in place: Laclau's intellectual intervention is aimed at the ontological ground of the social. The theoretical dignity restored to the categories of populism and of hegemony is an ontological dignity. These categories are not merely 'ontic' tools of social analysis (which they also are), but shed light on the mystery of the very institution of our social world: the nature of social being *eo ipso*.

Thirdly, this profound transformation of the Marxist problematic emerged from Laclau's serious engagement with poststructuralist and Heideggerian thought, which was applied to the field of politics and further developed into a qualitative method of political discourse analysis. In *Hegemony and Socialist Strategy*, deconstruction and Lacanianism were, for the first time in social theory, extensively employed as tools for political analysis.

In his later work Laclau would continue to reconceptualise many traditional notions of political thought from a post-structuralist vantage point, including the concepts of power, order, representation, universality/particularity, community, ideology, emancipation and, of course, the categories of politics, the political, society and the social. For Laclau, however, post-structuralism never was an article of faith. It was a resource that could provide theoretical tools as much as Gramscianism or phenomenology could. It was thus necessary to non-dogmatically combine these tools into conceptual 'war machines', as Deleuze would have put it. Laclau, quite similar to Deleuze, was not invested in theorising by resentment, i.e. criticising someone else's theory for the sake of indulging in the narcissism of minor differences, or of triumphing in an intellectual competition. Whenever he appropriated and reassembled conceptual tools of different origins, and whenever he criticised other theorists, it was dictated by the subject under discussion. As Laclau made clear, for instance, deconstruction – in order to be of use for political analysis – is in need of being complemented by a theory of hegemony. If the deconstructive operation consists in laying open the moment of ultimate undecidability inherent to any structure, hegemony provides us with a theory of the *decision* taken on such undecidable terrain (E 66–83).

Hence, with Laclau's work, post-structuralism encountered a decisively political turn. But again, I would like to direct attention to the fact that there was an ontic and an ontological component to this displacement. On the one hand, integrating post-structuralism into hegemony theory allowed Laclau to develop a discourse analytical framework that made it possible to engage in concrete projects of political analysis – as demonstrated by many empirical studies that came out of the Essex School (for example, Norval 1996; Howarth et al. 2000; Stavrakakis 2004; Howarth and Torfing 2005; Marchart 2013b; Stavrakakis 2014). On the other hand, the entire project of discourse analysis was premised upon an 'ontological' notion of discursivity – a notion that went far beyond a linguistic concept. The very being of the social world is, for Laclau, discursive. Not in the sense of speech or writing, of course, but in the sense of being ordered (in whatever medium, 'material' institutions included) along the two axes of equivalence and difference, which involves a notion of antagonism. Despite heavy criticism Laclau never abandoned this position. The title of his last, posthumous book, *The Rhetorical Foundations of Society*, points towards this ontological dimension of discursivity. The goal of rhetoric, in Laclau's view, is not simply to describe linguistic tropes or figures of speech; it is to describe the way in which social identity is constructed. Rhetoric is a way to capture the grounding principles of the social.

Laclau's Concept of Antagonism

Which leads me to Laclau's fourth and most decisive theoretical contribution: his conception of antagonism. The theory of antagonism was developed in *Hegemony and Socialist Strategy* (*HSS* 93–148) and later synthesised by Laclau in *New Reflections* (*NR* 3–85) and in a series of articles (*E* 36–46; *RFS* 101–25). Let us see what, in a nutshell, the argument is. According to Ferdinand de Saussure, the father of the structuralist school of linguistics and theoretical starting point for Laclau, the meaning of a given sign does not follow from the latter's relation to a referent outside language. Meaning emerges from *within* language; and language is conceived as a system of differences.[10] For meaning effects to arise, a minimal degree of systematisation is necessary, as otherwise differences would disperse and no coherent meaning effect could arise. We would be living in a psychotic universe. But how to bring about systematisation? Laclau argues that a system demands a limit, and a limit demands negation. For differences to assume a certain degree of systematicity, they must be brought into a relation of equivalence, which can only be stabilised vis-à-vis a common outside that cannot simply be another difference (as in this case it would not constitute a true outside but would be internal to a system of differences). The outside must be of a *radically* different nature: different, that is, from all internal differences. And this it can only be as a *non*-differential instance of radical negativity – named antagonism by Laclau:

> [I]f the systematicity of the system is a direct result of the exclusionary limit, it is only that exclusion that grounds the system as such. [. . .] The condition, of course, for this operation to be possible is that what is beyond the frontier of exclusion is reduced to pure negativity – that is to the pure threat that what is beyond poses to the system (constituting it that way). (*E* 38)

Negating the differential nature of a given system is the very precondition for its systematicity and, thus, for meaning to arise. Let us take the simplistic example of an alliance of political forces all of which have their own differential demands of, for instance, affordable housing, gender equality or the protection of the environment. There is no common ground intrinsic to all these demands. They are of an entirely differential nature. Every demand, before it enters a process of systematisation, constitutes a positive difference with a particular content. If a chain of equivalence is to be established, simply adding another positive difference would not do the trick. Their equivalence can only be established if a negative outside – defined as the political 'elite', 'neoliberalism' or the like – comes to serve as a common denominator. Not in the sense of a positive reference point, but as something that, in an entirely negative way, threatens the very positivity of every difference from outside. All forces in this alliance feel that their respective identity is blocked by an outside threat which, at the same time, serves as a *negative* reference point to their chain of equivalence. Hence, the only thing they have in common is something entirely negative.

Again, and as Laclau repeatedly insists, this logic – which describes the basic functioning of signification – is not restricted to political meaning nor is it restricted to linguistic meaning in a narrow sense. In fact, it covers all signifying systems, including, for instance, social and cultural ones such as the 'language' of fashion as described by Roland Barthes (Barthes 1990). All social order, to the extent that it is symbolically structured (and if it is not, it is not an order), is oriented to some degree towards such a radical outside. Every effect of meaning relies, if only to a minimal degree, on some form of antagonisation. This is because signification, as was established above, is in need of a certain degree of systematicity; and every system – by virtue of being one – is in need of a limit and, thus,

21

a constitutive outside. From here we have to conclude: if antagonism is our name for the political, and if antagonism is necessary for
the temporary stabilisation of meaning as such, then *all* meaning is,
at its root, political.

I will repeatedly return to this point as it lies at the basis of my
argument for an ontology of the political, but let me just add that
we should not be fooled by what Stuart Hall once called the 'linguistic metaphor' (Hall 1996b: 271) in social theory. No doubt,
the linguistic turn in which Laclau's approach was still very much
rooted has exhausted itself and we may ask how, given the recent
turn towards materialist and realist ontologies, the passage from
Laclau's theory of meaning to an ontological kind of theorising
can be envisaged. How to move beyond the linguistic turn without
pretending, naïvely so, to have found immediate access to 'reality'? I consider this to be a pseudo problem. Laclau's arguments
retain their validity when transposed from the linguistic field
to the field of a general ontology. Laclau himself was very clear
about this: hegemonic articulation does not take place 'just at the
level of words and images: it is also sedimented in practices and
institutions'. Discourse, for that matter, 'is never merely a verbal
operation but is embedded in material practices which can acquire
institutional fixity' (*PR* 106). Hegemony is very much ingrained
into the 'matter' of our social world.

Let me return to what is a second, complementary side to the
institutive function of antagonism. As a threatening outside to a
given order, antagonism institutes that order, but also prevents it
from totalising itself. Antagonism grounds a given system of differences only by simultaneously *undermining* the differential nature
of all the elements of the system, by subverting their 'positive' content and making them interchangeable:

> [A]ntagonism and exclusion are constitutive of all identity. Without
> the limits through which a (non-dialectical) negativity is constructed,
> we would have an indefinite dispersion of differences whose absence
> of systematic limits would make any differential identity impossible.
> But this very function of constituting differential identities through
> antagonistic limits is what, at the same time, destabilizes and sub-
> verts those differences, it makes them all equivalent to each other,

interchangeable with each other as far as the limit is concerned. [. . .] The system is what is required for the differential identities to be constituted, but the only thing – exclusion – which can constitute the system and thus makes possible those identities, is also what subverts them. (E 52–3)

The term 'antagonism' denotes this double-sided moment: the moment of original *institution* as well as the moment of original *destitution* of social order. It has an ontological – or, as Derrida (1994) would have said, 'hauntological' – character.[11] I suggest that it is here, in his political ontology, where Laclau's decisive achievement has to be located. Society is instituted politically, and being instituted politically means being instituted through the labour of the negative, i.e. antagonism. Since ontology is the science of being-qua-being, we can designate this assertion as ontological in the sense of constituting a claim about the antagonistic nature of social being *as such*, not merely about the nature of political affairs in the narrow sense of politics as a particular sphere or form of action. If taken seriously, this ontology will lead to a dramatic change in perspective. The social world starts to appear in a strongly political light. As a consequence, Laclau's theory of antagonism can redirect our attention to the fundamentally contested, conflictual and dislocated nature of all things social.

All other dimensions of Laclau's thought, I submit, coalesce around this ontological notion of the political. Take the case of populism. Why does populism constitute the 'royal road' to understanding the political? Because populism is not simply a form of politics among others. In encapsulating political rationality *tout court*, it enables us to catch a glimpse of the nature of the political. Populism is the clearest expression of the logic of antagonism, which, in turn, is the defining feature of the political. Similarly, the radical implications of Laclau's theory of signification are largely ignored. If they were fully accepted, however, we would have to recognise that the being of institutions, organisations, subjectivities and the like is constructed, linguistically or not, through the play between difference and equivalence, mediated by antagonism.

Towards an Ontology of the Political

Admittedly, such a radical political ontology is hard to digest and, therefore, tends to encounter resistance and denial. Laclau himself shrank back from the dramatic consequences of his thought. While knowing that the ontological framing of the concepts of antagonism and the political had the potential of shedding light on the institution of our social world and on the nature of social being *eo ipso*, he retreated from the idea that antagonism is of ontological primacy by introducing a further notion: *dislocation* (NR 39–51). 'Dislocation' – roughly equivalent to the Lacanian Real as that which disturbs the laws of the Symbolic (of language or society), but, just like the Lacanian Real, without political resonance – is supposed to be located on an even deeper ontological level. The ontological value of antagonism was thus reduced to a particular discursive response to a more prior dislocation. It was reduced to a political way of constructing a given source of dislocation as a political 'enemy'. Laclau described his shift from antagonism to dislocation as follows:

> When Chantal Mouffe and I wrote *Hegemony and Socialist Strategy*, we were still arguing that the moment of the dislocation of social relations, the moment which constitutes the limit of the objectivity of social relations is given by antagonism. Later on I came to think that this was not enough because constructing a social dislocation – an antagonism – is already a discursive response. You construct the Other who dislocates your identity as an enemy, but there are alternative forms. For instance, people can say that this is the expression of the wrath of God, that this is an expression of our sins and we have to prepare for the day of atonement. So, there is already a discursive organization in constructing somebody as an enemy which involves a whole technology of power in the mobilization of the oppressed. That is why in *New Reflections* I have insisted on the primary character of dislocation rather than antagonism. (Laclau 1999: 137)

I was never convinced by this shift to dislocation as something more primary than the political. Laclau had retreated from the 'radical breakthrough' achieved with his initial conception of antagonism in *Hegemony and Socialist Strategy*. Now, antagonism was given a narrow political meaning: the construction of an enemy. However, if my reading of Laclau's general theory of signification is correct, then antagonism is involved in the construction of every meaning system, not only of political discourses that construct their outside as 'the enemy'. Indeed, according to Laclau's theory of signification, if taken seriously, antagonism must be made the ultimate source of social dislocation, as every system is not only instituted, but will also be destituted by a threatening outside. But, even if it is conceded that there can be non-social sources of dislocation – such as natural catastrophes – their effects are always immediately inscribed into social or political frames of reference which, indeed, involve 'a whole technology of power'. Dislocation, no matter where it issues from, always occurs within a prior horizon of being: the social. Examples given by Laclau for seemingly non-antagonistic social practices prove to be far from being not political. To construct, for instance, a volcanic eruption or an earthquake as an expression of our sins and the wrath of God may be different from attributing it to a political enemy, but it does involve a technology of power, the Catholic Church for instance, which is politically instituted. At no point one can experience a dislocation that is not immediately reframed via the instance of antagonism. Whatever occurs in our social world, it has to pass through the medium of antagonism.

I would therefore resist attempts to reduce antagonism to a particular sub-species of non-political phenomena.[12] But even if we return to the model of signification elaborated in *Hegemony and Socialist Strategy*, what I propose to call an *ontology of the political* should not be conflated with this model. What Laclau seeks to explain is a political *logic* – or should we say: a political *onto-logic* – understood as a theory of the symbolic laws of difference and equivalence, of metaphor and metonymy, of the particular and the universal.[13] Indeed, the logic is premised on antagonism as a necessary function of an outside threat, but there is little engagement with the question of antagonism *per se*. This 'logic', by virtue of being a logic, does not allow to *think* antagonism. In fact, the split between his political ontology (or onto-logic) and what remains a merely implicit ontology *of the political* pervades Laclau's entire work. It may appear negligible at first sight. But the picture is blurred by Laclau himself who employs the same term – 'the political' – for both the 'logic' of hegemony and the instituting/destituting 'event' of antagonism and radical negativity, or, in Lacanian parlance, for both the laws of the Symbolic and a *political* ontology of the Real. The latter constitutes a 'hauntological' instance, a purely negative outside of the social, which is certainly necessary for establishing any symbolic order, but should not be conflated with a particular chain of equivalence established in a particular 'ontic' struggle.[14] In Heideggerian terms: the play between ground and abyss, through which antagonism is unconcealed, is located beyond the functioning of any determinable 'logics'.[15] The play between ground and abyss is not a hegemonic 'operation' (*RFS* 121), as it is described by Laclau; it is the temporal unfolding of being-as-difference. And the only equivalent of this Heideggerian notion can be found, within hegemony theory, in the very instance of negativity inscribed into the play of political difference. To claim, along Heideggerian lines, that antagonism 'grounds as a-byss', means saying that the social can only be grounded in the absence of a metaphysical foundation. And it is this absence, supplemented by antagonistic struggles for refoundation, that needs to be made a matter of thought.

Without doubt Laclau, as a post-foundationalist, would have agreed on the abyssal nature of any ground.[16] After all, it was his firm theoretical conviction that social identities are instituted, and undermined, by their constitutive outside. What I wanted to point out, though, was that his onto-logics of hegemonic politics does not strictly coincide with an ontology of the political. The logics of equivalence and difference, the empty signifier, the rhetorical figures of metaphor, metonymy or catachresis – all these technical categories to be found in Laclau's work are premised on, but not equivalent to a radical moment of negativity which makes itself felt in the differential play between the ontological and the ontic, the political and politics. Let us therefore recapitulate what differentiates the Laclauian project from our attempt at *thinking antagonism*: it is the fine line between these two kinds of ontology – one comprising the symbolic logic of equivalence and difference according to which all social order is structured, the other engaging with the very instance of antagonism presupposed by the former.

The Stakes Involved in Thinking Antagonism

I am well aware that debating problems of ontology will not nec-essarily be considered an affair of political urgency and militant engagement. But Laclau's life, in fact, attests to the contrary. It attests to what is called in this investigation a self-implicated form of thinking: a way of thinking the political on political terms, i.e. *politically*. Evidently, political thought – to the extent to which it is to be considered a political practice in itself – cannot take place exclusively within the academic discipline of philosophy. It will have to be practised *beyond* philosophy. If topographical metaphors are allowed, we could say that thinking is both 'above' and 'beneath' philosophy as an academic discipline. It is 'above', because it cannot be subordinated to the procedures of academic philosophy, let alone 'objective science', without producing anom-alies. By running against what is incommensurable to thought, i.e. antagonism, thinking exceeds philosophy. And it is 'beneath' phi-losophy, because at the same time thinking assumes the status of a political intervention: if the political is supposed to be thought *in a political way*, then the aim of thinking is to *politicise* philosophy and academic life.

Laclau himself may serve as an *exemplum*. Laclau, it seems, did not conceive of himself as a philosopher and remained silent with regard to the status of his theory (there is no Laclauian *discours de la méthode*) or the question of thinking. On one of the rare occasions when he did speak about the disciplinary affiliation of his theory, he expressed a certain scepticism with regard to 'politi-cal philosophy', a label that 'would assume the unity of an object of reflection, which is precisely what is in question' (*NR* 69); and once he remarked that he was writing 'as a political theorist rather than a philosopher in the strict sense of the term' (Laclau 1996b: 47). We can thus assume that Laclau sought to differentiate his own project – which is exclusively concerned with questions of politics and political theory – from the practice of doing philoso-phy in any disciplinary sense. His reluctance to present himself as a philosopher, let alone a political philosopher, might surprise given frequent references to Heidegger, Husserl, Gadamer and the later Wittgenstein. But Laclau, indeed, is not a philosopher in the

27

'strict sense of the term' for a very clear reason: his thinking passes through the realm of politics. In terms of practical experience it is Laclau's involvement with Argentinian populism and with the New Social Movements of the 1970s and 1980s that constitutes the background of his thinking:

> That's the reason why I didn't have to wait to read post-structuralist texts to understand what a 'hinge', 'hymen', 'floating signifier' or the 'metaphysics of presence' were: I'd already learnt this through my practical experience as a political activist in Buenos Aires. So when today I read *Of Grammatology*, *S/Z*, or the *Écrits* of Lacan, the examples which always spring to mind are not from philosophical or literary texts; they are from a discussion in an Argentinian trade union, a clash of opposing slogans at a demonstration, or a debate during a party congress. (*NR* 200)

It was the political experience of debates and demonstrations that taught Laclau his 'first lesson in hegemony' (*NR* 200). Antonio Gramsci's work later provided him with the means to translate this experience into a coherent framework of political theory and analysis – which, in turn, served as a theoretical base for his subsequent engagement in a project of radical and plural democracy (in *HSS* 149–94) and his public support for the 'pink wave' of Latin American left-wing populism and the Kirchner governments. Unsurprisingly, Laclau held that the separation between political theory and political practice 'is largely an artificial operation' since 'theoretico-political categories do not only exist in books but are also part of discourses actually informing institutions and social operations' (Laclau 1994: 2). Hence, it is important to notice that for Laclau, contrary to what some of his critics claim when they accuse him of formalism or excessive abstraction, the practice of theorising is far from being disconnected from practical politics. On the contrary, Laclau's practice brings together academic learning and political militancy.

In fact, this 'identity of the opposites' is what characterises Laclau's thought more than anything else (I will return to this point in the Conclusion). Yet, make no mistake, this is not to say that Laclau would be carried away with a political mission. Thinking evaporates when entirely merged with politics. Rather than following the outworn model of the 'engaged intellectual', Laclau in his own involvement with politics remained, at the bottom of his heart, a political militant rather than a university professor who would make his opinions publicly known from time to time. Conversely, although his theoretical endeavour was clearly motivated by political concerns, it stood on its own and was at the same time detached from concerns of political urgency. While his aim, on the theoretical plane, was to develop a coherent and systematic theory – what I have described as his political 'onto-logic' – it is also clear that this theory sprang from political intuitions. To generalise the point: thinking, on the one hand, means to implicate oneself in the force-field of a social world criss-crossed by antagonisms; and, on the other hand, it means to follow, as consistently as possible, a theoretical path leading to the point where philosophical certainties collapse.

Hence, practical stakes are involved in a post-foundational ontology of the political. At stake is the very way in which the social world is imagined – practically as much as theoretically. Do we consider our world to be built on irrevocable principles, necessary functional processes, rational calculations of interest, prophetic tasks, holy books, anthropological constants, genetic predispositions, economic laws – *or*, do we think of our world as being built on contingent political acts of institution, which must always be renewed, can be constantly questioned and are therefore essentially contested? Evidently, our answer will have practical implications. The world is full of fundamentalist reactions to the absence of first principles and final grounds – a potentially frustrating absence that is oftentimes greeted with resentment and aggression. As much as epistemic foundationalism is a defence reaction against the absence of a final ground of knowledge, political fundamentalism is a defence reaction against the absence of a final ground of being, against what we have named antagonism: the contingent as much as conflictual nature of all social facts. Foundationalists as well as fundamentalists seek to ignore, deny or disavow the conflicts and contingencies that constitute the very 'matter' of our world. To think antagonism is to remain attentive, not only to moments of political upheaval and social crisis, but also to the subcutaneous restlessness of social life, the unevenness of social relations, the micro-conflicts that incessantly unfold around us. The ontology of the political, as defended in this book, is an attempt at giving expression, in theoretical terms, to the politicality of social life. It has nothing to do with the outmoded idea of ontology as the science of a stable ground of being. Antagonism is a name for the essentially unstable and disputed nature of the social. It names, in Heideggerian vocabulary, an abyss that only finds a transitory form of presence in the interplay between a ground and what is grounded.

Plan of the Book

The following chapters, all of which take as a starting point the notion of antagonism, have as their aim to expand – in a variety of ways and fields of inquiry – on Laclau's 'primacy of the political' thesis, i.e. the idea of an ontological primacy of the political vis-à-vis the social. It is claimed, by radicalising Laclau's central intuition, that antagonism – perhaps the only truly political name of 'the political' – assumes the function of a groundless ground of social being. If this is the case, antagonism has to be allocated its rightful place as *the* key concept of social and political thought. As Slavoj Žižek clearly perceived after the publication of *Hegemony and Socialist Strategy*, the real achievement of the book resides in the concept of antagonism as a tool for social analysis, yet this breakthrough was 'of such a novelty that it was usually not even perceived in most responses to *Hegemony*' (Žižek 1990: 249). It is fair to say that, at that time, it may not have been perceived by Laclau and Mouffe themselves. And even today, as the Laclauian project is much better known and understood than in 1985, the immense importance of the concept of antagonism is still not fully realised within the field of social theory. I would not want to speculate as to the deeper reasons for such neglect; but as Žižek recognised, the concept of antagonism points to a 'traumatic impossibility' at the centre of the social, a 'fissure which *cannot* be symbolized' (249) – and the social sciences, given their deep-seated objectivism, are hardly prepared to cope with an ontology of social trauma. *Thinking Antagonism* is a response to that traumatic impossibility. The chapters that follow are meant to illustrate the philosophical as well as political fecundity of that response.

Now, the reference to 'politics' and 'the political' remains a game of empty phrases as long as we do not succeed in fleshing out the political difference in a convincing fashion. Therefore, an ontological account of the political-qua-antagonism will be developed first (Part I) and, subsequently, we will attend to an 'ontic' theory of politics compatible with this ontology (Part II), followed by an 'application' of our theory of politics to the question of thinking (Part III).

Chapter 2 will provide the reader with a historical genealogy of the concept of antagonism from the Kantian antinomies via the Hegelian labour of the negative and the Marxian antagonism between means and relations of production to the twentieth-century fusion of Hegel and Marx with Heidegger. While Laclau's theory of antagonism is reminiscent of the Marxian bet on the class struggle at the ground of social being, a close examination reveals that Marx's notion of 'antagonism' is not reducible to the struggle between classes (it is Marx's term for the very incommensurability between the forces and the relations of production which, by virtue of being a radical ontological discrepancy, serves as the actual motor of history). Antagonism, I will suggest, denotes an insurmountable blockage of society, an instance of radical negativity that simultaneously forces and precludes the closure of social differences into a totality. There is room for concrete conflicts – antagonisms in the plural – only because of a primary ontological instability that prevents society from coinciding with itself, thus provoking never-ending conflict around partial closure and foundation. Antagonism, hence, is not to be confused with ontic struggles.

For the same reason, a Marxist notion of conflictuality has nothing to do with a 'war-like' conception of politics. The point is clarified in Chapter 3 by way of a comparison between the ontology of antagonism and three polemological alternatives that employ metaphors of warfare to portray an all-pervasive struggle: (a) Michel Foucault's *genealogical alternative* where an eternal 'battle' assumes ontological value; (b) the *eristic alternative* of Bernard Stiegler, for whom the Greek *agon*, as rule-governed competition, is preferable to antagonism; and (c) the stasiological alternative of Nicole Loraux,

who develops a theory of *stasis* (or civil war) as the constitutive/
destitutive principle of the *polis*. A warning will be issued against
polemological ontologies and their dualistic interpretation of 'struggle'. The social, it was said, is not defined by struggles between
objectively given parties, but by a fundamental blockade named
antagonism. It would thus be misguided to imagine the social
world either in terms of a single unity (i.e. society as a self-sufficient
totality) or in terms of a warring duality. Society should rather be
conceived, in Adorno's words, as an 'antagonistic totality', or, as
proposed by Laclau, in terms of 'failed unicity'.

While the chapters of Part I are concerned with the ontological
dimension of the political, the chapters of Part II turn around politics (and the social world of institutions and identities) as the ontic
side of the political difference. What is clear, is that the notion of
antagonism does not simply refer to rare moments of revolutionary rupture when, in Chairman Mao's words, One divides into
Two. Antagonism, as referring to social being-qua-being, is deeply
ingrained in the finest capillaries of everyday life. Its micrological
effects, as demonstrated in Chapter 4, can be experienced everywhere: in the workplace, in the family, in our interactions with
individuals and institutions. There is no utopia unscathed by relations of subordination and hierarchy, inclusion and exclusion, or
the unequal distribution of economic and symbolic capital. This is
what Laclau calls the *unevenness* of the social. The cause of this
unevenness is, in the last instance, political – it is *the political*.
Every single social asymmetry can be traced back to a moment
of political institution in which historically available alternatives
were initially suppressed and then forgotten. But, to coin a phrase,
where there is power, there is resistance. While total inclusion is
impossible, and lines of exclusion will always be encountered, it is
contestable where these lines run.[17] There would simply be no need
for defence if there were no attacks. Ergo: politics is ineradicable.

While the ontology of the political has effects on our notion
of even the most minor, humble and private acts – which, it will
be argued, are an expression of the political, but the political
in another 'mode': the mode of the social – the fashionable title
'micro-politics' would be a misnomer. What can reasonably called
'politics' refers us to those moments in which conflicts are fought

out collectively and in the open (not in hidden, subcutaneous and individual ways). Politics, it will be argued, reveals antagonism in the form of protestation. To sustain this hypothesis, Laclau's perhaps most famous contribution to political thought – his theory of populism – will be discussed and contrasted with Birmingham Cultural Studies in Chapter 5. The claim will be defended that all politics is *protest* politics – the reason being that political articulation, as Laclau has shown, consists on the most elementary level in the construction of a chain of equivalence between different political demands (the demand, for Laclau, is the minimal unit of politics) vis-à-vis a radically negative outside force serving as a common denominator. To raise a demand, though, is to protest. It is to demonstrate the contingent nature of the given, the fact that things could be different.[18] Ergo: politics, at the moment of inception, equals protestation.

In Chapter 6 we will continue our voyage to the 'zero point' of politics. What I call 'minimal politics' is an attempt at reducing political action to its minimal conditions. What are the conditions to be met in order for us to reasonably speak about politics? The notion of minimal politics is directed both against defenders of 'micro-politics' (which in our view is not politics) and the traditional idea of 'grand politics', i.e. the politics of 'grand' historical actors (great individuals, parties, classes, peoples). Minimal politics, on the other hand, *is* 'macro-politics', but it is 'macro-politics' to a, perhaps, minimal degree. The conditions we will determine: collectivity (all politics is collective), organisation (all politics is organised), strategy (politics has to overcome obstacles and must therefore proceed strategically), conflictuality (politics will unfold along particular lines of conflict), partisanship (political actors will have to position themselves on one or the other side of such a line of conflict) and 'becoming-major' (politics is geared towards constructing a symbolic majority) – all these conditions must be met, if only to the most minimal degree. The argument is aimed at establishing a realist, practicable and entirely un-heroic idea of politics that would still be compatible with an ontology of the political. Even the smallest collective, I propose, can act politically if it acts in a somewhat organised, strategic, conflictual and partisan way with a view to becoming hegemonic.

33

After having navigated through both the ontological and the ontic side of the political difference, the chapters of Part III will be concerned with the question of 'thinking'. Based on our previous observation that philosophy and politics are inseparably intertwined in Laclau's work, what we call thinking, far from being an exclusively academic exercise, should be envisaged as a practice of *reflective intervention* by which politics is folded back onto philosophical terrain. As will be explained in Chapter 7, thinking, by politically implicating the thinker in what is to be thought, to a large part exceeds the metaphysical tradition of the *vita contemplativa* (as much as it exceeds, of course, current philosophising in the disciplinary academic sense). The task of thinking is to bend conflict into philosophy in order to reactivate the *doxa*, the canon and institutional procedures of the academy and to make visible their contested and contingent nature – as will be exemplified with Antonio Negri's reading of Descartes and Étienne Balibar's reading of Spinoza. The seemingly outdated discipline of 'ontology' may thus be rejuvenated as a placeholder for the political within the field of philosophy.

In Chapter 8 the necessity of bringing together Hegel and Heidegger, radical negativity and ontological difference is once more underlined. But an 'activist turn' is proposed with regard to the notion of being. As Reiner Schürmann reminded us: being, for Heidegger, *is acting* – but it is a rather passive form of acting. It is only with a Hegelian notion of radical negativity that political acting can be defined along more activist lines as the *negation of the given*. As a consequence, thinking, if it is to be political, must consist in the negation of the given (the *doxa*, the canon, the procedures). Not in a nihilistic sense, however. By negating the given, thinking, at the same time, means *affirming* the politicality of the world. Thinking, in this regard, is affirmative. It is a way of occupying the world in the mode of politics by actively engaging with conflict and contingency. Thinking antagonism, in other words, is an attempt at activating antagonism. Our ontology of the political will turn out to be based on a politics of ontology.

Part I
Thinking the Political

2 Marx on the Beach: An Intellectual History of Antagonism

'The Final Law of Being'

In August 1880 Karl Marx received a visitor in Ramsgate, the English seaside resort where Marx and his family spent their summer vacation: John Swinton, a reporter for the New York based journal *The Sun*. Surprisingly, in the article where Swinton presents his account of the meeting he has little to say about political issues. Perhaps he was all too overawed and humbled by his meeting with the famous revolutionary. Instead, Swinton reports impressions from Marx's family life in the form of a domestic tale. A key moment in this narrative is his depiction of a family picnic on the beach and of the events that followed. As the evening dawned, the male members of the Marx family went on a promenade walk with their visitor. After an hour of chatting Swinton worked up the courage to pose a question which, he thought, could only be answered by a 'sage' like Marx – a question regarding the very ground of being:

> Over the thought of the babblement and rack of the age and the ages, over the talk of the day and the scenes of the evening, arose in my mind one question touching upon the final law of being, for which I would seek answer from this sage. Going down to the depth of language, and rising to the height of emphasis, during an interspace of silence, I interrogated the revolutionist and philosopher in these fateful words, 'What is?' And it seemed as though his mind were inverted for a moment while he looked upon the roaring sea in front and the restless multitude upon the beach. 'What is?' I had inquired, to which, in deep and solemn tone, he replied: 'Struggle!' (Marx [1880] 1985: 443)

This, of course, is an entirely apocryphal Marx. We do not know with certainty whether Marx, on this summer evening in 1880, responded to the inquiry regarding the ground of being with the word 'Struggle!'. Nonetheless, the Swinton text is remarkable. It draws its importance from indicating to us the shape of a Marxian ontology, that is a Marxist theory of *being-as-being* (rather than the conventional Marxist anthropology of being-as-labour). In all likelihood Swinton knew about the importance of his report. The entire narrative of the article is clearly geared towards the ontological question. The ultimate target point of Swinton's superficial interview with Marx (whose replies are only reported indirectly) and the picturesque portrayal of his picnic with the Marx family is the only word by Marx that is relayed to us as a direct quote: 'Struggle!'. It brings the text to a close. Struggle, the 'final law of being', remains virtually the final word in this curious report – it could well be Marx's final word on ontology.

This single word, possibly uttered at the seaside of an English resort, confronts us with a fissure or seam where the most extreme margin of the Marxian œuvre – a single apocryphal word – is folded back onto its centre. The marginalia provides us with a glimpse of the conflictual ontology at the heart of Marxism. In the eyes of a Marxist (a Marxist of the 'Ramsgate School', as it were), all social being is determined by class struggle. The ontological character of class struggle is well illustrated by Swinton. In his idyllic scene our view glides over a landscape with children playing and adults strolling along the shore. This is certainly not a scene of smoking chimneys and workers' demonstrations. If class struggle defines *all* social being, then it occurs not only in the form of labour strikes and barricade fighting. It also occurs in the – apparently – most idyllic situations of social life. There is no place in society untouched by class struggle – neither the parliament nor the bathing beach, neither the factory nor the museum, neither the sweatshop nor the university. Whoever looks at a painting through the filter of the conflictual ontology of Marxism sees class struggle. Whoever listens to news on the radio listens to class struggle. Whoever visits a university lecture course pays a visit to the class struggle. Ramblers on the shore promenade class struggle. Children on the beach play class struggle.

For those who do not want to listen and do not want to see, such a claim is absurd. But it is just a realistic picture of the social. The studies of Pierre Bourdieu and his school, for instance, prove beyond doubt that the distribution of economic, but also of symbolic and cultural capital, contributes to reproducing class divisions – and these divisions are deeply inscribed into every individual in the form of habitus, bodily *hexis*, and colouring of speech. It may well be that the lines of class division appear more fluid and less obvious today than they did in the nineteenth century but this does not mean that class struggle has come to a standstill. From a Marxist perspective not only the contestation of social divisions but even their reproduction *is* class struggle. Subcutaneous forms of class struggle contribute to reproducing the conditions of exploitation as much as the distribution of symbolic capital. Society reproduces itself in and through class struggle. This is the Marxist wager formulated in the *Communist Manifesto* where Marx and Engels speak about a hidden civil war raging within society. If their claim is taken seriously, we have to accept that struggles rage even when everything appears quiet and peaceful, as, from a Marxist perspective, the denial of class struggle is very much *part* of class struggle.

There is one aspect of this account, however, that should make us pause. The answer reported was not class struggle – it was struggle. Why has 'class' disappeared? Did Marx, in a weak moment after a bottle of wine, give in to the temptation of mythologising class struggle into a natural law, a Heraclitean war at the heart of all things? Did Swinton suppress 'class' because it sounded too radical? Or, perhaps, it was a simple misreading of Marx along the lines of Social Darwinism?[1] Whatever the answer is, freed from the determinate attribute of 'class', struggle assumes an even more important role. Provided it is located at the level of the very being of society (and not the being of nature), the marginalia may guide us to the core not only of the Marxist problematic, but also of the problematic of a post-foundational theory of the political.

The Post-Marxist Wager: Laclau's Theoretical Revolution

Indeed, a post-foundational reconstruction of Marxism cannot take as a starting point what generations of orthodox Marxists have presented as the imaginary centre of Marx's œuvre – the economic theory proposed in *Capital*. In opposition to the orthodox view, I have proposed reconstructing the Marxist ontology from the outermost margin of Marx's œuvre: the apocryphal word '*Struggle!*' For what appears as a lapsus by either Marx or Swinton – the disappearance of the attribute 'class' – serves as an entry point to a Marxism freed from economic determinism. On the theoretical plane a post-foundational Marxism has to be informed by our contemporary experience and will be based on an ontology of the political rather than a set of economic formulas from the nineteenth century.[2] This, at the same time, means that the conventional theory of class struggle has to be elevated to a more sophisticated level, which is only possible if the concept of struggle is detached from the determining attribute of class (or any other determining attribute) – an operation which, in turn, necessitates a thorough retheorisation of 'struggle'. What we are looking for is a concept of social struggle that is firmly located beyond all forms of (a) technological or economic determinism; (b) positivistic objectivism, as in bourgeois conflict sociology; or (c) 'bellicism', as in the polemical models of the political in Schmitt or Foucault.[3]

The post-Marxist conception of antagonism, proposed by Ernesto Laclau and Chantal Mouffe in their seminal *Hegemony and Socialist Strategy* (*HSS*) and further developed by Laclau (in *NR*, *E* and *RFS*), is the only serious contender for this role. It is one of the main conceptual innovations in social thought of the last decades. This is not to say that, as post-Marxists, Laclau and Mouffe simply abandoned the Marxist legacy. On the contrary, among all post-foundational thinkers of the political Ernesto Laclau is the one most loyal to the conflictual ontology of Marxism. In what follows, I first delineate Laclau's genealogy of his concept of antagonism. I then propose a slightly heterodox reading of the theoretical sources of the concept thus relativising Laclau's anti-Hegelianism. This will allow us to bring together, in the concept of antagonism, a Heideggerian notion of radical difference with a Hegelian notion of radical negativity.

Where should we start with our theoretical genealogy of the concept of antagonism? Let us first consider how this revolutionary epistemic object entered the philosophical stage on Laclau's own account before providing an alternative account of its intellectual history. As a close reader of the founder of structuralist Marxism, Louis Althusser, Laclau was convinced – as Althusser was – that the Hegelian baggage, which weighed heavily on Marxist theory, had to be left behind.[4] But Laclau had also encountered, and accepted for some time, a critique of Hegelian Marxism that preceded Althusser and his school: the Italian debate of the 1950s and 1960s around the nature of social contradictions and antagonisms. In this debate, the Hegelian 'logical' account of social struggle, symptomatic of the mainstream of Italian Marxism at the time, was criticised by Galvano Della Volpe and his school. Their declared goal was to reconcile Marxism with modern science (Della Volpe 1956). To achieve this, the abstruse idea of a 'dialectical' constitution of social or physical reality had to be discarded. Hegelian Marxists, in Della Volpe's critique, had diluted the materiality of actual conflicts into dialectics and, thus, into logics. The conflicting relation between labour and capital should not be mistaken as a logical or dialectical contradiction; rather, it was to be assimilated to a form of contradiction described by Kant as real opposition (*Realrepugnanz*), first in his pre-critical work and later in his remarks on the amphiboly of the concepts of reflection in his first critique (Kant [1781] 1983: 285–306 [A 260–92]). The model of real opposition had to replace, in the view of the Della Volpians, the model of dialectical contradiction. So, where do we locate the difference between these two models? While every pole of a dialectical contradiction $A : Non\text{-}A$ can only constitute itself qua negation of its opposite pole, in the case of a real opposition $A : B$ both poles collide, but nonetheless have their independent, positive existence (as in the case of two colliding physical objects).

Translated into the Marxist problematic, this meant that, for the Della Volpe school the relation between labour and capital had to be understood as real opposition, not as dialectical contradiction. The move was not meant to deny the antagonistic character of society, but to demystify antagonism in order to integrate it into a more 'scientific' theory. This required, in turn, that the social had to be cleansed of all negativity (present, but gentrified in Hegelian approaches), which led to the return of social objectivism. For if social conflicts are real oppositions, no radical form of negativity is imaginable, and in this case antagonisms could only emerge between positively given objects of reality.[5] Laclau eventually became highly critical of Della Volpian scientism. He came to realise that there is nothing antagonistic in the collision between two objects (two vehicles, for instance). It remains a mystery 'how a theory of the specificity of social antagonisms can be grounded upon the mere opposition to logical contradiction that it shared by a clash between two social forces and a collision between two stones' (*HSS* 123). However, the concept of dialectical contradiction does not fare better as it runs into the same objectivist impasse. What is assumed in *both* cases is a relation between real objects as 'full identities':

> In the case of contradiction, it is because A *is fully* A that being-not-A is a contradiction – and therefore an impossibility. In the case of real opposition, it is because A is also fully A that its relation with B produces an objectively determinable effect. (*HSS* 124–5)

So, Hegelian 'logicism' does not evade the charge of objectivism. We have to consider the possibility that a radical concept of antagonism has nothing to do with either logical contradiction or real opposition.

As is clear from this discussion, Laclau and Mouffe's theoretical intervention aims at the disruption of the objectivist problematic in the social sciences. They not only deny that antagonism describes an objective relationship between already existing entities; they even claim that it is, precisely, the effect of antagonism which makes every presumably objective identity unachievable. In this sense, as I will argue, antagonism assumes the ontological – or, à la Derrida (Derrida 1994), *hauntological* – function of a (negative) ground of society. Let us consider their example of a farmer who is expelled from his land by the land-owner. The relation between both agents is antagonistic. But it is not antagonistic because of their 'objective' social identities as either farmer or land-owner. Antagonism shows itself in the fact that the farmer is hindered by his antagonist from developing a self-enclosed identity. The 'objective being' of the land-owner becomes a symbol of the 'non-being' of the farmer: 'the presence of the "Other" prevents me from being totally myself. The relation arises not from full totalities but from the impossibility of their constitution' (*HSS* 125). The example once more illustrates that both real opposition and logical contradiction will not get us any further in our attempt at describing the working of antagonism: they are *objective* relations, while 'antagonism constitutes the limits of every objectivity, which is revealed as partial and precarious *objectification*' (*HSS* 125). Antagonism introduces an ineradicable moment of negativity into social positivity.

Marx's Hidden Theory of the Incommensurable

To envisage antagonism as the limit of all objectivity brings the concept in close proximity to Lacan's notion of the Real, as that instance which escapes and subverts the register of the Symbolic, i.e. of language and social institution. After the publication of *Hegemony and Socialist Strategy*, Slavoj Žižek immediately recognised the analogy between antagonism and the Lacanian register of the Real (Žižek 1990). Laclau reacted to Žižek's intervention by specifying his concept of antagonism and differentiating it from what he termed *dislocation* – an ontologically more radical phenomenon which appears to become Laclau's now depoliticised version of the Lacanian Real. I have already registered serious concerns about this distinction between antagonism and dislocation – which in my view tends to domesticate the radical nature of antagonism by turning the latter into a variant of an even deeper ground untouched by the political. Let me focus here on the philosophical genealogy of the idea of antagonism as a moment of pure negativity which undermines any attempt at establishing an objective and self-identical social whole. The decisive question is the following: should we seek to trace back this radical notion of antagonism in intellectual history to Marx's concept of class struggle, as Laclau occasionally does (with the proviso that struggle should be detached from actors which are exclusively determined economically)? Or, is there another, more structural concept in Marx that cannot be reduced to any form of empirical struggle but serves, similar to the Lacanian Real (but with a political twist), as a name for a fundamental incommensurability at the ground of the social? Is there a name in Marx for the self-discrepancy of the social that sets struggles into motion in the first place? If so, then the passages where Marx speaks about class struggle might not be the most promising place to begin.

My claim is that such a fundamental notion of social negativity is, in fact, hidden where it is most obvious: the actual forerunner of a post-foundational notion of antagonism is no other concept than, surprisingly, Marx's concept of antagonism. Why should this be a surprise? To understand it, one has to remind oneself of the fact that Marx, as a rule, does not employ the term 'class struggle' (*Klassenkampf*) as a synonym for antagonism. These two things easily get mixed up in the reception of his work. Laclau too when speaking about 'class antagonism' tends to obliterate the distinction.[6] Yet, a precise structural function is reserved by Marx for antagonism. In most cases the term does not refer to a duality (a real opposition) between objective forces; rather, it indicates a fundamental incommensurability. The point of the matter is that not every contradiction has to be antagonistic, as not every contradiction involves such fundamental incommensurability (for instance, the contradiction between use value and exchange value is not antagonistic, as both sides of this pair can very well be fused within a single commodity). Without doubt, the most important case of an antagonism in Marx is that between the material forces of production and the relations of production as described in the preface to his *Critique of Political Economy* (Marx 1961).

Curiously, this appears in the very passage which has always been read as the apogee of Marx's economic determinism. As Marx explains in this famous text, it is the economic base which determines the politico-juridico-ideological superstructure. Although the picture is slightly more complex, since the economic base is, in turn, socially produced, it nonetheless appears to serve as a stable foundation for the rest of society. The conventional architectonic metaphor of the building – with its base and superstructure – is typical for foundationalist discourse since at least Descartes. This model can hardly be made congruent with the idea of a universalised struggle as proposed by the apocryphal Marx on the beach, as struggle, in the economistic model, is confined to the political superstructure. It is thus degraded to a mere epiphenomenon and stops being a feature of social being as such. However, the other side of the picture is that something else takes over the ontological function, thus serving as the actual motor of social change.

This function is taken up by what at first sight appears as a purely economic contradiction unfolding, with the certainty of a natural law, in the predestined direction of capitalism's self-abolition. This fundamental contradiction is operative within a given mode of production (such as feudalism or capitalism) between, on the one hand, the productive forces, most importantly the technological means of production, and, on the other, the social relations of production (especially concerning the ownership of the means of production). According to the standard reading, at some point in the course of their development the productive forces, due to technological progress, will break up the established framework of the relations of production – an idea which must have appeared as self-evident in the nineteenth century when belief in technological and social progress was still unbroken.[7] Now, in light of this standard reading, which is also Laclau's reading, the passage appears as a straightforward case of economic and technological determinism where agents of social struggle are made into puppets of a higher structural necessity. At first sight Marx's operation appears unambiguous: the ubiquitous spook of struggles is derived from a solid economic ground.[8] Struggles, it seems, are caused and their direction is determined by laws of motion that unfold with the certainty of natural laws. The moment in Ramsgate, when Marx was haunted by a struggle that cannot be confined to any level of the social, that threatens to break out and spill over on its own terms, is forgotten. If the apocryphal Marx were to start a debate with the orthodox Marx, it would turn out that a generalised notion of struggle cannot be integrated into this model, or so it seems.

There is, however, another and radically heterodox way to read the passage. Observed from a slightly different angle, it turns out that Marx's solution, meant to provide history with a foundation, can only work by presupposing an even deeper-reaching instability. The economy can only play the role of a causal ground of historical development because of a fundamental contradiction, *within* the economic base, between forces of production and relations of production. History is driven forward, if this is considered carefully, not simply by the irresistible progress of the technological means of production. Nor is history decelerated by the relations of production. Rather, it is the *mere discrepancy* between these two dimensions – their *incommensurability* (reminiscent of what Lyotard has described as 'the incommensurable') – which leads to explosive jumps from one mode of production to another. Social change, in other words, is founded upon antagonism. But what a strange foundation this is: a foundation that consists of nothing other than a mere incommensurability. 'Social being' – the economic base – does not provide class struggles with a positive ground, but, in turn, is grounded on an entirely negative instance. Hence, in the reading proposed, social change is instigated not by a positive, ontic instance but by an ontological discrepancy without any content of its own. The economic base turns out to be grounded on an abyss.

Evidently, Marx could not leave it at this point. Once more he had to ground this abyss upon a new, positive ground. This is the actual reason why Marx has to give a determinate direction to the driving force of antagonism. The contingent ground of the social has to be chained to laws of historical necessity for otherwise there would be no guarantee that the proletariat eventually emerges as the victorious class. It is clear that this operation is Hegelian through and through. Already in Hegel contradictions are meant to propel a process whose stages are entirely predetermined (they could not progress in any different order), resulting in the final synthesis of the totality of the system. This totality cannot be put into question by a particular contradiction. There is no contradiction that, at the end of all days, would not be resolved. That theoretical constructs like these are extremely precarious is demonstrated by the fact that a simple chirurgical intervention suffices to make them collapse. For what happens if the thin band which, in Marx, connects antagonism to a metaphysics of history is cut through? What if antagonism was not chained any more to the higher principles of teleological necessity? Our elevation to the state of grace of a peaceful and liberated society would be rendered impossible. But then, the benefit would be that antagonism is set free to stand on its own. Unrooted from a deeper and more solid ground, it would become its own ungroundable 'ground'. In this case, though, we will be winding up with Heidegger rather than Marx – or, with a Heideggerianised Marx. For it was Heidegger who, in the course of his tireless destruction of Western metaphysics, insisted that there is no ground of the ground and that, therefore, 'the ground grounds as a-byss' (Heidegger 1994: 29).

The Historical Sources of Laclau's Concept of Antagonism

Marx's foundationalism it seems is historically untenable. His forecasts are disproven by historical reality, even as some die-hard Marxists may still be waiting for the collapse of capitalism and the emergence of the proletariat as a universal class. The history of late Marxism and post-Marxism – from Adorno via Althusser to Laclau and Mouffe – is a history of emancipation from Marxist foundationalism (a history not always, but often, inspired by a more realistic picture of politics). This history is characterised by recurrent attempts at disarticulating negativity from the logic of teleological necessity. More and more space was granted to Hegel's 'labour of the negative' (Hegel [1807] 1999: 18). Step by step, the term 'antagonism' was rebuilt from a figure of necessity into its opposite: a figure of contingency. At the end of this trajectory, where we stand today, antagonism does not point to a deeper economic objectivity any more. It has become a synonym for the incommensurable: the ungroundable ground of social negativity. This does not mean, in terms of a mere *anti*-foundationalism, that *all* grounds have vanished into thin air. While the economic ontology of orthodox Marxism is largely defunct today, there is still space for its conflictual *hauntology*. What I propose to describe as the post-foundational turn within the Marxist trajectory results in a conceptualisation of antagonism as a name for the very 'being' of society and history; a 'being', however, which confronts us with the impossibility of the foundationalist Being or *being-as-Ground*. This turn was premised on a critical examination of the Hegelian roots of negativity by, among others, Adorno and Althusser. In a comparable, but non-Marxist sense, this critique of Hegel's notion of negativity was in fact anticipated by Heidegger who had accused Hegelian philosophy of ignoring the questionable (*das Fragwürdige*) of negativity, thereby defusing the latter and incorporating it. According to Heidegger (2009: 24), Hegel did not take negativity as serious as he should have (a charge that, as we will see in Chapter 8, could be turned against Heidegger himself). Post-Marxist critiques of later years echoed this accusation. Nonetheless, the conception of negativity – transmitted via Hegel and Marx – remained an indispensable element of late Marxism and post-Marxism.

We have now to determine where this short reflection on the theoretical history of antagonism leaves us with respect to Laclau's notion of antagonism. If Marx, who started as a left Hegelian, moved on and beyond Hegel, something similar must be said about Laclau. Indubitably, Laclau would have dismissed all Hegelianism, as he vociferously did in a debate with Žižek when he recommended that we 'forget Hegel' (*PR* 148). But it is important to understand that this verdict only applies to the Hegelian logic of teleological necessity. It does not apply to the Hegelian labour of the negative. The latter is needed, more than ever perhaps, in order to differentiate the ontological dimension of antagonism from the (neo)liberal idea of conflict as rule-governed competition. The latter, historically prefigured in the Greek *agon*, reduces antagonism to 'ontic' conflict (see Chapter 3), an idea which also dominates conflict sociology and even Bourdieuian field theory. What makes the situation even more complicated is the frequent confusion, in the literature, between antagonism and class struggle. Against received wisdom, I have insisted that, in Marx, social change is prompted by a hauntological incommensurability as the very ground of society. The name for this incommensurability is not class struggle which is of an entirely ontic nature. The name is antagonism, which marks an insurmountable blockage that makes it impossible for the social to coincide with itself.

For the record of intellectual history it should be noted that, as a figure of radical negativity, this notion of antagonism is neither originally Marxian nor is it originally Hegelian. If one were to determine the precise historical location of its invention, one would have to trace it back to Kant. Curiously, and this might come as another surprise, the source in Kant is *not* the place where the term 'antagonism' literally appears. In his *Idea for a Universal History from a Cosmopolitan Perspective*, 'antagonism' – designating the famous 'unsocial sociability' of man – does not go beyond the liberal idea of conflict-as-competition. In order to find the source of the radical concept of antagonism, one would have to turn to Kant's discussion of the antinomies of reason in his *Critique of Pure Reason*. It is this discussion which inspired the young Hegel of the Jena period to develop his idea of dialectical contradiction. In other words, the prototypes of today's radical notion of antagonism, including Laclau's notion of antagonism, are the Kantian antinomies. Their prototypical role is arguably most obvious with regard to the mathematical antinomies, the discussion of which forestalls today's debate as to the (im)possibility of a social whole. The discussion was framed by Kant in terms of the more traditional question as to whether propositions on a cosmological whole were possible. Kant refutes the endeavour of so-called rational cosmology, a sub-discipline of traditional metaphysics, the goal of which was to synthesise all phenomena that can be experienced into an integral totality (of the world). As Kant explained, any attempt of reason to come up with such an *unconditional* instance will produce an antinomy. Kant sets out to show that reason, by itself and with necessity, will produce the metaphysical thesis of an absolute unity of the world. This does not prove anything, however, as with equal justification the antithesis can be formulated. While we cannot escape the metaphysical exigency, Kant's discussion of the antinomies destroyed our certainties with respect to the existence of a first beginning, a totality of the world, causality on the basis of freedom, and a necessary being.

This, at least, was how Kant's discussion was received by his contemporaries. In their eyes, he had proven the self-defeating nature of any search for a first principle. He had deprived metaphysical foundationalism of a solid ground.[9] One should not forget that the *Critique of Pure Reason* led to all sorts of individual 'Kant crises' and nervous breakdowns among his contemporaries – Heinrich von Kleist was one of the most prominent victims. Hegel was still in accordance with this common appraisal of Kant as the *Alleszermalmer* who has 'scrunched everything'. In Hegel's eyes Kant's teaching on the antinomies of reason provoked the breakdown of traditional metaphysics. But Kant, for Hegel, did not go far enough. He restricted himself to proving the antinomic structure of the four categories (quantity, quality, relation and modality). In Hegel, on the other hand, *every* category of his system consists of two antinomic sides. More than that, every side of an antinomy – thesis as well as antithesis – already contains within itself its counterpart, that is, the opposite. An internal diremption is at the basis of every single concept, driving a concept to transgress itself. The radicality of this principle is, however, subordinated to Hegel's philosophy of identity, his teleological necessitarianism, as every single stage in the self-development of the system is always already determined from the perspective of finality of the fully developed system (it therefore can only be reconstructed *ex post* by the philosopher, which, at the same time, explains why for Hegel a system can only be a seamless totality). Yet, the whole process that leads to this totality is not based on a positive ground, but instead on the antinomic labour of the negative.

Historically, this idea of a radical incommensurability spread from Kant to Early Romanticism and German Idealism. Not only Hegel, but also Fichte, Hölderlin, Schlegel, Novalis, and many others developed their own versions of contradiction, paradox, or antinomy (Arndt 2009). They collectively forged a modern idea of radical negativity, or incommensurability, which was later politicised by the young Hegelians and continues to secretly inform today's notion of antagonism. Historically, they reacted to the dissolution of a final ground, something that could not be ignored in a world where state bureaucracy increasingly gained power, the social field became differentiated into functional systems, the pauperisation of ever larger sections of the population could not be ignored, and the French Revolution had shown a way out of political regimes that claimed to be based on transcendent grounds of legitimation. The experience of fragmentation and division was now elevated into an object of theoretical reflection. At the same time, though, all the paradoxical tropes of negativity, invented by philosophers and poets with unbelievable ingenuity, were increasingly dissolved into tropes of reconciliation, identity and systematicity. The radical moment of negativity – which pointed back to the experience of the ultimate ungroundability of the social – had to be recaptivated philosophically. At the end-point of this course the 'struggle of the opposites' was subjected by Marxism to 'objective laws of development'. The hauntological figures of conflict were turned into figures of necessity – which, in turn, explains why late Marxist and post-Marxist approaches, by disassociating themselves from the postulate of teleological necessity, came to liberate the notion of antagonism, freeing the latter from the chains of economic objectivity and turning it, once more, into a synonym for the ungroundable ground of negativity.

A Short History of Nothing

It is not until the first half of the twentieth century that we can witness a recovery of the radical moment of negativity. Initially, however, the latter did not so much re-emerge within the field of Marxism, as negativity was reinserted into the field of a newly established ontology. With the Kantian antinomies of reason, the dominant paradigm of epistemology had encountered its limits. Now, these limits, it seems, reappeared as an intrinsic element of epistemology's great, and largely forgotten, rival paradigm: ontology. For this reason, the introduction of Hegel and Heidegger into French philosophy in the 1930s was to a significant degree directed against the dominance of Cartesian rationalism, which in France had assumed the role of a quasi-official state doctrine (Roth 1988; Janicaud 2001). However, ontology did not re-emerge in full glory, as a return to the pre-critical, 'pre-modern' stable ground of being. By the time of its return, the category of being had turned into something intrinsically precarious, something haunted by the spectre of its own absent ground. For this reason, today's ontology cannot any longer be understood in terms of, to use Heidegger's words, traditional *onto-theology*, in which the role of being was to provide us with a stable ground. Again, this move of reviving, and at the same time post-foundationally subverting, the traditional discipline of ontology was prepared to a significant extent by Heidegger's work. He pointed out that the onto-ontological difference – the relation of ontic beings to their ontological beingness (the realm of being-qua-being) – has always been interrogated in the history of metaphysical thought. The central question for Platonism, for instance, was how ontic beings relate to their 'idea' (the answer was: through some sort of mythical participation of *methexis*). Or, in the medieval Aristotelian framework, it was the relation between essence and existence which was at the centre of reasoning. As long as the metaphysical framework remained operative, the ontological side of the difference was always supposed to deliver an explanation for the very beingness of beings. What was forgotten, though, is what Heidegger calls the 'grounding question': What about the difference between the ontic and the ontological *as difference*? In the radical Heideggerian understanding of *difference-as-difference* (Heidegger 1957), being cannot be located on one or the other side of the difference, but unfolds through the never-ending play between the ontological and the ontic. Hence, being in the most radical sense – or, as Heidegger anachronistically writes to signal this differential dimension, *beyng (Seyn)* – should be understood as the play which simultaneously unites *and* separates the ontic and the ontological (the realm of beings and the very beingness of these beings), thus introducing an irresolvable difference into being that amounts to a constitutive deferral of every stable ground of being.

But, while this aspect of Heidegger's work turned out to be formative for later philosophies of difference (of which Jacques Derrida and the early Gilles Deleuze may well be the most prominent proponents), what was of immediate importance as a source for subsequent theorisations of *negativity* was the early Heidegger's notion of finitude which lent itself to a Hegelian reading. According to Heidegger's *Being and Time* (Heidegger 1953), the *Dasein* of man is intrinsically temporal because it is finite: the being of *Dasein* is being-towards-death. Although death cannot be experienced directly (we can only witness the death of others, but not our own), it still makes itself felt within our life as an absence, which has a very real presence. Finite being is thus held out in a *Nothing* that is not at all neutral or indifferent. For if Nothing, as Heidegger puts it, 'were only something indifferently negative, how could we understand, for example, horror and terror before the Nothing and nihilation' (Heidegger 1998: 45)?

It was during the perhaps single most important academic event of the twentieth century that the Heideggerian notion of finitude was folded back into Hegelian dialectics, thus producing an 'anthropological' theory of negativity, lack and desire that should prove to be the starting point for subsequent political ontologies. Alexandre Kojève's seminar on Hegel's *Phenomenology of Spirit*, held at the École Pratique des Hautes Études between 1933 and 1939 and visited by, among others, Bataille, Queneau, Aron, Breton, Merleau-Ponty, Hyppolite, Éric Weil and Lacan (even Hannah Arendt paid the seminar an occasional visit), was silently devoted to the Heideggerianisation of Hegel (Kojève 1980). Hegel is celebrated by Kojève for having introduced into ontology the fundamental category of negativity, yet by assimilating that category to the Heideggerian notion of finitude, Kojève proposes an 'existential' or anthropological version of Hegelian dialectics, whose field of application is now entirely restricted to the realm of human affairs, thus excluding the realm of nature. As a result, Kojève can define negation as the constructive act by which man, under the sign of his own finitude (or death), freely creates history. To define negativity in terms of a free and creative form of human *action* allows Kojève to simultaneously abandon the more contemplative approach of Heidegger and radicalise the Hegelian idea of historicity (the Kojèvian idea of action will be taken up in Chapter 8). In Hegel's dialectics between lord and bondsman, Kojève detects a fundamental antagonism at the heart of history. Lord and bondsman are bound together by their negatory struggle for recognition. Initially, the lord is not the one who is more powerful but the one who is prepared to accept his finitude and risk his life in the struggle for recognition – thus forcing the bondsman to recognise him as lord. However, *forced* recognition can never be *full* recognition. Full recognition can only be achieved if it is mutual, which would imply the ultimate 'sublation' (*Aufhebung*) or dissolution of negativity, and the final resolution of struggle. But, if the struggle for recognition functions as the motor of history, then the achievement of a state of universal and reciprocal recognition of all individuals would be tantamount to the end of history. As is well known, Kojève was more than happy to draw that conclusion.

To presume such final sublation and reconciliation of historical struggle does not fit easily with the Heideggerian trend of Kojève's argument. In Heidegger, as already mentioned, 'finitude' should in no way be confused with the 'end' of our life, because our own death can never be reached as such (we cannot experience our own death, only our own dying). No wonder that subsequent ontologies would insist on the irresolvability of negation. Jean-Paul Sartre was one of the first who in this respect would take up and radicalise the Kojèvian model. It is in Sartre's *Being and Nothingness* (Sartre 1956) that the traditional ontological question regarding being-qua-being is most explicitly reworked into a theory of being-qua-*lack-of-being*. Like Kojève, Sartre starts from a clear-cut separation between the subjective realm of consciousness or being-for-itself (*être-pour-soi*) and the objective realm of natural being-in-itself (*être-en-soi*). While the latter is a sphere of pure positivity and plenitude, the former, that is conscious human being, is permeated by *nothing*: it always is what it isn't, and it isn't what it is. Since consciousness necessarily means consciousness *of* something, it is always incomplete and in need of an outside object. Now, insofar as being-for-itself is characterised by such irresolvable *lack-of-being* (*manque-à-être*), the conscious subject can never entirely overlap with the realm of objective being, nor can it ever overlap with itself. This lack of self-identity lies at the very core of subjectivity and, according to Sartre, has to be fully accepted. An imaginary future totality towards which consciousness may project itself is unreachable; the for-itself will never become in-itself-for-itself, no ground of being will ever be attained. In this way, lack-of-being turns into a source of human freedom; not least because the for-itself, equipped with the power of negation, is able to disengage from the realm of causal and determinate being. For this reason, negativity has to be understood, not as a nihilistic, but as a *productive* category – and in Chapter 8 we will see that political acting, which consists in the negation of the given, is an equally productive category: it is the 'source' of social being.[10]

Differentialised Negativity, or, the Highest Point of Heideggerian Marxism

In political thought, Laclau is arguably the most sophisticated heir to the tradition of left Heideggerianism. By articulating negativity with difference Laclau managed to deeply politicise the Heideggerian notion of the ontological difference. In doing so, he brought the two forces of Hegelian negativity and Heideggerian difference to converge. In this precise sense Laclau's post-Marxism can be described as the highest point of Heideggerian Marxism. Let us, therefore, continue our trajectory and see how Laclau's own combination of the ontological difference with a moment of radical negativity significantly expands on twentieth-century left Heideggerianism (for the latter see Wolin 2001; Janicaud 2001). The picture, however, is complicated. On numerous occasions where Laclau resorts to a Heideggerian notion of the ontological difference the latter is employed in a merely heuristic, if not metaphysical, fashion along the lines of a simple form/content distinction. A hegemonic relation is frequently described in terms of a particular ontic 'content' (a particular hegemonic project) taking over the ontological task of incarnating the universal form (Laclau 2000a: 58). With regard to a mere form/content distinction, Laclau's theory remains within the ambit of occidental metaphysics, while the Heideggerian notion of difference-as-difference refers to a much more radical play of 'differencing' far remote from any Platonic *methexis* of the ontic in the ontological.

On the other hand, though, Laclau makes clear that 'no ontic content can ultimately monopolize the ontological function' (71). No particular ontic order will ever succeed in fully hegemonising the very ontological principle of ordering, no particular hegemonic project will manage to fully incarnate the place of universality. Any kind of *methexis* is bound to fail. And it is bound to fail because of a primordial lack or negativity. As Laclau explained in an interview:

> If we had a dialogical situation in which we reached, at least as a regulative idea, a point in which between the *ontic* and the ontological dimensions there would be no difference, in which there would be

a complete overlapping, then in that case there would be nothing to hegemonize because this absent fullness of the community could be given by one and only one political content. (Laclau 1999: 135)

But, if the fullness of any ontic being, including the fullness of social agents and of society at large, 'is unreachable, this split in the identity of political agents is an absolutely constitutive "onto-logical difference" – in a sense not entirely unrelated to Heidegger's use of the expression' (*E* 61). This is clearly a post-foundational way of framing the ontological difference beyond any metaphysi-cal form/content distinction. The play between the ontological and the ontic (the ground and what is grounded), precisely because it cannot be arrested, points to what Heidegger would have por-trayed as the a-byss of the (non-)ground (Heidegger 1994). And it is this notion of difference-as-difference (supported by a notion of lack or negativity) that secretly underpins Laclau's otherwise 'metaphysical' use of the ontological difference. If the latter use is part of his political ontology (his 'onto-logic' of the functioning of hegemony), the former may pave the way for a post-metaphysical ontology of the political.

Unfortunately, there are only a few places in Laclau's work where he sets out to directly engage with this fundamental dimen-sion of the political *eo ipso*. The only extensive discussion can be found in an article jointly written with Lilian Zac, in which social negativity is explicitly discussed in terms of the onto-ontological difference. This article, largely neglected among Laclau scholars, can serve as a key to clarifying the relation between radical nega-tivity and ontological difference that, otherwise, remains obscure in Laclau's work.[11] In their article, Laclau and Zac differentiate between, on the one hand, ontic nothingness as the source of par-ticular beings that – within a given historical epoch – are absent but could very well be present under different conditions, and on the other, ontological nothingness, which they describe with reference to Reiner Schürmann's work as the 'pull towards absence that per-meates presence to its very heart' (Schürmann 1990: 141). Now, if we want to conceptualise the difference between beings and being, what is required is a 'passage' through ontological nothingness (Laclau and Zac 1994: 29), for the latter is the 'very condition of access to Being' (30). Radical negativity, in other words, must not be conceptualised in the form of mere indifference: the 'nothing' Laclau speaks of – a 'nothing' which simultaneously relates *and* subverts the field of positive differences – has a very real presence comparable to Heidegger's notion of 'horror and terror before the Nothing and nihilation' (Heidegger 1998: 45).

It is clear that this idea of a radical 'nothingness' touches at Laclau and Mouffe's conception of antagonism. In *Hegemony and Socialist Strategy* they affirm '*that certain discursive forms, through equivalence, annul all positivity of the object and give real existence to negativity as such*'. What makes full presence impossible – the 'impossibility of the real – negativity' – 'has attained a form of presence' (*HSS* 129). The constitutive outside of a given system of beings, even as it does not *exist* on the level of beings as one more being, very much *insists* in that it subverts ontic being through a process of absencing/presencing. If we managed to completely erase ontological nothingness, we would destroy the very fabric of the social, thus producing something of the order of a Parmenidean *One*, a closed totality of the social, a state of pure identity and presence: a state of pure Being. So, that the ontological and the ontic are 'irremediably split' has two consequences:

> [T]he first is that the ontic can never be closed in itself; the second, that the ontological can only show itself through the ontic. The same movement creating the split, condemns its two sides (as in all splits) into mutual dependence. Being cannot inhabit a 'beyond' all actual beings, because in that case, it would only be one more being. Being *shows* itself in the entities as that which they are lacking and as that which derives from their ontological status as mere possibility. Being and nothingness, presence and absence, are the mutually required terms of a ground constitutively split by difference. (Laclau and Zac 1994: 30)

As emphasised in this passage, the split between the ontic and the ontological must be radical, otherwise it would be internal to the ontic. Or, in terms of Laclauian discourse theory: it would be part of a system of differences as simply one more difference. To call the ontic and the ontological 'irremediably split', as Laclau and Zac do, means exactly this: that the radical difference between the ontic and the ontological is *necessary* for a differentiated world of beings to exist. And yet, a world of positive and self-sufficient differences (without any degree of equivalence) is rendered *impossible* by the very same instance – radical negativity – which makes it possible. Obviously, the latter cannot be directly approached in conceptual terms, nor cannot it be empirically nailed down – which is why we assume, in this investigation, that it can only be *thought* by way of keeping attention to that which manifests itself in moments of conflict and contingency within the field of the ontic. Precisely because 'nothing' is not mere indifference but insists as an absent presence, it can only show itself within the realm of beings through their failure to fully constitute 'the system as pure Being' (*E* 39). This revelatory moment of antagonism sets in when gaps, breakdowns and interruptions are experienced on the ontic level of beings. The dislocatory event is thus accompanied by an effect of unconcealment: the ontological dimension, which cannot show itself directly, presents itself as lack in the ontic level: 'It is this effect of unconcealment that splits the opposing forces between their "ontic" contents and the character of mere possibility – that is, inception, pure Being – of those contents' (Laclau and Zac 1994: 30). Thinking is an attempt at remaining attentive to these effects of unconcealment.

Flirting with Nothingness

As was to be expected, Laclau's conception of radical negativity was met with fierce criticism. Fred Dallmayr, in an early critique of *Hegemony and Socialist Strategy*, perceived in it a prime example of what he termed '[f]lirtation with nothingness' (Dallmayr 1988: 45). He did not ignore that, for Laclau and Mouffe, inside and outside of a signifying system, that is, the ontic and ontological, are completely imbricated, for otherwise the system would be either totally open or totally closed. But the point of the matter is that we cannot have radical difference *without* radical negativity. What Dallmayr sees as a deficiency in Laclau and Mouffe's argument – their insistence on the radical, negatory character of the outside – is actually an indispensable part of it. Only under the

proviso that the system's outside assumes the role of an antagonistic limit vis-à-vis the inside can we speak about an outside at all
and, hence, about a fundamental play of difference between inside
and outside. A 'passage through negativity' (*NR* 213) – which is
nothing other than the passage through antagonism – is required
in order to account for relative and always hybridised systematicity. Otherwise, a mere differencing between the ontic and the
ontological would result in nothing other than a self-identical
mess without antagonism: the night in which all cows are grey. If
there are systemic cracks through which the light shines in, these
cracks are the result of radical negativity. Popularised accounts of
postmodernism that present meaning in terms of an unrestrained
pluralism or a happy-go-lucky play of signification tend to obfus-
cate the instance of radical negativity (which is, strictly speaking, beyond the realm of meaning, language or sense). This is the
gulf separating Laclau from those who tend to celebrate hybrid-
ity or 'third spaces'. From the perspective of Laclauian political
ontology social 'being' is not unitary, nor is antagonism premised
on the duality or the plurality of conflicting parties. Rather, antagonism, as we will see, is nothing other than a name for the *failed
unicity* of being: the failure of the social to ever reach a state of
self-same unicity.

This is a far cry from what Dallmayr suspects to be 'a Sartrean
kind of antithesis' between being and nothingness (Dallmayr 1988:
45). A state of full being can never be reached – which is why we
never encounter an entirely systematic system, or, for that matter, an entirely structured structure, a fully instituted institution, a
totally organised organisation, a completely self-identical identity,
or, in philosophical terms, a fully existent being, i.e. a being whose
essence is its existence – all of which would amount to a state of
pure positivity. Nor will we ever encounter, on the other hand, a
state of pure negativity (such as a psychotic war of all against all).
For what Laclau says about social being – that it cannot be reached
as such – must also be said about this very outside: it is inaccessible
as outside. In Laclau and Mouffe's approach, being and nothingness, therefore, do *not* stand in a relation of antithesis. In fact,
Laclau's theory of signification implies that complete closure of a
signifying system is as unachievable as complete openness of that

system. This must not prevent us from relating to 'nothingness' in an, indeed, flirtatious manner by 'waving' at something which can only show itself indirectly, in the dislocation of the ontic order of beings – a dislocation effectuated by the labour of the negative. This is the reason why the latter is not hypostasised to a black hole or antithesis to being. Laclau and Mouffe do not adhere to any form of 'negative ontology', let alone 'negative theology' – which would just be a mirror image of metaphysical foundationalism:

> To assert, as we have, the constitutive nature of antagonism does not therefore mean referring all objectivity back to a negativity that would replace the metaphysics of presence in its role as an absolute ground, since that negativity is only conceivable within such a very framework. (*NR* 27)

In other words, negativity must not be conceived in terms of a mystical abyss that would only be the mirror image of an equally mystical ground of total presence. An ontology of antagonism, when conceived post-foundationally, will have to envisage negativity through the lens of difference and vice versa.

So, what Dallmayr takes for flirtation with nothingness is in fact an attempt at *thinking antagonism* – but perhaps, why not, in a flirtatious manner, as antagonism is both radically inaccessible and yet always present to the extent to which no ontic being exists in the social world that would not be distorted in some ways by an outside force of negativity. Thinking means to follow the traces of distortion with obstinate rigour. It is not about 'discovering' the final 'law' of being – as antagonism is not a law in any meaningful sense. It is what lies at the ground of, and makes operative, the laws that can account for the production of concrete antagonisms (in the plural). These laws were discussed by Laclau, at different stages of his work, under the title of discourse, hegemony or rhetoric. They describe, in the restricted sense of a political ontology, the working of politics[12] – which must not be confused with the political: antagonism. The latter has more to do with the Heideggerian and post-Heideggerian category of the 'event' or, as said before, with all the paradoxical figures of negativity developed in the post-Kantian tradition of German Idealism and the philosophical thought of Early Romanticism. We can experience it in our daily life, and, on a politico-theoretical plane, we can try to think antagonism.

Laclau's Question

Thinking antagonism involves, as explained in the previous chapter, a moment of self-implication. Thus, a process of thinking is in place whenever we actively follow the traces of conflicts and dislocations encountered in the social realm, whenever we decide to respond to the experience of antagonism by inferring, extrapolating and working out the consequences of our encounter. This is not to argue against Laclau's insights into the political logic of social being – which remain perfectly valid. My critique is meant to push further these insights onto the philosophical terrain of an ontology of the political which would be slightly more – and slightly less – than a political ontology. This will require us to remain faithful to what could be called *Laclau's question* 'What is an antagonism?' (Laclau 2014: 102) – only that my proposal on how 'to advance on the theoretical front' was to ask the more fundamental question: What is *antagonism*? Once again the political difference – as the difference between politics and the political – may help to grasp the different dimensions of antagonism. If *Laclau's question* is aiming at the political 'onto-logic' of hegemony, discourse and rhetorics, and if the social sciences tend to restrain the concept of antagonism to the ontic dimension of empirical struggles, the question 'What is antagonism?' aims, precisely, at the differentiating play *between* politics and the political – a grounding play which, at the same time, remains abyssal. Rather than being a logics of social articulation, antagonism, by virtue of being involved in the moment of social institution and being presupposed by the symbolic logic of hegemony, should be conceived of as an all-pervasive *dimension* of the social, *a continuous movement of de- and re-grounding* or what, in a more Deleuzian vein, one may want to describe as a process of *becoming* – which is also the reason, by the way, why there is no incompatibility between an ontology of negativity or lack and an ontology of abundance or excess.[13]

I am well aware of the potential dangers of this approach. Asking, in such Heideggerian mode, about antagonism-as-being rather than the functioning of *an* antagonism must not distract our attention from the 'ontic' level of political struggles and confrontations. However, I do not consider this a real danger. Quite the contrary, the ontology of the political may direct our view to the ubiquitous emergence of conflicts at any time and any place. In this respect, such Heideggerianism of the political remains firmly located within the Marxist tradition. Precisely because, as will become clearer in the course of the subsequent chapter, it is not chained any more to a polemological notion of 'class war' or other 'objective' conflicts, the ontological ground of antagonism will have to realise itself ontically in the form of concrete social struggles. The Marxian notion of antagonism – understood correctly as a radical incommensurability at the heart of the social – turns out to be immensely productive for social analysis. The Marxist wager is, and has always been, that history is a perpetual process of struggles. In our daily life we are unaware of most of these struggles, as most struggles are rendered invisible within a given hegemonic formation. Yet it is highly unlikely that any regime will ever succeed in suppressing even the remotest memories of struggle. There is always the danger, in the eyes of any regime, that struggles pass from a 'latent' to a 'manifest' stage. And, given such danger, even phases of apparent tranquillity will be perturbed by a certain restlessness: by the background noise of struggles. These struggles originate from an absent source of radical negativity – antagonism – which impedes the pacification of society into a state of harmony and closure.

3 Beyond the 'War Hypothesis': Polemology in Foucault, Stiegler and Loraux

Thinking *Polemos?*

In the previous chapter we traced back the Marxian name for being – 'Struggle!' – to its roots in German Idealism: radical negativity. The latter was described in terms of a fundamental blockade, an unsurpassable incommensurability at the ground of society. It is evident that such a notion of antagonism is much more demanding than any conventional idea of social conflicts. Antagonism cannot be absorbed into the image of two opposing camps as would be typical for conflicts of war or class struggle. This new notion of antagonism, hence, differs from any empiricist or objectivist setting of conflicts between social groups, as would be typical for bourgeois conflict sociology. It is far away from any kind of social objectivism. As a figure of the incommensurable, to repeat what was established in the previous chapter, antagonism must not be confused with, in Kantian terms, a 'real opposition' between two objectively given opponents – the bourgeoisie vs the proletariat, the Romans vs the Carthaginians, the Confederates vs the Unionists, or any other binarism of that order. As a name for the absence of any final ground of the social, antagonism is not conflict, it is that which engenders conflicts (and their preliminary pacification), for the impossibility of total closure will forever engender disputes about partial closure. The advantage of such an ontological conception, as opposed to a purely ontic one, is clear. It allows us to affirm the foundational nature of social conflictuality without falling into the trap of a violent 'bellicism' by either envisaging the political according to the Schmittian friend–enemy criterion (if friend and enemy are understood as objective terms) or by presuming a perpetual war of all against all. Antagonism, as a figure of the incommensurable, opens a perspective onto the deeply conflictual structure of the social, but is not in itself identical with 'ontic' disputes, wars and struggles.

To call attention to this fact, I have proposed to differentiate between political ontology (or 'onto-logic') and the ontology of the political. If the former is aimed at the, ultimately, political *laws* of constitution of politics or social institution (described by Laclau under the rubric of discourse, hegemony or rhetoric), the latter is an exercise in thinking the political as the ontological instance grounding these laws. In the intellectual tradition that spans from the Kantian antinomies via German Idealism and Marxism to Laclau and Mouffe's post-Marxism, one of the names for the political in the latter sense is antagonism. In this tradition, thinking the political means thinking antagonism. Yet, no doubt, there are other contenders for the role of the political, and there are alternative names for an ontological instance of all-pervasive conflictuality. Before we continue on our journey of thinking antagonism – a route that will take us back to a closer engagement with politics in Parts II and III – it is advisable to revisit some of these alternatives. This will not only allow for a clearer picture of the ontology of antagonism, but will also demonstrate its advantage over approaches that tend to conflate the ontological with the ontic, the political with politics.

In this chapter, the ontology of antagonism will be compared with rival ontologies, which I categorise as the *genealogical*, the *eristic* and the *stasiological* alternatives. As it is impossible to paint a comprehensive panorama within the limited space of this book, I will focus on a single proponent respectively. After critically discussing the genealogical ontology of Michel Foucault, I present the eristic ontology of Bernard Stiegler and then continue to the stasiological ontology of Nicole Loraux. All three approaches represent what, from our perspective, constitutes a particular misunderstanding of the conflictual nature of social being, a certain reification of antagonism, i.e. a diminution of the latter to one or the other kind of 'real opposition'. They also rest upon a fantasy of bellicism: the phantasmatic idea that a *war* is raging at the ground of society.[1] This ongoing war, or *polemos*, is stylised by Foucault in his genealogical phase into a subcutaneous, eternal 'battle' (Chevallier 2004). For Stiegler, who is presented as an exponent of agonistic theories of politics, this everlasting *polemos* has to be legally tamed into *eris* or civic strife; while in the model reconstructed from ancient Greek sources by Loraux, the logic of external war is, as it were, folded back into the city in moments of *stasis* or 'civil war' when society is split into two oppositional halves and all efforts at domesticating conflict fail. To the extent to which all three alternatives are oriented towards war as the anarchic principle of social relation, all three could be described as polemological.

Thinking antagonism, however, means thinking beyond the 'war hypothesis'. As will become apparent from the discussion, taking the imaginary of war as a reference point produces theoretical and practical effects which differ greatly from those produced by the ontology of antagonism. Let me, for heuristical reasons, illustrate the matter in Lacanian terms: polemological approaches will ultimately remain locked in the register of the Imaginary, in the binarism of a mirror game between friends and enemies, thus bypassing, if not completely ignoring, the registers of the Symbolic (the 'logic' of equivalence and difference as described by Laclau, i.e. political onto-logic) and of the Real (the ontological moment of radical negativity). As long as our approach remains confined to the imaginary register, we will not be able to either touch a more scientific base or start envisaging a process of thinking what remains beyond the realm of either science or fantasy. The originality of the Laclauian conception of antagonism becomes all the more impressive when compared with these polemological alternatives.

The Genealogical Alternative: Foucault's Ontology of War

Michel Foucault's work as a genealogist is arguably the most prominent example for a polemological approach.[2] Similar to a post-foundational ontologist of the political, the genealogist is opposed to foundationalist metaphysics. The genealogist sees what the metaphysician, by searching for a stable ground of order, cannot perceive. Where the latter sees eternal truths, the former sees a throng of ancient errors. Where the latter sees necessary laws and universal principles, the former sees the play of chance. Where the latter would presume the most sublime values, the former seeks to trace back these values to their base, ordinary and perhaps farcical origins. To make metaphysical foundations crumble, the genealogist has to follow the accidental turns of history with a view to clarify the historical conditions of possibility of truth. What then comes to light through the cracks in these foundations are violent collisions. On the ground of society there is a battle raging on. When you say power, you have to say power struggle. The idea is already present in the later stages of Foucault's so-called archaeological phase but comes to the fore with *Discipline and Punish* and his subsequent plans to write a genealogical history of the disciplinary institution of the military. In terms of empirical investigation, the latter project remained unrealised, yet Foucault further investigated into the methodological – and, I would claim, secretly ontological – principle of genealogy. The latter can be condensed in what he calls the Nietzschean and also Clausewitzian hypothesis: 'Power is war, the continuation of war by other means' (Foucault 2003: 15). By inverting Clausewitz's famous proposition Foucault arrives at a conception of politics as the continuation of war by other means. For some years Foucault seems to be fascinated by the possibility of analysing power through the lenses of polemology. All power struggles, according to this hypothesis, have to be analysed as episodes of a displaced and latent battle that continues raging subcutaneously. Power, thus, becomes a metonymy of warfare, a function of an all-pervasive *polemos*. 'The struggle is everywhere', as Foucault puts it – inadvertently echoing the Marx of Ramsgate – when describing his aim of bringing to the fore 'this perpetual agitation' (in Fontana and Bertani 2003: 280).

It is evident, though, that by framing the question along these lines, the self-declared nominalist Foucault comes to make ontological claims about the (polemical) nature of the social *eo ipso*. As he cannot allow himself, at this stage, any form of ontological reasoning, he pursues the only way out available to a genealogist:

he sets out to 'genealogise' Nietzsche's hypothesis, that is, to recon-struct a *genealogy of genealogy*. His lecture course held at the Collège de France in the years 1975–6 under the title 'Society Must Be Defended' was explicitly devoted to testing the 'war hypothesis', which is said to have three implications. The initial meaning of it is that politics 'sanctions and reproduces the disequilibrium of forces manifested in war' (Foucault 2003: 16). A particular relation of forces, emerging from an initial, but largely forgotten historical battle, is constantly reproduced during a peacetime 'silent war'. It is reinscribed, as Foucault points out, 'in institutions, economic inequalities, language, and even the bodies of the individuals' (16). Secondly, while the balance of forces shifts and is modified during this process, the political struggles that modify and condense the relation of forces into a political system should also be seen as a continuation of war: 'We are always writing the history of the same war, even when we are writing the history of peace and its institutions' (16). And finally, the hypothesis implies that the out-come of struggle cannot be adjudicated by law or political author-ity. It can only be decided in a 'trial by strength in which weapons are the final judges' (16). If the perpetual battle had an end (by way of a final battle), not only war, but any exercise of power would be suspended.

Now, that a genealogy of genealogy is a perfectly circular enter-prise does not seem to be a matter of concern for Foucault. When asking, 'Who saw war just beneath the surface of peace; who sought in the noise and confusion of war, in the mud of battles, the principle that allows us to understand order, the State, its institu-tions, and its history?' (47), it does not seem to cross his mind that it was *him*, Foucault, who had started from precisely this question. Foucault cannot allow himself to openly draw ontological conclu-sions; so, instead of explicating his self-implication in the question – which would have forced him to rephrase it along the lines of our starting question: 'What's going on with Being?' – he seeks to reconstruct the war hypothesis historically.[3] Anyway, he arrives at a startling result. That politics is the continuation of war is a hypothesis that *precedes* Clausewitz – and it was Clausewitz who inverted the prior hypothesis. In the seventeenth and eighteenth centuries, a 'historico-political discourse' had emerged in which such a binary model of society was proposed. In a key passage of his lectures, the main features of this discourse are described by Foucault as follows:

> War is the motor behind institutions and order. In the smallest of its cogs, peace is waging a secret war. To put it another way, we have to interpret the war that is going on beneath peace; peace itself is a coded war. We are therefore at war with one another; a battlefront runs through the whole of society, continuously and permanently, and it is this battlefront that puts us all on one side or the other. There is no such thing as a neutral subject. We are all inevitably someone's adversary. (Foucault 2003: 50–1)

This new discourse is fiercely opposed to the 'philosophical-juridical discourse' of law, contract and monarchical sovereignty, understood as principles of social unity. Sovereignty, in the eyes of politico-historical thinkers, results from violent usurpation or conquest. It follows that there are always *two* historical narratives: the history of the victors and the history of the vanquished. Despite, or because of, its binary format, this discourse proves surprisingly flexible by changing ideological sides repeatedly. It emerges in the politics of the Levellers and Puritans of revolutionary England in the 1630s. Half a century later, oppositional aristocracy under Louis XIV makes use of it against the jurists and magistrates of the court. In the 1820s, Augustin Thierry interprets the French Revolution along the lines of this historico-political discourse. Revolutionary practice, theory and history-writing always aim, as Foucault stresses, at reactivating a subcutaneous war. Their aim is to discover 'beneath the forms of justice that have been instituted, the order that has been imposed, the forgotten past of real struggles, actual victories, and defeats which may have been disguised but which remain profoundly inscribed' (Foucault 2003: 56). Explaining social and political norms from below, rather than from above, 'means explaining them in terms of what is most confused, most obscure, most disorderly and most subject to chance' (54). It is not human rationality or higher laws that govern history:

[It] is the confusion of violence, passions, hatreds, rages, resentments, and bitterness; and it is the obscurity of contingencies and all the minor incidents that bring about defeats and ensure victories. This discourse is essentially asking the elliptical god of battles to explain the long days of order, labor, peace, and justice. Fury is being asked to explain calm and order. (Foucault 2003: 54)

Only, the order of fragile rationality, that appears to arch over the battle zone, makes us believe that the clash of arms has ceased.

Clearly, Foucault's own genealogical project has to be located within this genealogy. Only this explains why his historical account, in many passages of these lectures, tends to turn into a paean of praise. Foucault concedes his own fascination at the beginning of his lecture of 28 January. However, in the course of his lectures it becomes increasingly clear that the historico-political discourse eventually proves indefensible as the polemological binarism was biologised in the nineteenth century and the constitutive function of war re-envisaged in medical and biological terms. The 'war hypothesis' was reframed by social Darwinists as a struggle for survival, which implies a fundamental conversion of the logic of conflictuality. A social binarism turns into a biological monism. There are not two 'races' any more (in the pre-biological sense of national groups such as Franks vs Gauls) that face each other, but a single 'race' is differentiated into an 'over'- and a 'sub'-race. The latter threatens to infect and decompose the social organism as a whole. Society has to be defended, that is, cleansed from everything that is perceived as heterogeneous to its totality. With his genealogy of state racism at the end of his lectures, Foucault has manoeuvred his genealogical project into an impasse. If the war hypothesis converts itself into racism, it can impossibly be retained as a methodological principle for further research. The genealogy of genealogy has led to the dissolution of genealogy (as polemology).[4] Not without good reason. To conceive of social conflictuality in terms of war is politically problematic and intellectually misleading. I would describe this fantasy on the verge of a sociological bellicism as *pseudo-radical*. It is pseudo-radical not only because it involves phantasmatic violence, but, more than that, because it does not go to the ontological *roots* of social conflictuality. It stops short of being truly radical. For what would be encountered on the very ground of social conflicts if not antagonism? Or, to paraphrase Heidegger, the ground of conflict – antagonism – is nothing conflictual.

Nonetheless, it is hard to ignore a certain vicinity to a post-Marxist perspective. Foucault, similar to Laclau, starts from a critique of the Marxist theory of power, including political power, as merely a function of the economy. And, like Laclau, he becomes increasingly interested in detaching struggle from economic denominators such as class. As he pointed out in an interview, the Marxist tradition does not provide us with a theory of struggle:

> What I find striking in the majority – if not of Marx's texts then those of the Marxists (except perhaps Trotsky) – is the way they pass over in silence what is understood by *struggle* when one talks of class struggle. What does struggle mean here? Is it a dialectical confrontation? An economic battle? A war? Is civil society riven by class struggle to be seen as a war continued by other means? (Foucault 1980: 208)

Here, again, the inverted Clausewitz makes an appearance as a potential solution to the riddle of social conflictuality. As Foucault came to realise at the end of his genealogical trajectory, polemology was the historical source of the Marxist theory of class struggle. The latter emerged as a sideline of the idea of biological 'race war'. Marx himself conceded that he had found the idea of class struggle in the work of Thierry. In turn, the idea of class struggle – or, more adequately, 'class war' – could, thus, be modulated in a racist direction. In orthodox Marxism, nonetheless, this danger was relatively low as long as 'class' was determined in strictly economic terms. Yet in other cases, especially in anarchism, Blanquism and the Parisian Commune, a racist tendency took hold when attempts were made to construct the enemy in mythical and essentialist terms. This conclusion to Foucault's genealogy of the war hypothesis is not without a certain inadvertent irony. Wasn't it Foucault himself who had experimented with the dissociation of struggle from class? Is every non-economistic conflict theory in danger of becoming complicit with state racism? This would be a far-fetched argument for someone as critical of Marxist economism as Foucault. But Foucault, by clinging to his objectivist theoretical framework, cannot find a way out of this dilemma. While his (self-)criticism of a war-like conception of social conflictuality is accurate, he cannot allow himself to deobjectivise struggle. What, from a post-foundational perspective, would be the only alternative – an ontology of antagonism – is simply not on the agenda for a self-declared nominalist. Eventually, Foucault feels forced to abandon his genealogical project of historico-political research rather than complementing it with an ontological dimension: the dimension of the political.

The Eristic Alternative: Stiegler's Ontology of Strife

Bernard Stiegler's work stands in a line with the work of other post-foundational an-archists such as Jacques Rancière, to whom Stiegler often refers in his more political writings, or Miguel Abensour and Reiner Schürmann. Yet with Stiegler, a quite different light is shed on the debates in post-foundational thought as Stiegler has devoted his work to the philosophical refoundation of the question of technics or technicity. The absence of an ultimate ground for action, or in Heidegger's terms: the intertwining between ground and abyss, is reconceptualised in terms of an originary technicity premised upon what Stiegler defines as an originary de-fault of all origin. The reason for this de-fault lies in the existential structure of human *Dasein*. The human being, for Stiegler, is what in philosophical anthropology would be called an uncomplete creature or *Mängelwesen* (Gehlen [1940] 2016). The mortal is marked by an original flaw, lack or handicap 'for which he has need of prostheses to supplement this original flaw, or more exactly to defer (and differ from) it [*le différer*]' (Stiegler 2003: 156). If the mortal is a being by de-fault, or in more technical Heideggerian terms: if the existential structure of *Dasein* or 'being-there' is, at its most fundamental level, a 'being-in-de-fault' or a 'being-through-de-fault' (on the premise that *Dasein* is necessarily characterised by *Endlichkeit* or finitude), then the only thing such a founding myth founds is the very absence of an ultimate foundation, named by Stiegler 'the originary de-fault of origin' (Stiegler 1998: 199). Before this fault, before the lack of origin, 'nothing had happened' (189) – which is, of course, why

71

it is originary. For this reason, we would be completely misled to assume a positive origin which, after having existed at some point in the past, fell apart and became unreachable.[5]

And yet, even though this de-fault of origin is in itself originary, its status is not purely negative since the absence of foundation calls for 'positive' supplements. Precisely because both origin and end are always deferred and an ultimate ground will never be reached, the latter will have to be supplemented, and these supplements are conceived by Stiegler in terms of *technical prostheses*. Technics, as 'elementary supplementarity', is nothing but '(the relation to) time (différance)' (183), i.e. the supplementary relation towards the endless deferral of ground and origin. By applying Reiner Schürmann's term to this idea, we can conclude that the 'anarchy principle' (*le principe d'anarchie*) has found a new name: *technicity*. This is where the originality of Stiegler's account lies: in his reformulation of ontological an-archism in terms of an originary *techne* or technicity.[6]

Once again, the post-foundational nature of such a claim comes to light: if every *episteme* is already tainted by *techne*, then philosophers will search in vain for an epistemic ground or a foundational truth for their activities. There is no *episteme* that would not, from the start onwards, be *technical* to some extent. And this claim can be expanded by adding that there is no language, no discourse, which is not already, in and by itself, deeply technical, i.e. *rhetorical*, given that no ultimate ground will ever be available for discourse to once and for all fix the flow of meaning. As one would expect, such a claim must have consequences for our thinking of politics as a particular *art*, *skill*, or *techne*. In fact, a striking parallel between Stiegler's rehabilitation of the rhetorical and Laclau's rhetoricised political ontology can be determined. Stiegler's claim that politics is to be understood as a particular *techne* can find support from an Essex School perspective. Yet there is also a significant difference. In Stiegler's view, particular techniques, including rhetorics and the art of politics, have to be differentiated from a more general or ontological *technicity*, not, as in Laclau, from an ontological politicality. As a result, it could be argued, not only the dimension of *the political* or *antagonism* is pushed out of focus (not completely though; we will return to this aspect in a moment), but also politics is attributed a derivative status with respect to technicity.[7] By granting technicity the role of an originary supplement to the de-fault of origin (i.e. the absence of an ultimate ground), the fundamental status of antagonism, as so often before in political thought, is once more disavowed. With the same move by which our attention is directed to the philosophical 'forgetting' of technicity, our attention is drawn away from the political. From a Laclauian perspective, however, 'the political' is not simply a name for the rhetorical *techne* of strategic action but designates a primordial antagonism without which no space for strategic action would arise to begin with. In other words, while the conflictual dimension of politics is taken into account by Stiegler, it remains restricted to the ontic level. This will become all the more evident when we now turn to Stiegler's conception of conflictuality.

In Stiegler's account, the artefact that comes to supplement *Dasein*'s originary de-fault of origin 'brings disorder (*eris, polemos*). Consequently mortals fight each other and destroy themselves' (Stiegler 2003: 156). Mortals are forced into a fundamental war against themselves by their originary 'protheticity', by the fact that every technology may be turned into a weapon (Stiegler 2004: 35). Politics is an attempt at pacifying this general war induced, in the last instance, by the technologically supplemented absence of origin. But how is political pacification possible? Given the necessary character of technological supplements, politics will have nothing to rely on except, again, technological supplements. It is what Stiegler calls 'mnemotechnics' which serves as a precondition for all political pacification. The mnemotechnics of scripture allows for the literal fixation of the law, thus providing the material means for the pacification – by way of institutionalised memorisation – of politics (80). And yet, it appears that for Stiegler a state of fundamental conflictuality, of 'war', cannot be overcome entirely. Even though war can be pacified with the help of mnemotechnics, every pacificatory effort will at some point run aground. Hence, politics will remain 'the *agora* of a struggle, an agonistic, an eristic, an art of dispute. In times of peace as in times of war, *polemos*, of which *eris* is the civil or policed version, is the law of all things: the law of becoming' (36). Consequently, politics can be defined as the pacification of war by means of a judicial (and eventually mnemotechnical) affirmation of a *we* that nevertheless retains a polemical relation towards itself.

From *Polemos* to *Stasis*: A Short Detour via *eris*

Do we have to conclude that Stiegler *does have* a notion of fundamental antagonism (tamed ontically or agonistically by means of law and 'mnemotechnics')? For two reasons this is not the case: firstly, because *polemos* cannot be considered fundamental as long as it remains derivative of a more originary technicity or 'prostheticity'. And secondly, what Stiegler describes as *polemos* does not capture the double-sided nature of the political, understood as antagonism. The latter involves both a moment of grounding and of degrounding. To explicate this point we will have to turn towards a third term – *stasis* – whose relevance is openly denied by Stiegler. As the French political theorist Étienne Tassin has pointed out, as others have before him, one has to clearly differentiate between war or *polemos* in the sense of an external conflict between city states, and a form of conflict internal to the City (Tassin 2003). The latter form is identified in Greek as *stasis* – a name for civil war. Despite the fact that in the passages where Tassin develops his theory of *stasis* he relies on some passages in Plato's *Republic*, in actual fact he positions himself in the tradition of Machiavelli and of Claude Lefort for whom the City is based on an irreconcilable internal strife (Lefort 2012). Tassin is taken to charge by Stiegler for mixing up the concept of *stasis* with that of *eris* – the Greek goddess of civic discord – as only the latter implies, according to Stiegler, that diverse interpretations of law will be accepted – a diversity of discord which is precisely what Plato aims at expelling from the City (Stiegler 2004: 117, 190–2). Here, Stiegler, by expelling the ontological dimension of antagonism (presented in the ancient guise of *stasis*) from the City, falls into the same trap as most agonistic theorists of politics. As Chantal Mouffe has argued, antagonism tends to be neglected by theorists of agonism like Hannah Arendt, William Connolly or Bonnie Honig

(Mouffe 2013: 9–15). Stiegler's eristic version of agonism does not fare much better. But, as Mouffe sustains, it 'is only when division and antagonism are recognized as being ineradicable that it is possible to think in a properly political way' (14).

We can therefore conclude that Stiegler's 'conflictual' notion of politics remains inconsequential as long as even the remote possibility of *stasis* – or antagonism – is expelled from the inner life of the City. Contrary to what he assumes, the intrinsic and inseparable link between the ontic dimension of politics and the ontological of the political is cut off by such a move. Yet there is no politics that would not have to pass through or reactivate the dimension of the political, no agonism that would not work according to the logic of antagonism, no community without potential *stasis*, i.e. without a certain degree of *internal polemos* with its double-edged logic of unification/division. What is more, to expel the aspect of *stasis* from politics also means that radical political action – for instance, in terms of populist mobilisations or in the form of revolution (which is but a particular version of civil war) – is deemed impossible. Of course, the degree of diversity, plurality, or singularity within a given community is certainly reduced, if we return to Laclau, by the construction of chains of equivalence. Yet to reduce the play of differences is the only possibility for us to arrive at a politics that will not be entirely absorbed by the differential structure of social institution and administration – of, in Jacques Rancière's terms, a 'police' distribution of the sensible. Stiegler is not prepared to live politically with this unificatory function of antagonism, even though he considers *eris* a vital ingredient of political life. And while his emphasis on the rhetorical, that is, strategical dimension of the art of politics is a timely and more than welcome contribution to political thought, his denegation of the fundamental status of the political in the form of antagonism produces a series of depoliticising effects within his discourse. One of these effects is the disappearance of radical politics (be it in the populist or in the revolutionary register), instead of which one finds, in his more political texts, appeals to regulate the media or to protect and reform educational institutions in order for citizens to learn to take 'care' of themselves and others, or to regulate *eris* with a sense of Aristotelian *philia* or love and friendship among citizens (Stiegler 2010).

Stiegler's moralistic proposals of an eristic governmentality seem to be rooted in his ontology of technicity. Not that a particular ontology would imply, in the deterministic sense, a particular form of politics or analysis. But the possibilities of thinking and acting politically are hampered, to say the least, if orientation is sought in a depoliticised ontology. By turning technicity into the an-archic principle of being-as-being, we may easily be seduced to analyse the empirical realm of ontic beings in 'technological' rather than political terms. And consequently, we may be seduced into seeking solutions by merely submitting our proposals to the administrative sectors of the state rather than reactivating more antagonistic forms of politics and shifting the hegemonic field of forces. This argument does not amount to a wholesale refutation of Stiegler's philosophy. He is certainly right to claim that politics is always technical – in the sense of strategy – but we need to add that political strategies are employed with the aim of attaining a goal through the construction of a particular 'we', through giving a certain degree of unity to a collective.[8] It is therefore not a merely academic question, an eccentric philosophical family quarrel among post-foundationalists, whether ontological primacy is granted to technics or the political. This decision will influence the way in which we think about and act upon our social word. For this *political* reason, and not because there is a third and firm rational ground to rest our decision upon, the political should be posited as the an-archic principle of being, and politics as the necessary supplement to the originary de-fault of origin.

We can thus conclude that, from a perspective rooted in the Machiavellian tradition, Stiegler is half right and half wrong. On the one hand, there is a necessity for *politics* as a *techne* (as agonistics) because there is no *arche*. The endless deferral of an ultimate ground, the originary de-fault of origin, will necessarily lead to political attempts at partial grounding, at establishing less than ultimate principles. Some grounds, some principles will have to be established through strategic means. On the other hand, though, the very absence of an ultimate ground or origin – the an-archic nature of being – can be said to be an *effect* of the political if by the latter we understand, pace Laclau, antagonism as the condition of possibility *and* impossibility of society. Even though Stiegler is fully justified in claiming that politics, in its strategic mode, can only be conceived in terms of technicity, it cannot be technicity that supplements the absence of an ultimate ground. For whatever assumes, at least partially, the function of an origin or principle will have to be instituted antagonistically (against other principles); and to be instituted antagonistically means to lose the function of an origin or principle. It means to be in de-fault *by principle*: the principle of the political. What is more, Stiegler's defence of *eris* against *stasis* does not pay sufficient tribute to the paradoxical nature of the latter term. Nicole Loraux, as we will now see, pointed out that the Greek concept of *stasis* does not refer to the struggle between some among multiple factions (all of them composing the eristic unity of a *polis*, as Stiegler sustains), but refers to a binary discord which does not add up to a complementary harmony. The Greek concept of *stasis* remains fundamentally ambiguous, if not paradoxical, in signifying two contradictory moments: the agitational movement of insurrection on the one hand (of, in modern terms, 'revolution'), and, on the other, the 'static' moment in which inimical forces confront each other in a frozen and immotile state of paralysis. It is this coincidence of oppositional determinations – a paradoxical bond of conflict that simultaneously constitutes and threatens to undermine community – that comes closest to a modern ontology of antagonism.

The Stasiological Alternative: Loraux's Ontology of Civil War

The science of *stasis*, or civil war, is the variant of polemology that comes, perhaps, closest to an ontology of antagonism. We can call this science, with a term introduced by Giorgio Agamben (Agamben 2015), *stasiology*. Of course, class struggle or the 'race war' imagined in the politico-historical tradition can be readily subsumed under the category of civil war. However, *stasis*, the Greek term for civil war, has somewhat paradoxical implications that may allow to see in *stasis* a predecessor of the 'hauntological' concept of antagonism. Let us see in what respect the term anticipates a concept of the political that would direct our view to the ground and abyss of the social. Our key witness is Nicole Loraux – a collaborator of Jean-Pierre Vernant, who belonged to the circle around the Paris Centre de Recherche Comparée sur les Sociétés Anciennes – who has written what is arguably the philosophically most viable study of the concept of *stasis*. She expanded the historico-anthropological approach of the school most significantly with a series of feminist studies on the culture of ancient Athens. Her *magnum opus* on the divided city – the *cité divisée* – is dedicated to the Greek, and in particular the Athenian, idea of civil war (Loraux 2006). We should not, however, limit ourselves to reading Loraux's work as that of an ancient historian. It is a genuine work of political theory, as Loraux in fact presents a contemporary theory of the political via the medium of historical anthropology. For this purpose, she employs the difference between the terms of 'politics' and of 'the political', using the first term for political routine work, i.e. the ontic side of the political difference, while the second term denotes its ontological side: a fundamentally conflictual nature of the *polis* (155).

With regard to *this* idea of the political, Greek politics certainly does not appear to be tolerant of conflict. Quite the opposite is, in fact, true: the politics of the *polis*, as Loraux discerned, followed a basic dictate of consent and served ideas of a closed society. The hegemonic discourse of the *polis* was Platonic in the sense that Plato's *politeia* aimed to bring together all citizens into a communal whole. The ties of political society must, as Loraux stresses, be woven tightly. The politics of the *polis* was driven by the constant fear that these ties could break, and the *polis* be afflicted by the spectre of civil war:

> It is necessary to knot, bind, weave, and regulate civil peace each and every day because the threat of a tear always looms: the slightest loosening of the knot, the tiniest split in the fabric, and the rift dividing the city gapes open. This would be the end of the One, the breakup, the return to multiplicity – in short, a catastrophe. In order to banish the very thought of it, the bond of community must be made ever tighter, so that no disagreement (*diaphora*) may arise and so that no hate and *stasis* can slip through. (Loraux 2006: 94)

Beyond the agonistic façade of public competition there looms the rule of forced consensus. The Greeks felt unease at any failure to achieve unanimity in their assemblies. Majority decisions were accepted, but they never lost their touch of the illegitimate. The principle of the political – antagonism – was therefore not out in the open, but can best be reconstructed only at the hands of the negative impression it left in the political discourse. That is Loraux's very goal in her description of a political that is evacuated from itself:

> [I]n claiming that the political is evacuated from itself, I am constructing an ideality of the political that would be the missing link in existing analyses. Conflict is this missing link, this hidden dimension, which I tend, if not to identify with the political as a whole, at least to see as indispensable to any thought about its workings. (Loraux 2006: 52)

Loraux locates that negative impression which is able to reveal the political in the Greek *polis* in the bugbear of civil war – *stasis*. From the Greek point of view, *stasis*, the struggle of the City with itself, can only result in utter self-laceration. Civil war turns the closest relatives and best friends into antagonised strangers. The internal war vaults the walls of houses, cuts through family ties and shatters the barrier between the public space of politics and the private sphere of *oikos*, relinquishing any possibility of reconciliation at a later date. In this bugbear of warring *stasis*, as drawn up by Plato among others, we can recognise a polemological understanding of antagonism: a war against an (internal) enemy to be destroyed.

Nonetheless, some aspects of this war could suggest that a proto-Laclauian variant of antagonism did indeed exist in ancient Greece, namely where 'the spectre of *stasis* takes the terrifying form of a curse' (Loraux 2006: 40). This 'hauntological' figure goes beyond the image of an empirical inner-city *polemos* insofar as it brings into being a paradoxical conception of universal conflict. As Loraux explains, *stasis* is a word that entails an inner juxtaposition. On the one hand, it connotes standstill and an uprightness degenerated into rigor. In the semantic field of politics, it can therefore denote the *position* taken by a party or faction. On the other hand, *stasis* is used as a synonym of the Greek term *kinêsis*: motion. This meaning leads us to the political concept of uprising and civil war. Together, the word therefore transports the inner juxtaposition of a *static motion*. *Stasis* has always been *kinêsis stasimos*: motion in standstill. What induced the Greeks see movements of political uprising as being nothing but standstill? What made them consider convulsion and paralysis as synonymous? Loraux suggests that, in a moment of *stasis*, the *unity* of the *polis* can be experienced *through its very division*, because the division is one into two juxtaposing halves of *the same polis*. Yet, paradoxically, this 'unity in division' is precisely what arrests the motion of conflict: 'civil war is *stasis* inasmuch as the clash between two equal halves of the city erects (just like a *stele*) conflict in the meson' (106). Thereby, the civil war draws up a front 'that introduces into the city the paradoxical unity that characterizes the simultaneous insurrection of two halves of a whole' (108).

English has a term that approximates the notion of motion in standstill: the *standoff*. Countless Hollywood films are set in this empty space-time, in which neither of the sides will step into action – the entrenched hostage-taker on the one side, the police lying in wait on the other. In situations like these, suspension creates suspense. The passage to action is delayed, but remains latently present as a looming threat (the building being stormed, the entrenched person attempting to break out). The situation threatens to escalate. Robin Wagner-Pacifici, in her brilliant study *Theorizing the Standoff*, investigated a whole series of such situations, of which the uprising of the Davidian sect in the Texan town of Waco is probably the most well known. According to Wagner-Pacifici's definition, *standoffs* are 'situations of mutual and symmetrical threat, wherein the central parties face each other, literally and figuratively, across some key divide' (Wagner-Pacifici 2000: 7); finding, in her perspective from the field of cultural anthropology, that social life is usually defined by an attempt to avoid *standoff* situations. It nevertheless remains true that 'there's something of the standoff lurking, contingently, behind every social situation' (6). The concentrated accumulation of conflicts creates the danger that rule-led social processes degenerate into a kind of self-blockade. Although this is in fact an infrequent occurrence, the possibility of a *standoff* remains in attendance at all times. Or, speaking with Loraux: *stasis* continues to lurk in the background even at times of apparent social harmony. At the same time, and this constitutes the punchline of Wagner-Pacifici's research, in moments of *standoff* we become aware of the contingency of rule-led processes. The *standoff* allows us to experience *Contingency in Action* (the subtitle of her book). The concept of the *standoff* is – just like that of *stasis* – a contingency concept.

'Failed Unicity', or, the Co-Originality of Contingency and Conflict

Stasis, standoff, antagonism – these terms point, in their most fundamental dimension, to what could be described as the quasi-transcendental condition of society: the co-originality of contingency and conflict. Whenever social securities are undermined, we come to experience the fundamental contingency – the absence of an ultimate ground – of the social. As far as the social cannot remain without *any* foundation (or could only remain so within an anti-, not within a post-foundational framework), conflicts over the provisional refoundation of a dislocated ground immediately set in and, conversely, make all the more apparent the very contingency of social affairs. If antagonism, as was argued in the previous chapters, is the name that was given to the phenomenon of social negativity in the tradition of German Idealism, Early Romanticism and Marxism, we can now see why it was in this historical period, described by the German historian Reinhart Koselleck as *Sattelzeit* (a watershed period between 1750 and 1850), that the experience of social negativity gained ground and began to universalise itself (Koselleck 1972). That all social being is both contingent and conflictually established (or can be challenged through conflict) came to be the typical experience of modernity. Due to a series of interlocking historical developments, through which everything that was solid melted into thin air, social conditions were no longer considered necessary or irrevocable. Contingency and conflict, emerging from the same source, became what one would call the reflective determination of the social in its totality: where every social fact can be experienced as contingent, conflicts are bound to arise over its redesign; in turn, where every social fact can be changed by way of conflict, it is possible to experience its essential contingency. This reflective determination of all social facts as necessarily contingent and necessarily conflictual allowed for the development of a post-foundational political ontology according to which the absence of a final ground generates disputes over the partial refoundation of the social. Therefore, at the end of a long intellectual development, the notion of antagonism emerges as a fit name for the doubly reflective determination of conflict and contingency. Antagonism, as we can now define it, is the single name for the double experience of conflict and contingency in modernity. It is the key word of an ontology of the political that corresponds to our modern experience of ubiquitous conflict and contingency.

Where does this leave us with regard to (pre-modern) polemological alternatives? It is evident that the genealogical alternative of the 'war hypothesis' is ultimately indefensible. Antagonism, ontologically understood, must not be confused with an actual, if only subcutaneous, war between friends and enemies. Also the eristic alternative is modelled upon a war-like image of society, only that moments of *polemos* and of *stasis* have to be expelled from the city. Thereby, eristic theorists not only, as Mouffe has criticised, exclude the very ontological dimension of antagonism (leaving us with the ontic level of *eris* or *agonism* and the institutional procedures for domesticating antagonism), they also deprive us of a political explanation – in the sense of *the political* – of how a certain degree of unity of the City is established and, in the same stroke, subverted. In this respect, the stasiological alternative seems to have a clear advantage over other polemological approaches. The ground on which society rests, and cannot rest, is torn apart by an irresolvable tension between unity and division, movement and standstill, agitation and paralysis: two oppositional features bound together by one and the same logic. Thus, the Greek concept of *stasis* proves to be at least relatable to a modern theorisation of antagonism.[9] What is certainly comparable is the idea that *stasis* encroaches from the *polis* of citizens onto the entire city, and thereby is a form of conflict that touches upon and at the same time questions the social totality, i.e.: society. *Stasis*, in its 'paradoxical' dimension of a 'bond of conflict', emerges as the dangerous flip-side of society as a whole.

However, there remains an important difference.[10] The modern notion of antagonism goes beyond this antique notion because of its radical hauntological dimension of a negativity that is no longer expressed by way of the paralysing clash of *two* objectively given parties (which suggests an ultimately 'ontic' understanding of conflict), but in the very breakdown of any form of unicity. The antagonism that is revealed and hidden in the game of political difference is not only beyond the One, it is even beyond the Two. In the case of *stasis*, the unity of the City is thought and experienced in terms of duality – this is exactly the paradox detected by Loraux. Yet, Laclau's understanding of antagonism-as-Real diverges from any dualistic understanding of conflict. Given the 'grounding role' he attributes to negativity, he cannot, Laclau insisted, 'assert the unicity of Being' (Laclau 2004: 324), but neither can he assert pluralistic ontologies or, for instance, Badiou's ontology of the multiple:

> For me the starting point – once accepted that what is is not the One – is not multiplicity but *failed unicity*. This means that the ontological task for me is different than for Badiou: it consists in finding in every identity the traces of its contingency – i.e. the presence (in a way to be specified) of something different from itself. (Laclau 2004: 325)

In as far as the traces of contingency are also traces of conflict, the ontological task – to bring out the consequences of the Laclauian approach – is to identify the traces of antagonism in any social fact under analysis.

But let us not ignore that the same argument must apply to society as the totality of all social facts. A post-foundational approach cannot simply abandon this notion without turning into some postmodern, anti-foundational 'anything goes' approach to the social. Society, from our perspective, must not be dissolved into a number of monadic individuals or some sort of social pluralism, as liberals would propose; nor is an ontology of multiplicity – in the sense, for instance, of Hardt and Negri's 'multitude' – helpful in determining the political logic of unification. There can be no politics without the construction of chains of equivalence, and, consequently, a world of pure multiplicity would be a world devoid of politics. For this reason, we have to hold on to a notion of society as totality, even as society cannot be closed into a *full* totality. It should now be clear why, as Laclau claimed, the only form of social unicity that can be reached, and must be pursued, is failed unicity. Society will always remain an impossible (and yet necessary) object because the social world can only be totalised through the instance of an incommensurable outside which, through radical negation, constitutes and, simultaneously, subverts social order (see also *NR* 89–92; for an extensive engagement with society as an impossible, and yet necessary, object see Marchart 2013a). If the radical nature of negativity is taken seriously, then the social world is grounded on the partition between society itself and its outside, which can only be experienced in the negative. This is to say that the totality of social being, which by way of convention is entitled 'society', is instituted at the very moment at which it is negated, and thereby remains marked by the *inherently external* threat it is exposed to. To borrow a technical term from Jean-Luc Nancy: antagonism, as an outside which makes itself felt from within all social being, stands to society in a relation of *transimmanence*. And, if the principle of its grounding is identical to that of its degrounding, society will *never be fully* foundable, but neither can it remain entirely unfounded, which is precisely the reason why the play between the two sides of the political difference, politics and the political, will not come to rest. We will now turn towards the side of politics.

Part II
Thinking Politics

4 The Restless Nature of the Social: On the Micro-Conflictuality of Everyday Life

Traits of the Political

One cannot get around the unbridgeable chasm between science and thinking. 'Science does not think' – Heidegger's infamous verdict was meant to be intentionally shocking. But it was not intended as an outright attack against the sciences (Heidegger 1968: 8). While the social sciences provide us with important tools for describing and understanding our social world, they also tend to avoid thinking – which has to do with their 'ontopolitical' interpretation of the world. Even as social scientists may consider themselves defenders of positive knowledge, the baggage of metaphysics weighs heavily on their shoulders. The main remainder of metaphysical thinking within the social sciences is social objectivism: the metaphysical assumption of 'social facts' as objectively given. In his theory of populism, as we will see in the next chapter, Laclau was highly critical of group-sociological approaches that would presuppose the pre-existence of social actors. He was equally critical of approaches that would disperse political agency in the functional processes of society. Any attempt at anchoring social phenomena in a prior and grounding 'objectivity' (an objective agent, social structures, functional imperatives, economic laws, etc.) can be called metaphysical. Is there a post-foundational alternative imaginable? What can be said with certainty is that social constructionism – which is considered the main contender to objectivism – would not fare much better. A simple constructionism à la Berger and Luckmann, for instance, amounts to no more than an anti-foundationalist mirror image of social objectivism. What we have to account for when – correctly – assuming the constructed nature of social facts are the *limits* of construction (Stavrakakis 1999: 66–7). We have to account for that remainder of negativity which cannot be constructed but, in turn, operates as the source and limit of all construction.[1]

We will now start exploring some of the implications of the ontological approach elaborated so far. In Part I, I have concentrated on the ontological side of the political difference. Questions regarding its ontic side – the side of politics and of the social – have largely been neglected and still require sufficient theorisation. Otherwise it could appear as if the conceptual innovation of the political had displaced its complementary partner, politics. This imbalance has to be corrected by increasingly shifting focus towards the realm of political and social practices and institutions. If the political difference is taken seriously *as* difference, this 'ontic side', inextricably intertwined with the political, must not be ignored. What we call thinking requires a constant effort to acknowledge the play of political difference and the persistence of social negativity. It requires us to follow the traits of the political as they lead through social theory, but, as a rule, remain neglected and disavowed. Thinking means to confront these traits and to awaken objectivists from their dogmatic slumber.

In the present chapter, the Laclauian model of the social will be expounded via Edmund Husserl's early critique of scientific objectivism. Not only was Husserl's critique path-breaking, it also provides Laclau the conceptual means to differentiate between the two modes of social 'sedimentation' and political 'reactivation' – which, I propose, should be interpreted as two modes or aggregate states of a single ontological force. In other words, the social and the political have to be seen as different (if not *self-differencing*) aspects of one and the same phenomenon: antagonism.[2] By following the inner logic of Laclau's thought, his political ontology can thus be pushed to the point where it turns into an ontology of the political: a theory about the political nature of *all* things social. Being-in-the-World, as was argued from a left-Heideggerian perspective, should be understood as being-in-*the-political*.

Such a shift in perspective will allow us to extend our previous critique of polemological models of the political by proposing a more sophisticated way of affirming the ubiquitous nature of social conflictuality. There is no secret war raging 'under the surface' of an apparently pacified social formation. A post-foundational notion of ground would anyway sit uncomfortably with any metaphysics of depth. There is nothing to be discovered deep down 'under' the surface. In this regard, the social is only surface. Antagonism will always be right there, in front of our eyes, on the surface of every social institution, of every social identity, of everything that presents itself as social fact. Being transimmanent to the social, antagonism makes this 'surface' tremble from within. It does not make much difference, at the ontological level, whether we think of institutions, groups, organisations, functional systems, structures, interactions, classes or identities. Antagonism is what undermines their very objectivity. Such a claim, of course, instigates a fundamental alteration of our image of the social world. We are now forced to bring into view the contingencies and conflicts that are at the basis of the apparently most stable social formations. Not only have these formations emerged from conflicts, from which they could just as well have emerged in different forms. Exposed as they are to the withdrawal of their own foundations, they are never fully institutionalisable. Day by day they must be stabilised and reproduced anew – which would be expendable if they were not battled over. As simple as this consideration is, as far-reaching its consequences are. On an empirical level, and precisely because the ubiquitous traces of antagonism – the traits of conflict and contingency in every social identity – are not mysteriously hidden, but are only forgotten, ignored or negated, these traces can be recovered and empirically studied. The micrological approach proposed in this chapter is meant to direct our attention to the traits that are blindingly obvious. And if, on a theoretical level, a political task can be attributed to the ontology of the political, then it will be that of thwarting the appearance of apparent stability and helping the restless motions of the social – and thereby antagonism – to become visible. This is the task of *thinking antagonism*: to *reactivate* the sedimented routines of philosophy and the social sciences. It is an attempt to make science think.

Husserl's Critique of Objectivism: Institution and Reactivation of the Social

Before developing our argument as to the restless nature of the social we have to make a brief detour via Husserl. There are good reasons for this detour. Hegemony theory, as developed within the Essex School paradigm, has as one of its most central theoretical goals the development of a non-objectivist conceptualisation of the social. Apart from the philosophical resources of post-analytic philosophy and post-structuralism, it therein draws on the phenomenological tradition. As Laclau relies in his critique of objectivism on Husserl's *Crisis* (see Husserl 1962), first published in 1936 as *Die Krisis der europäischen Wissenschaften und die transzendentale Phänomenologie*, we have to revisit for a moment the Husserlian critique of objectivism. According to Husserl, all modern positive science is dominated by the idea of objectivity as originally developed in the natural sciences. Their objectivism is traced back by Husserl to its original institution (*Urstiftung*) by Galileo, by which nature came to be mathematically idealised. But such mathematisation and, eventually, technicisation of the natural sciences came at a price. As long as only the mathematically idealised entities were taken for real, it was ignored that even the ancient discipline of geometry did possess a foundation in the sensual realm of the life-world. Objectivism started by taking 'for *true being* what is *method*' (Husserl 1962: 52), while the most important questions of mankind were banished from the scientific realm: the *doxa* appertaining to the life-world was devaluated by scientific *episteme*.[3]

This critique of modern objectivism turned out to be fruitful for Laclau, who develops a notion of the social which relies on aspects of Husserl's theory of the life-world. In particular, Laclau relies on the Husserlian distinction between *original institution/reactivation* and *sedimentation* in science, only the latter is associated by Laclau with the realm of the social and the former is determined as the moment of the political:

> For Husserl the practice of any scientific discipline entails a routinization in which the results of previous scientific investigation tend to be taken for granted and reduced to a simple manipulation, with the

result that the original intuition which gave rise to them is completely forgotten. At the end of his life, Husserl saw the crisis of European science as the consequence of a growing separation between the ossified practice of the sciences and the vital primary terrain in which the original or constitutive intuitions of those sciences were rooted. The task of transcendental phenomenology consisted of recovering those original institutions. Husserl called the routinization and forgetting of origins 'sedimentation', and the recovery of the 'constitutive' activity of thought 'reactivation'. (*NR* 34)

Thus, Laclau proposes to think of the social as the terrain of sedimented practices. These practices – no matter whether they manifest themselves in rituals, in cultural identities or in functionally predetermined rules and institutions – gain objectivity because they can be anticipated on the basis of their repetitive nature. What constitutes an institution is the high degree to which operational sequences are sedimented. The life-world examples used by Laclau are telling: the post being delivered every morning, buying a cinema ticket, having dinner at a restaurant, going to a concert. In all these cases it can be anticipated, to a large degree, what is going to happen. Even though sedimented practices like these may allow for some degree of variation, we will still expect the postman to deliver the post, we will expect the concert to take place in accordance with the schedule, and we will expect to be served in the restaurant where we have reserved a table. All this might, under particular circumstances, very well not happen, yet the social would be an unliveable place without such institutionalised sequences with little variance and a high degree of predictability. This is what constitutes the sedimented layers of social objectivity.

This conception of the social as a space of sedimented practices has to be qualified in two respects. First, all social sediments can be traced back to the moment of an 'original institution' or *Urstiftung* – herein Laclau follows the Husserlian terminology. The original institution assumes a grounding function by repressing alternatives that were equally available at the moment of institution. For this reason, every sedimented practice is based on a moment of exclusion which, in the course of the sedimentation, sinks into oblivion:

> Insofar as an act of institution has been successful, a 'forgetting of the origins' tends to occur; the system of possible alternatives tends to vanish and the traces of the original contingency to fade. In this way, the instituted tends to assume the form of a mere objective presence. This is the moment of sedimentation. It is important to realize that this fading entails a concealment. If objectivity is based on exclusion, the traces of that exclusion will always be somehow present. What happens is that the sedimentation can be so complete [. . .] that the contingent nature of that influence, its *original* dimension of power, do not prove immediately visible. Objectivity is thus constituted merely as presence. (*NR* 34)

Since every sedimented layer of the social came into the world through an original moment of exclusion, social objectivity could have been constructed differently. In other words, social sedimentations are contingent, because they could have been instituted in a dissimilar form.[4] It is through processes of sedimentation that the contingent, historical and power-ridden nature of the original institution falls into oblivion. What is more, we not only tend to forget the concrete historical alternatives once available, we also forget the aspect of radical negativity at the ground of all social relations: their *antagonistic* character, as expressed by the unavoidable struggle raging over the question as to which alternative should in a given moment be ruled out.

Nonetheless, the moment of radical negativity attached to the original institution cannot be completely erased from the field of sedimentations. Social positivity will always be tainted by traces of original negativity – traces of contingency, historicity, power and conflictuality – since *total* sedimentation would be a logical impossibility. A world consisting of repetitive practices without any room for deviations would be a self-propelled machinery, a *perpetuum mobile*, not a social world. No institution can be total.[5]

This leads us to the second qualification of the above-said. For as long as a trace of original negativity remains, latently at least, within the sphere of social objectivity, it will always be possible to remind ourselves of it. This, according to the Laclauian lexicon, constitutes the moment of 'the political', when the contingent, ungrounded nature of social objectivity becomes fully visible

(*NR* 35). Laclau's term for this is *reactivation*. For Husserl, it was the philosophers' obligation – as 'functionaries of mankind' – to return to the moment of original institution and its variations within later institutions and reactivate them by questioning their sedimented forms (Husserl 1962: 72). What is to be reactivated for Laclau is not so much the original instituting moment as such. We do not have access to the concrete historical alternatives once available but now gone forever. What can be reactivated only is the contingent and antagonistic character of social sedimentations, the *groundless nature of the social through newly emerging antagonisms*: 'Reactivation does not therefore consist of returning to the original situation, but merely of rediscovering, through the emergence of new antagonisms, the contingent nature of so-called "objectivity"' (*NR* 34–5). And, for Laclau, it is not so much a matter of philosophical insight that would allow us to reactivate forgotten origins. It is a matter of politics. Only on the basis of newly emerging antagonisms can we become conscious of the original range of available alternatives: 'this rediscovery can reactivate the *historical* understanding of the original acts of institution insofar as stagnant forms that were simply considered as objectivity and taken for granted are now revealed as contingent and project that contingency to the "origins" themselves' (*NR* 35). It is through the collision of antagonistic forces that we become aware of the contingent nature of sedimented routines. Only then do we become conscious of the fact that things could be different – historically, at present, and in the future.

Time, Space and Human Geography

This argument has the potential to change the way we imagine temporality and space. Laclau argues that in order to anticipate an event within a given routine sequence the temporality of the event has to be reduced. All practices that can be predicted because of their repetitive structure are by nature *spatial*. To the extent to which differences are articulated into a relational structure they can undergo a cartographic mapping. For instance, sedimented

routines within a given institution can be 'spatialised' into an institutional organogram. If differences were to remain in an entirely
unstructured state, they would be subject to a continuous flow.
In such a psychotic universe we would be buried under an ava-
lanche of the unexpected. But as soon as they are fixated spatially,
they enter a process of sedimentation. Social objectivity emerges
from the synchronisation of differences into relational structures.
What Laclau calls 'space' is precisely the outcome of differences
arranged into a relational whole: 'As we know, spatiality means
coexistence within a structure that establishes the positive nature
of all its terms' (*NR* 69). Every form of relationality produces
space. It follows that social objectivity is by nature spatial.

Conversely, the same approach leaves us with a completely
reshuffled conception of temporality. If any 'repetition that is governed by a structural law of successions is space', then the relation
of successive temporal moments or any *cyclical* representation of
time – such as, for instance, the Polybian *anakyklosis* of regime
forms – would also be spatial (*NR* 41–2). As said, sedimentation
emerges from the repetition of an original moment of institution;
and repetition creates space. However, Laclau, an attentive reader
of Derrida, is very well aware of the fact that mere repetition of the
identical is quite simply impossible (Derrida 1988).[6] Laclau aims at
this idea with his conception of *dislocation* – a term that refers to
the Latin *locus*, and thus to a place within a topographical structure that has been pushed 'out of place'. Seen from the perspective
of the sedimented structures of the social, dislocation is perceived
as an event that cannot be integrated into the horizon of expec-
tations: it is something we did not expect and which therefore
threatens the sedimented routines and processes of social institutions. To the extent that the social in its sedimented state is spatial, this event must be ontologically different from space – which
leads Laclau to his definition of dislocation as the true form of
temporality. Only an event which is of essentially temporal nature
will be able to dislocate the spatial arrangements of the social.
Conversely, the temporal aspect of the event will get eliminated
to the extent to which it is inscribed into the repetitive processes
of sedimentation. Laclau exemplifies this point with the *fort/da*

game Freud (1999: 12–13) observed with a little child who aimed to get to grips with the absence of his mother through inventing a repetitive game for himself. In this way repetition allowed the child to inscribe absence into the space of presence (Laclau 1990: 41).[7] The social can thus be defined as a relationally articulated spatial structure whose original institution resulted from an act of radical negativity (i.e. antagonism) which later became forgotten, but in any moment can be reactivated through the experience of dislocation, i.e. time.

This theory was met with fierce criticism by human geographers.[8] In particular, Laclau was charged by Doreen Massey with holding onto an outmoded notion of space. In the 1960s and 1970s, as Massey recounts, spatial theories in human geography underwent the same constructivist turn that other social sciences had experienced. The canonical slogan of the time was that space had to be conceived as socially constructed. It is not an unchanging substance or foundation on which society rests; rather, the specific structure of space is taken to be the result of social, economic and political processes – a perspective nicely captured by Timothy Luke: '[s]pace does not exist as such; it too must be fabricated continuously in the production and reproduction of society' (Luke 1996: 120). However, from the 1980s onwards, this approach was radicalised to the point of nearly being inverted. Not only is space now seen as socially constructed, the general understanding is, inversely, that the social sphere is also *spatially constructed*. It is now claimed, according to Massey, that the spatial institution of the social sphere affects the way in which society works, as the latter will continuously be transformed through processes of spatialisation. While in the earlier account space was still conceptualised as an entirely passive entity, i.e. as the outcome of processes of social construction, in today's view it is space itself which assumes the role of a social agent. As Massey claims in *For Space* (Massey 2005), space must be envisaged as something open, multiple, and heterogeneous by nature; not only is it constantly being made and remade, there is also a certain disruptive quality to it. Only in a second step is this disrupting and constantly changing force of space tamed and ossified, for

95

instance, through mappings and other forms of representation. Laclau is taken to task by Massey for remaining within the first paradigm, thus misconstruing space as a static realm – the reason being that Laclau allegedly positions the category of space in binary opposition vis-à-vis the category of time, thereby reproducing an old philosophical narrative according to which it is temporality that plays the part of agency, not space.

The Social as a Mode of the Political

This critique would be entirely justified if only Laclau held such a dualistic view. To assume so means to ignore the inner logic of his argument. Of course, given Laclau's definition of dislocation as temporal, it may seem at first sight that Massey was correct in her criticism of Laclau's 'passive' conception of space. But what if space and time were not conceived as binary opposites by Laclau? In fact, their relation is much more complex and I am prepared to defend the following interpretation of Laclau's spatial theory: contrary to the simplistic picture of a binarism of space/time, passivity/activity, or closedness/openness, we have to come to an understanding of time and space as entirely intertwined, as indeed *the same thing in a different mode*. And what, exactly, is it that can appear in the two different modes of time and space? I have hinted at it already. I submit that it is precisely what we have sought to think all along as antagonism. Certainly, Laclau himself does not go that far in his spatial theory, yet I would claim that it follows from his assumptions if we are prepared to work out their radical consequences. For if antagonism lies at the very moment of original institution of sedimented social practices, then it cannot be the opposite of the latter. As their instituting moment it remains present in a state of oblivion and, as Laclau showed, can be reactivated at any time. For this reason, the social is antagonistic by nature. Indeed, 'the social' is but a name for antagonism *in a 'sleeping mode'*. On an experiential level we become conscious of this fact whenever antagonisms are reactivated. In other words, there exists no dichotomy between sedimentation and institution/reactivation, between social construction and political dislocation, between space and time. Every attempt at constructing and reconstructing the social will necessarily produce effects of dislocation – because in any case it will to some extent have to rely on the articulation of antagonistic frontiers.[9]

How could it be otherwise – given the underlying Heideggerianism of Laclau's theory? Radical negativity, it was claimed in Chapter 2, is always mediated *through difference*. It never appears as such, but only within the ontic field of the social. The impression of a simple dualism between space and time is evidently false.[10] Space and time, the social and the political, are not two separate spheres. We have to think of them as two modes of one and the same instance: antagonism, through which the spatial and the temporal, in their respective degree of spatialisation/temporalisation, are modulated. In terms of what seems to function as a 'time/space modulator', antagonism not only (de)grounds sedimented social routines and institutions but, what is more, presents itself in the illusory shape of (seemingly) pacified and frozen social relations.

This idea is less eccentric than it may seem. We must not forget that, from a Marxist perspective, what appears as the absence of class struggle is but a particular stage of class struggle (indicating the hegemonic dominance of the bourgeoisie). Similarly, what in the eyes of a Marxist of the 'Ramsgate School' appears as the absence of the political is merely a particular mode of the political: the mode of socially sedimented antagonism – but nonetheless antagonism. The political, to be sure, is not the opposite of the social. But neither is the social simply the product, effect or outcome of an instituting moment that later became entirely separated from its initial ground. Massey is right, it would be misguided to conceive of the social in metaphysical terms as a pre-given passive 'matter' that was actively formed by the political. But she is only right because there is not much difference between the social and the political – except their difference *as* difference. The social, I have proposed, has to be envisaged as nothing other than the political in an *instituted mode*.[11] It is the political itself perceived – i.e. experienced – from a different angle. This, perhaps, counter-intuitive claim directly ensues, without being developed by Laclau himself, from his 'primacy of the political' thesis:

Any advance in the understanding of present-day social struggles depends on inverting the relations of priority which the last century and a half's social thought had established between the social and the political. This tendency had been characterized, in general terms, by what we may term the systematic absorption of the political by the social. The political became either a superstructure, or a regional sector of the social, dominated and explained according to the objective laws of the latter. Nowadays, we have started to move in the opposite direction: towards a growing understanding of the eminently political character of any social identity. To use Husserlian terminology: if the social is established through the *sedimentation* of the political, through the 'forgetting of origins', the *reactivation* of the original meaning of the social consists in showing its political essence. (*NR* 160)

If the passage is read attentively, it becomes evident that the political, rather than being simply the opposite of the social (in the sense of a metaphysical dualism), is what grounds and ungrounds social relations. But this function does not issue from the transcendent position of an unmoved mover. If there is such a thing as a 'political essence' of the social, then the political, given that every social phenomenon is subject to a constant play between ground and abyss, must be conceived as *transimmanent* to the social. Differentialised negativity is transimmanent negativity; the radical outside of a given identity only makes itself felt within this identity.

Zooming into the Micrological, or, How to Make Science Think

It could be argued that such a conception of antagonism remains abstract philosophy and cannot possibly be translated into empirical research. I do not think so. The ontology of the political may provide us with an outlook that should influence empirical research. As soon as the essentially antagonistic nature of social space is taken seriously, any given social topography starts to appear in a strongly political light, and one will have to study the contingent, historical and power-ridden moments of its originary institution. What is more, our view will shift towards the dislocatory struggles that are constantly taking place around the shaping and reshaping of the social. In this sense, the category of antagonism – in its two modes of the social and the political (i.e. in terms of a constant play between the instituted and the instituting side of radical negativity) – may prove to be as much of philosophical as of analytical value. Furthermore, it will produce something of the order of an 'estrangement effect' with regard to social life. In empirical research we must always ask: How can the political nature of a given social fact be reactivated? How can a sense of the contingency and conflictuality of what appears as solid and unalterable be recovered? In other words, how can we, in our research practice, *think* antagonism? The ontology of the political, as I propose to conceive it, thus initiates a change in perception that reaches down to the micrological level of the social. It has effects on our notion of even the most humble and private routine acts. These acts too have to be conceived as an expression of the political, but the political in another 'mode': the mode of the social. This understanding constitutes a fundamental shift in our view of the social world.

Perceived through the lens of our ontology, relations of power and force appear to permeate the entire social world. To this day, most social scientists will seethe at such a statement. If everything is political, runs the counter-argument, then nothing is political. This counter-argument misses the ontological status of the concept of the political. Of course, not everything is political in the sense of the social subsystem of politics. However, there is no social relationship that is not at the same time also a relationship of conflict, power and exclusion. This insight emerges not only from Laclau's thoughts, of course. Foucault too sees a presence of the political, even if he does not call it by this name, creeping even into the smallest crevices of the social. He speaks of thousandfold minor conflicts between the sexes, between parents and children, between those who are imputed to have knowledge and the others. The social therefore presents itself as a large swarm of tactical micro-actions. In this, Foucault argued ontologically – even if that is hardly reconcilable with the declared positivism and nominalism of his approach. Countless places in Foucault's writings imply, as we have seen, the primacy of the struggle. In *Discipline and Punish*, the microphysics of power is based on the model of an everlasting battle (Foucault 1977: 308; Chevallier 2004). For the historico-political discourse, which Foucault himself philandered with for a while, war is posited as a condition for the existence of society. At the basis of might: the fight.

Obviously, from the viewpoint of the post-foundational ontology, as it has been advanced here, this fundamental struggle does not go by the name of 'war' or 'battle', as in the genealogical Foucault, but by the name 'antagonism'. Foucault's polemology reveals itself to constitute a short-circuit, an inadmissible 'ontisation' of antagonism. Foucault will not permit himself to leap from his polemology to an ontological condition of antagonism (which has nothing to do, as I have argued, with the warring relationship between friend and foe). He is hindered both by his blanket rejection of the negativistic tradition of Hegel and Marx and by his own nominalism, sometimes bordering on social objectivism, which prevents him from differentiating between an ontic and an ontological dimension of the social. Yet, in its consequences, his suggestion is not so far removed from the 'Ramsgate School'. From Marx's point of view, class struggle institutionally settles not only in factories, but in all institutional sediments. The police, the law, the family, the opera, the social security, the church, the university, the football club – all of that *is* class struggle. The only difference is that from a post-Marxist perspective, all of these institutions consist *not only* of the struggle between 'classes' but equally importantly also of the struggles for the equality of the genders or the inclusion or exclusion of migrants, etc. The removal of social struggles from the main agent of class leads to a far-reaching politicisation of social structures.

Against Micro-Politics: The Absolute Restlessness of the Negative

There is one aspect to be adopted from Foucault, however: the sense for the micrological, which Marxists tend to miss (exceptions like Adorno, Bloch and Benjamin are a confirmation of the rule). Laclau also largely lacks a micrological sensorium. What is required is a sense for the most minimal restlessness in the social, the most minute conflicts and contingencies. Those who have such a sense see the social begin to flicker before their very eyes, hear it buzz in their ears and feel it wobble underneath their feet. The hauntological work of the present-absent instance of antagonism can be recognised by the high-frequency oscillation of conditions that, up to this point, had been considered stable. The social begins to oscillate as soon as it is touched by antagonism. It oscillates when radical negativity is set in motion by the play of difference. This phenomenon is still far removed from politics in the stricter sense (even from what we will call minimal politics). It does not matter whether we find ourselves on the beach with Marx, outside the asylums and prisons with Foucault or at the museum with Bourdieu – there is always some struggle to watch, which will cast unease over even the greatest idyll. The political expresses itself, after all, not only in the large upheavals but also in the secret conflictuality of daily life – the minor and barely visible tectonic shifts of social sediments.

The conventional term of 'micro-politics' is, as will be argued in the subsequent chapters, a misnomer, for what we are dealing with at this micrological level of social vibrations, effectuated by antagonism, has nothing to do yet with 'politics' in any meaningful sense. It is the most minimal form of appearance of *the political*. And as the hauntological labour of the negative cannot easily be entered on a micro/macro scale, one should perhaps abandon the qualification 'micro' altogether or only retain it for heuristic reasons. From the vantage point of this 'hauntology' of the political, it would be wrong to order antagonisms by their size. If the distortion of the relational space of the social is a phenomenic form of appearance of antagonism, then the question of scale is not important. Antagonism, as an ontological concept, is beyond the scalable. Its modulations reach from revolution to the fight over housework, from the general strike to skiving off.[12] Antagonism – as opposed to ontic politics – cannot be grasped by a sociological differentiation into micro and macro. It is not quantifiable; it is merely possible to experience its intensity – or more precisely: experience it *as* intensity.

This differential play of negativity, as it occurs throughout the social on diverse levels of intensity, is nicely captured by Hegel's notion of 'the absolute restlessness of becoming' (Hegel [1813] 1999: 384). This phrase, when read with and against Hegel, is able to appropriately capture the flickering nature of social phenomena. Adorno had recognised in what he called the *non-identical* the very 'restlessness' of identity, 'that Hegel calls becoming: it shudders within itself' (Adorno 1975: 160). In a significant study, Jean-Luc Nancy (2002) pointed out in particular the micrological dimension of this restlessness, which is nothing other than the 'restlessness of the negative'.[13] Thus, Hegel is portrayed by Nancy as a post-foundationalist:

> The Hegelian *ground* is neither fundament nor foundation, neither groundwork nor substrate. It is the depth in which one is submerged, into which one sinks and goes to the bottom. More precisely, this ground founds only to the extent that it sinks in itself: for foundation should be a hollowing out. Thus thought is not grasped in its depth without being such a hollowing out. Still further: this hollowing neither attains nor brings to light a secure groundwork. It hollows out the point of passage, and the point itself is such a hollowing out: work of the negative, but right at the surface. (Nancy 2002: 15)

Following this reading of Hegel, the labour of the negative would be the labour of splitting identity or, rather, differentiating it from itself, thus undermining every first principle and every firm ground, but by doing so enabling, even necessitating, further regrounding. The Marxian idea of antagonism as a social blockade between the forces and the relations of production is then, from this point of view, but an imaginary exaggeration of those upheavals that grasp every order, no matter how well grounded, always and everywhere, in all degrees of intensity. The model to think negativity is not, then, the grand revolutionary breach, but the minute, hardly perceptible oscillation of social relationships: this latter is the norm, and a revolution is merely an occasional peak of amplitude. The term Nancy uses for this hardly perceptible work of the negative is *trembling*: 'Negativity makes all determinateness tremble, all being-all-to-itself: it injects with a shudder and an unsettling agitation' (Nancy 2002: 45). What appears stable – the sediments of the social – in actual fact trembles. It is the force of antagonism, which – in the phenomenic appearance of absolute restlessness – drives the unstoppable process of constitution and destitution of the social. The post-Marxist ontology of radical negativity would then prove to be, *because* of its Hegelian inheritance, a hauntology of micro-conflictuality: of an antagonism that does not always make the petrified conditions dance, but always tremble.

Towards an Affectology of Antagonism

Every society experiences moments when forgotten struggles, rendered unthinkable by a given hegemonic formation, make themselves felt in whatever displaced way. As soon as the social ground under our feet starts trembling, we tremble with it. What Nancy, via Hegel, calls 'trembling' is what, in the Laclauian lexicon, is called dislocation. It is important to understand, however, that a political conception of dislocation is not simply deconstructive. Laclau does not just provide us with another term for the endless deferral of *différance*. For Laclau dislocation, in its political mode, retains an intrinsic connection to antagonism: 'every identity is dislocated insofar as it depends on an outside which both denies that identity and provides its condition of possibility at the same time' (*NR* 39). What this quote makes clear once again – a conclusion largely disavowed by Laclau himself – is that antagonism is *primary* with regard to dislocation as the latter clearly derives from the antagonistic outside to a given identity. This is also where our ontology of the political departs from a simple political ontology. Precisely because the instance of antagonism is effective only as a *threat* to social practices, it also dislocates the order of the social, and dislocation therefore must be seen as a function of antagonisation, not the other way around. Any social order emerges from a necessary passage through radical negativity. But this passage will, by necessity, make the social tremble. The problem, from an epistemological perspective, is: How can we know this? But the question is ill-posed. Of course, we cannot 'know' it in the sense of positive knowledge gained by way of, say, statistically measuring the degree of dislocation of a given order. That would obviously be nonsensical. Yet we haven't made the detour through phenomenology without good reason. In our everyday life we *do* know about the trembling of the social – not through conscious cognition, but in an experiential way.

So, even if we cannot gather positive knowledge about the ontological register of antagonism, we do *experience* its dislocatory effects within the ontic world of being that surrounds us. As a rule, experiences of this kind are made pre-consciously. In fact, we encounter the effects of antagonism every day in our experiences of subordination, exploitation, exclusion or precarisation, but also of withdrawal, stubborn subversion and silent resistance. In any pre-, or rather: proto-political confrontation – with the boss, with the police, with the family – we can experience, without necessarily being consciously aware of it, that the structure of our life-world is grounded on and modified by struggles. Such an encounter with the very limits of the social – whether it takes place in micro-conflicts or in the sedimented institutional guise of, for example, the glass ceilings we encounter on our professional trajectory or the manifold forms of structural exclusion – can manifest itself in a number of affects. These include resentment, jealousy, panic, anger, fear, aggression, resignation, despair, pride, arrogance, stubbornness, defiance, excitement, and so on. A doctrine of affects of the political – a political affectology – has, as far as I am aware, not yet been written: attempts to do so within the tradition of social phenomenology have had only limited success.[14] A combination of the resources provided by the late Foucault, the Spinozist tradition of political theory (for a Spinozist theory of politics as *ars affectandi* see Lordon 2016, 2013) and post-Marxism could, however, serve as a starting point, but is certainly beyond the reach of the present investigation.

Let us merely note that antagonism is experienced in the affective shocks we feel as a result of us, as it were, hitting the limit of the social. Such an encounter with the instance of radical negativity manifests itself in a multitude of bodily affects of all kinds. Even with ears and eyes most firmly shut, the body will register the repercussion and produce an effect of pre-conscious self-reflection. Something of the order of an affective 'self' emerges whenever the effects of antagonism inscribe themselves into the perceiving body regardless of whether experiences are made consciously or not. The self we are talking of here is not the subject of a lack, meaning the gap in the social which Lacanian social theories speak of and, in Laclau, depicts a structural condition for the development of new social and political identities (we will return to this kind of subject in Chapter 6). It also has little to do with a process of political identification as outlined by Laclau, or even with technologies of governmental self-subjectivisation or antique practices of the self as described by Foucault. In this sense, it is utterly a-subjective. When a self interiorises itself, it does so because it is *inflected by antagonism*[15] – the 'outside' of the social which, from a post-Marxist perspective, is constantly folded into the social. The social space of relations and sedimentations institutes itself only in the constant folds of inside and outside, i.e. in the infinitesimal interleaving of totality and negativity. In other words, the social texture consists of the oscillation between society, as an impossible totality or 'failed unicity', and antagonism as that which both unites and dislocates the social.

An affectology of the self not only would have to cope with the topological model of the fold (the affective folding inwards of the self; see Deleuze 1992), but must also be able to phenomenologically capture the micrological flickering and trembling of the self. Hegel's famous 'absolute restlessness of becoming' was translated by Nancy into the micrological, and we in turn must translate Nancy into the political. From the perspective of an ontology of the political, if the latter is to explain our very being-in-the-World as a being-in-the-political, it is the real and a-subjective force of antagonism, which – in the form of an *absolute restlessness of becoming* – drives the unstoppable process of constitution and destitution of the social as much as the folding of its limits into a self. Such a hauntology of antagonism would explain not only the flickering and eerie appearance of a social space peopled by ghosts of struggles past and present. It would also explain *our own trembling* as soon as we are touched by antagonism and experience the eeriness of this space ourselves. Because '[t]he self has its unity in trembling of itself' (Nancy 2002: 44), in the passive action of an 'act of being affected':

The self trembles at being touched, awakened, roused; it trembles as much at the feeling of its fragility as in the desire for its freedom. Its emotion is its own, and its trembling is a trembling of *itself* because it is thus that it comes to itself – thus that it comes and it goes away, that it comes in the same way as it goes: trembling. (Nancy 2002: 44)[16]

The Trembling Mob

Antagonism sends out shock waves that capture every single body, albeit with differing force. It is certainly true that the limits of the social are not always experienced in the form of open pro-test and revolt, but sometimes they are. Let us therefore not for-get, amid the political affectology of the self, the older meaning of restless motion: *turmoil* and *insurgence*. Social 'movements' carry it in their name until now. In French, the Latin word for movement, *motus*, is still there in *émeute*, meaning insurgence or popular uprising; it is also there in the German *Meute* and *Meuterei* (Sardinha 2010: 124–5), in the 'mutiny'; and it is there in the 'mob' (from Latin *mobile*). On the ontological plane of affec-tology, 'a mob' is just any movement of intensified and synchro-nised trembling. An ontology of the political must retain a sense of such collective restlessness. For what needs to be explained is not only the enfolding of antagonism into the social, but also the *unfolding* of the social into an antagonism. By unfolding, I mean nothing other than the politicisation of a social situation. Here, political and social movements appear as catalysts. They bring to light struggles that are subdued or subconsciously taking place in the course of daily life – for example, between the sexes, between the classes, between majorities and minorities – and make it pos-sible to transform them into politics. Contingency and conflictual-ity are thus experienced at the hands of the struggles brought to light by social movements. The same is true for the self. When the outside of society – antagonism – is folded into our bodies in the form of the self, then it can also be *unfolded* back into the social by way of politics. That presupposes, of course, the collectivisation of those shocks and affects which hit every singular body. Typically, this happens in protest. Protests do not emerge from discursive calls in the vein of 'Time for Outrage!' Affects, in contrast to mere political emotions, cannot be motivated by discursive interpellation (Massumi 2015). After all, they are caused by nothing but the encounter with antagonism, which – as an instance of a society's outside – does not belong to the register of the Symbolic.[17] It does not matter how many calls are published for a mass of bodies to join a demonstration – and the medium of the street protest is, after all, the human body (Butler 2015) – the mere issue of a call will not suffice. The absent cause of the protest is not the call, but the eruption of an antagonism, which cannot be voluntaristically forced nor verbally conjured up.

Of course, affects can collectivise in a range of forms. They can cause an amalgamation into a single fascist collective body or into marauding gangs. They can also compact in the 'multitude' of agglomerated individuals or in liberal-democratic protest communities. There is just as little to be said of the size of protests. A hunger strike of the few can be as important a form of protest as a demonstration by hundreds of thousands (see Chapter 8). In all cases, however, collectivisation means the linking and reinforcement of singular affects. The amplitude of the 'trembling' of individuals is heightened and synchronised into a movement – *a mob*. For this effect of reinforcement to occur, the *mutual* affectation of the protesting bodies is vital. That is one of the reasons why (unlike a putsch or a *coup d'état*) upheavals, revolts and revolutions – all these fluctuating movements on the undulating surface of the social – take place in the public sphere and presuppose the physical co-presence of protesting bodies.[18]

An order's ability for consent and consensus – and every hegemonic order is discursive and somatic at the same time – shatters not least due to the antagonised bodies of its subjects. Of course, the conditions need to be given. Hegemony needs to have been lost already, even if nobody noticed. Only then can insurrections and revolutions – one may think of the fall of the Iron Curtain or the Arab Spring – gather support and attract the masses. The extent to which a hegemonic formation is already fractured (or is reforming itself) cannot, however, be predetermined by scientific means. Of course, to the surprise of those who may want to accuse us of presenting an over-politicised metaphysics of antagonism, it must be said that, even though the ontological instance of antagonism escapes scientific measurement, the micro-conflicts of everyday life can indeed be studied empirically with the methods of, for instance, ethno-methodology or conversation analysis; and so can social movements be empirically studied. It is even possible, as we will see in the following chapter, to lay out the 'onto-logic' of political mobilisation. But the test is the protest. The ontology of the political, which has here been developed, is not meant to provide a scientific foundation for political practice. It is meant to provide a political basis. It therefore places a bet on the unstoppable movement of the social, which is put into motion by its own outside – an outside that appears in a manner of prism-like diffusion: the flickering of antagonism. We will now leave the microphysics of the political behind and turn to Laclau's theory of populism. Because it is in his theory of populism where we can find a general theory of *protestation*.

5 Politics and the Popular: Protest and Culture in Laclau's Theory of Populism

The Political Ontology of Peronism

Every theory that purports to explain a general field of phenomena will nevertheless pass through a particular historical experience. In the case of Ernesto Laclau's political ontology, it is the Argentinian experience of Peronism which forms the background against which Laclau's whole thinking of the political, including his theorisation of antagonism and of populism, emerged. As an activist of the Argentinian Socialist Party and the Peronist student movement, and later as a member of the political leadership of the Socialist Party of the National Left, Laclau was deeply involved in the Peronist struggle. Therefore, it should not come as surprise that with his hugely influential book *On Populist Reason*, published in 2005, Laclau took up theoretically the question of populism, thus returning full circle, after nearly thirty years, to his first book-length publication *Politics and Ideology in Marxist Theory* (Laclau 1977) with which he had introduced himself as one of the foremost theorists of populism. Yet, *On Populist Reason* is not simply a book on populism if by the latter we understand a more or less marginal political phenomenon; rather, the logic of populism, unravelled by Laclau, holds the key to any correct understanding of politics *as such*. The Kantian allusion of his title, 'On Populist Reason', seems to be hinting at the wider theoretical implications of populism. In fact, it can be assumed, given the hidden Kantianism of his title, that what Laclau sets out to develop is not simply an empirical account of current or historical populist movements, but a quasi-transcendental inquiry into the *conditions of possibility* of populism and, as he holds in his first sentence, of 'the nature and logics of the formation of collective identities' at large (*PR* 9). For this reason, Laclau's book on populism can be expected to provide important insights for the study not only of populism, but of politics in general, particularly of protest politics.[1] Seen from this perspective, *On Populist Reason* has to be read as a contribution to a political and cultural theory of mobilisation, not only to the study of populism in the narrow sense. As the 'royal road' to an understanding of politics at large, the discussion of populism – or the logic of populist articulation – will allow me, after having expanded on the previous chapter's discussion of social sedimentation and institutionalisation, to make good on the promise to shift focus towards the ontic side of the political difference: the side of politics.

If the social, as we have seen, is defined as the field of sedimented differences, then Laclau goes a significant step beyond the Saussurian notion of differences by assuming the fundamental 'brokenness' of that sphere. From Laclau's post-foundational perspective, the groundless nature of every socio-cultural identity implies that no identity will ever be fully enclosed in itself due to the effects of antagonism. For the same reason, a potential space for politics opens up right at the heart of the social: politics can thus be understood as the constant – yet ultimately unsuccessful – attempt at *regrounding* an identity fundamentally characterised by lack, dislocation and incompleteness. It is at this 'ontological' level of Laclau's theory where the need for political articulation is explained as a necessary precondition of society. But, how exactly, on the ontic level, do we have to imagine the reactivation of the social by the political *through politics*? Laclau's theory of populism could hold the key to a better understanding of the functioning of the political process of reactivation. I submit, taking as my starting point the Laclauian theory of political articulation, that *any* politics in the strict sense of the term (i.e. any practice that is touched by the political) will have to undergo a moment of *protestation*. Politics, at the moment of reactivation when social sedimentations are dislocated by the political, is, in its essence, *protest politics*. In a first step I will substantiate this claim by exploring the

Laclauian conceptions of political articulation and of its minimal unit, the demand. In a second step I will turn to theories of micro-politics, especially in the Birmingham Cultural Studies tradition, which will prepare the terrain for an alternative theory of *minimal politics* that will be presented in the subsequent chapter.

The Demand: The Elementary Unit of Politics

Laclau's theory of populism helps to shed light not only on all forms of populist mobilisation, but also on the very logic through which the social becomes dis- and re-articulated by politics. So let us consider the precise meaning of the concept of 'articulation' – a key term in Laclau's 'onto-logic' of hegemony and of post-foundational discourse analysis (Marttila 2015).[2] According to Stuart Hall's famous analogy, articulation can be compared to the English notion of an 'articulated lorry', where 'the front (cab) and back (trailer) can, but need not necessarily, be connected to one another' (Hall 1996a: 141). What is stressed by Hall is the contingent nature of any articulated unity, as his aim is to break with any form of class essentialism or economic reductionism that would derive the unity of a political subject from the subject's position within the relations of production.[3] However, Stuart Hall's analogy of the articulated lorry might be misleading as it does not exclude the possibility of imagining an articulated unity of elements that exist in advance of their articulation (in the same way in which the cab and the trailer already exist *as* cab and *as* trailer and only later may or may not get articulated into a lorry). When we speak about discourse, or the discursive unity of any cultural-political identity or subject, the case is different because every element we encounter will always already be the outcome of an articulatory process. And, what is even more important, the nature of the articulated elements will be significantly altered in the process of their articulation. The reason for this is easily understood: if a cultural-political identity is the result of the linking up of different elements, then the identity of these elements will not remain unaltered by the process of articulation. By entering a political alliance, for instance, everyone will have to adjust his or her own identity to some degree if the alliance is to be upheld. The political identity of the members of an alliance will thus be modified. They will not be able to encapsulate themselves within a purely particularistic state of 'interest politics' – in what Gramsci would have called the *corporative stage* – but will have to broaden their political outlook in order to accommodate some of the demands and ideas of their allies.

So, one of the most radical implications of a Laclauian theory of articulation is easily overlooked if one starts with a model of prefabricated 'trucks' and 'lorries'. Given the premises of this theory, the identity of a social agent or subject, be it the agent's cultural identity or political identity, can only be the *result* and not the source of an articulatory effort. Discourse is a process without a voluntarist subject pulling the strings behind the articulation process.[4] This argument puts into question the whole notion of group as the starting point of analysis. Laclau makes it sufficiently clear that to start with the group in an analysis of populism would be deeply flawed because, in this case, a fundamental reality beyond or before the process of discursive articulation is assumed. So we are confronted, right from the outset of any analysis, with a paradigmatic decision:

> A first decision has to be taken. What is our minimal unit of analysis going to be? Everything turns around the answer to this question. We can decide to take as our minimal unit the group as such, in which case we are going to see populism as the ideology or the type of mobilization of an *already* constituted group – that is, as the expression (the epiphenomenon) of a social reality different from itself; or we can see populism as one way of constituting the very unity of the group. (*PR* 72–3)

The alternative is clear: in the first case, the group will be the starting point of the analysis, in the second the group will be the outcome of a process of discursive articulation; and it goes without saying that Laclau opts for the second alternative which is the only one consistent with a post-foundational approach in discourse theory. It is through the discursive articulation of protest that the identity of the protesters is articulated in the first place. Yet this account still leaves unanswered the question as to the minimal unit of political discourse. If it is not the group, what is it? Here, Laclau provided in his later work on populism what must be considered one of the most significant advances since *Hegemony and Socialist Strategy*. What he proposes to do is 'to split the unity of the *group* into smaller unities' that he calls *demands*, while, conversely, the unity of the group turns out to be 'the result of an articulation of demands' (*PR* 9). In order to better understand this concept of demand as the minimal unit of analysis, a more extensive quotation from Laclau's book is in order – a passage crucial for any analysis not only of populism in the narrow sense but also of all forms of protest discourse:

> So what are these smaller units from which our analysis has to start? Our guiding thread will be the category of 'demand' as the elementary form in the building up of the social link. The word 'demand' is ambiguous in English: it has, on the one hand, the meaning of *request* and, on the other, the more active meaning of *imposing* a request – a claim – on somebody else (as in 'demanding an explanation'). (Laclau 2005b: 35)

Having laid out this distinction between (weak) request and (strong) demand, Laclau proceeds with the following example:

> [A] group of people living in a certain neighbourhood want a bus route introduced to transport them from their places of residence to the area in which most of them work. Let us suppose that they approach the city hall with that request and the request is satisfied. We have here the following set of structural features: 1) a social need adopts the form of a *request* – i.e. it is not satisfied through self-management but through the appeal to another instance which has the power of decision; 2) the very fact that a request takes place shows that the decisory power of the higher instance is not put into question at all – so we are fully within our first meaning of the term demand; 3) the demand is a punctual demand, closed in itself – it is not the tip of an iceberg or the symbol of a large variety of unformulated social demands. If we put these three features together we can formulate the following important conclusion: requests of this type, in which demands are punctual or individually satisfied, do not construct any chasm or frontier within the social. On the contrary, social actors are accepting, as a non-verbalised assumption of the whole process, the legitimacy of each of its instances: nobody puts into question either

> the right to present the requests or the right of the decisory instance to take the decision. [. . .] They presuppose that there is no social division and that any legitimate demand can be satisfied in a non-antagonistic, administrative way. (Laclau 2005b: 36)

Let me briefly comment on this first part of the example given by Laclau. We are still at a stage here where a certain claim (in this case for public transportation) does not yet truly amount to a demand in the strong sense of the term, but remains at the level of request. In this respect, we are stuck in the second stage of a three-stage process: Step (1) consists in some social need emerging out of the dislocation of a certain social or cultural identity (the identity of a, say, neighbourhood is put into question to some degree and due to the emerging lack of identity a certain need to fill the lack emerges). (2) A request is made to an outside power, the City Hall for instance, considered to be a legitimate instance for appeals of this kind. This is the stage of request. Whether we move to stage (3), the stage of demand in the strict sense, depends on whether the request will be met by the City Hall or not. If it is met, it is most likely that everything ends here until another lack is experienced, so that the request will not be transformed into a demand. But what if the request cannot be accommodated by the higher instance? As Laclau explains:

> Let us suppose that the request is rejected. A situation of social frustration will, no doubt, derive from the decision. But if it is only *one* demand that is not satisfied, that will not alter the situation substantially. If, however, for whatever reason, the variety of demands that do not find satisfaction is very large, that multiple frustration will trigger social logics of an entirely different kind. If, for instance, the group of people in that area who have been frustrated in their request for better transportation find that their neighbours are equally unsatisfied in their claims at the levels of security, water supply, housing, schooling, and so on, some kind of solidarity will arise between them all: all will share the fact that their demands remain unsatisfied. That is, the demands share a *negative* dimension beyond their positive differential nature. (Laclau 2005b: 36–7)

These reflections are crucial for a full understanding of the moment of protestation at the ground of all reactivatory politics. A transformation has to take place of a frustrated pre-political request into a political demand. This demand might, under the right circumstances, link up with other unsatisfied demands. And what all these demands will have in common is not a common substance; in fact, they do not necessarily have to have *anything* in common at the level of their claims' positive content. And still, they will have to have 'something' in common, even as this 'something' must be of an entirely negative nature: it is that outside instance which is considered to be responsible for the shared feeling of frustration. Now, as I said before, in order for an alliance between these demands to be established, they will have to be linked up somehow: and here the logic of hegemonic articulation enters the picture. As such, the diverse demands for transportation, schooling, etc. constitute a set of differences where every differential position has a positive content. In the moment of articulation, these differences have to be arranged or articulated into a relation of equivalence. Consequently, the logic of equivalence is defined by Laclau as:

> [O]ne in which all the demands, in spite of their differential character, tend to re-aggregate themselves, forming what we will call an *equivalential chain*. This means that each individual demand is constitutively split: on the one hand it is its own particularised self; on the other it points, through equivalential links, to the totality of other demands. (Laclau 2005b: 37)

Such a chain of equivalence is only effectuated vis-à-vis a common negative outside, a moment of pure negativity to which the antagonistic relation of equivalence gives expression. And in order to express, or rather, *represent* the totality of a chain (the unity of the protest movement), a common element will have to be established, a particular demand – defined by Laclau as an *empty signifier* – will therefore take up the role of universal representation. Yet this demand will be torn apart as well. On the one hand, it will retain some of its particular aspects (it will be one element in the chain); on the other hand, it will have to incarnate the whole of the chain. Let us think of the slogan 'Free Nelson Mandela' at the time of the South African apartheid. On the one hand, the slogan did have a concrete aim and content: releasing Nelson Mandela from jail. On the other hand, the slogan was meant to signify a

115

much wider demand: the abolition of apartheid as such, and thus, a whole system change within South Africa. What served as an empty signifier keeping together anti-apartheid mobilisation was, at the very end of the day, the name 'Nelson Mandela', an empty signifier *par excellence* (E 36–46).

'Going Macro': Birmingham Cultural Studies and the Essex School

Populism may be the 'royal road' to a better understanding of the functioning of what we have called Laclau's political onto-logic, but, as we have seen, every traveller on this road will have to pass through an experience of negativity and antagonism. Therefore, to fully comprehend the logic of articulation it is important to once more highlight the necessary passage through negativity: in order to mutually link up in an equivalential chain entirely disparate elements have to experience a common threat. As Laclau has clarified already in *Hegemony and Socialist Strategy* and in *Emancipation(s)*, the experience of such a moment of negativity, as a common outside, is a necessary precondition if differential 'positive' elements are to be articulated into a wider chain of equivalence. With this strong notion of antagonism (and equivalence) Laclau departs from the Saussurian model: 'Saussurian differences still presuppose a continuous space within which they are, as such, constituted. A notion of constitutive antagonism, of a radical frontier, requires, on the contrary, a *broken* space' (PR 85). The Laclauian discursive space is broken because the seemingly harmonious continuity of the social will be dislocated *ab initio* by a lack of ground and an initial experience of that lack. That is to say, the fullness of the social is not simply lacking – the fullness is *experienced*, especially in moments of crisis and dislocation, *as lacking*. This experience of an absent fullness, an experience which emerges due to a gap that opens within the whole way of life of a dislocated social or cultural identity, may produce a request and, if not met, a demand, directed at an outside instance, to bridge that gap. This is what I would call the moment of protest, and what Laclau calls the construction of a 'people' from a plurality of subject positions:

> So from the very beginning we are confronted with a dichotomic division between unfulfilled social demands, on the one hand, and an unresponsive power, on the other. Here we begin to see why the *plebs* sees itself as the *populus*, the part as the whole: since the fullness of community is merely the imaginary reverse of a situation lived as *deficient being*, those who are responsible for this cannot be a legitimate part of the community; the chasm between them is irretrievable. (*PR* 86)

At this point, two implications of the aforesaid have to be underlined. Firstly, while politics, at the moment when a social request is transformed into a political demand, always involves a dimension of protestation, demands constitute what we can now designate as the *elementary units of protest* and, concurrently, the minimal units of political articulation. The universe of politics, at the very instance when the social is touched by the political, is a universe of articulated demands. And secondly, the process of their hegemonic articulation confronts us with what I am tempted to call the logical stage of 'going macro'. A part of the social (a 'plebs') presents itself as the whole (a 'populus') by way of integrating an increasing number of demands and representing the totality of these demands vis-à-vis a common though negative outside.

By now turning, for the rest of this chapter and the subsequent chapter, to this second implication we immediately have to add that, of course, no automatism exists for a process of 'going macro' to start in the first place – this is simply a conjunctural matter of articulation. While a signifier like 'worker', as Laclau comments, 'can, in certain discursive configurations, exhaust itself in a particularistic, sectional meaning', in other discursive configurations, like in the Peronist case, 'it can become the name *par excellence* of the "people"' (*PR* 87). The mere dislocation of a given identity does not provide sufficient reason for a process of 'going macro' to be instigated. There will have to be an accumulation of frustrated requests as well as an articulation of those isolated requests into connected demands. Needless to say, no part will ever be able to incarnate the whole once and for all. The universal horizon to be incarnated by a particular social force will have to accommodate competing forces struggling over the hegemonic function of incarnating the whole. As a result, the hegemonic process will never come to a halt and a process of 'going macro' might very well be followed by the reverse process of losing hegemonic amplitude, i.e. of 'going micro'. Chains of articulated demands can disintegrate and the degree of antagonisation may decrease due to a more differential reading principle of a situation gaining ground against the equivalential one. For instance, some of the neighbourhood demands for housing, schooling, etc. could be met by the local council which will have a disarticulatory effect on their equivalential relation vis-à-vis the remaining demands. In this case, many unfulfilled demands will return to the stage of request, or might even be experienced again as simple social needs without being articulated at all. Other demands might change sides and become articulated with political forces and discourses of completely different, perhaps opposite provenance. This is what happened in the case of current right-wing forms of populism where demagogues of the political right effectively managed to integrate leftist demands for social security and the defence of the welfare state into their xenophobic discourse.

It should by now be clear why Laclau's account of populism – combined with his earlier theorisations of discourse and hegemony – presents an important contribution to the field not only of discourse theory and political science but also of anthropology, (micro-)sociology and Cultural Studies. From a political perspective, most approaches in these disciplines are barely able to describe in a satisfactory way the precise nature and logic of processes of 'going macro'. While they are well equipped theoretically and methodologically to analyse micro-political forms of subordination and resistance, they exhibit a certain degree of negligence regarding macro-political formations, and, what is more, they do not provide any account of the missing link between the micro- and the macro-level of politics, between a 'politics of culture' and the 'politics of politics'. Yet Laclau's theory of the passage from need to request and, eventually, to demand can help to delineate the traces of this missing link. As soon as translated into the categorial framework of these approaches, Laclau's theory of populism can provide us with a frame of explanation that allows us to think the passage from the social to politics in a more precise way. Since there is no space here to elaborate on all aspects in detail – although many arguments can easily be extrapolated from the above-said – I will restrict myself to a couple of remarks regarding possible lines of mutual translation between the Essex School paradigm of post-foundational discourse theory and the Birmingham paradigm of Cultural Studies.

In fact, the Birmingham School, whose most distinguished proponent was Stuart Hall, shares many family resemblances with the Essex School approach. This is hardly surprising given the reliance of both paradigms on Gramscian hegemony theory. Nonetheless, Cultural Studies practitioners have shown a certain reluctance to enter the field of political research.[5] And there is a clear reason for this reluctance. Cultural Studies had to establish themselves precisely by drawing a clear line of demarcation vis-à-vis a more traditional understanding of politics in order to enlarge the space of the political beyond the political system and include the micro-political sphere of the cultural and the everyday. In a movement reminiscent of the famous feminist slogan, Cultural Studies set out to prove that 'the cultural is political'. The legacy of Gramsci's hegemony theory proved to be of great help in politicising, at the micro-end of the scale, the sphere of everyday life ('common sense') and culture, yet, concomitantly, the same movement tended to occlude the macro-political side of any hegemonic project (McRobbie 1994: 51). So, while a certain vicinity to Laclau was sometimes acknowledged, many Cultural Studies practitioners deliberately abstained from engaging with a Gramscian-informed study of politics in the perhaps conventional, but no less important sense of the term, thus reconfirming a breach between the political micro- and the macro-level that Cultural Studies initially had set out to deconstruct. Early Subcultural Studies in the Birmingham tradition may serve as an analogous example for the deliberate evasion of the macro-political. As is well known, subcultures, according to this classical approach, do not challenge hegemony directly and openly but rather obliquely, through style and rituals (Hall and Jefferson 1975). While such resistance may be called a form of *cultural* protest, to the extent that it is articulated through style, it cannot reasonably be called *political* protest in the macro-sense of the term as it lacks any spelled-out political agenda and does not raise any explicit political demands. In other words, in cases of 'oblique' protest, where it remains largely unclear who protests against what and why in the first place, the link to macro-politics remains necessarily severed. No wonder that Dick Hebdige's *Subculture* (Hebdige 1987), *locus classicus* of the so-called 'resistance through style' paradigm, displayed a symptomatic aversion to explicit forms of political protest, an aversion expressed by the author's eagerness to distinguish subcultures from 'counter culture' – by which Hebdige understood 'the amalgam of "alternative" middle-class youth cultures – the hippies, the flower children, the yippies – which grew out of the 60s, and came to prominence during the period 1967–70' (148). These macro-political forms of youth-cultural action were not only discarded as middle class, the whole discussion of counter-cultural, i.e. *political* strategies of protest, was even relegated by Hebdige to a footnote whereby the discussion of the macro-political became, literally, marginalised.

Neither our understanding of the 'politics of culture', nor our understanding of the 'politics of politics' will be enhanced by an approach that relegates to the margins the macro-political side of protest, displaying no interest whatsoever in the very *passage* from the micro- to the macro-political. At the same time, and despite the unquestionable influence Laclau's early theorisation of populism and articulation exerted on Cultural Studies, Laclau found himself at the margins of a Cultural Studies *doxa* increasingly evolving in the form of readers and introductory volumes (Slack 1996: 120). Far from being coincidental, such partial neglect seems to result from a deep-running discomfort in macro-politics. This is all the more regrettable as the macro-political option remained open all the time with Stuart Hall's work on populism, for one should not forget that Hall's thoroughly Gramscian and, indeed, Laclauian answer to Thatcherite authoritarian populism consisted in his appeal to construct a counter-hegemonic project – a populist project from the Left – against the Thatcherite power bloc. As Hall reminds us: 'The only way of genuinely contesting a hegemonic form of politics is to develop a counter-hegemonic strategy'

(Hall 1988: 11). And while the scale of such a strategy certainly should not be restricted to politics in the narrow sense, the counter-hegemonic strategy nevertheless will have to be played out on the macro-political field, rather than being constrained to the – most likely entirely disparate – tactics of everyday life resistance. Only by way of macro-political, i.e. strategic forms of reaggregation, will micro-political tactics add up to a counter-hegemonic project. And the name for this aggregational logic – of the transformation of dispersed tactics into more coherent strategies, of micro-political resistance into macro-political protest, of the subordinate into the hegemonic, and, eventually of the particular into the universal – is, precisely, populism.

It is for this reason that populism became the *shibboleth* for Cultural Studies as a *political* project.[6] The notion of populism marks a crossing-point where a decision has to be taken either to disavow populism (and thus to by and large ignore the macro-political), or fully to flesh out a theory of populism for the sake of Cultural Studies' larger political aims. The second road was taken by Stuart Hall, who took an interest in political populism – an interest not widely shared by those who chose the first road – with the aim of contributing theoretically and analytically to the construction of a socialist (counter-)hegemony. Yet in many quarters of the field of Cultural Studies populism was, together with Laclau's name, relegated to the footnotes of Cultural Studies' collective memory.[7]

When Subordination Becomes Oppression

As we have seen, there was a time when the main ambition of approaches located in the fields of feminism, micro-sociology and Cultural Studies was to blur the line between the social, in particular the cultural, and the political, between subcultural resistance 'at a level beneath the consciousness of the individual members of a spectacular subculture' (Hebdige 1987: 195) and self-conscious counter-cultural or political action, that is to say, between the micro- and the macro-aspects of politics. And it certainly was necessary at that time to direct our attention towards the *latent* political aspects of popular culture. Yet even at the heroic high-point of this paradigm it made no sense to do away completely with the line between micro and macro and to ignore the moment when the socially or culturally latent becomes politically explicit. The problem was that, as a rule, no account could be given of *the passage* from the cultural to politics as long as one was caught in the heroic myths of micro-political resistance. Thus, one stopped at an analysis, which is of course necessary but not sufficient, of sedimented micro-political common sense (what Gramsci would have called *senso comune*) instead of studying the political moment of the latter's reactivation. What is needed today is an analysis of the passage between culture and macro-politics, that is, an analysis of the process of 'becoming macro', because it is via this process that popular common sense is recoded politically (as progressive, conservative, reactionary, resistant, or revolutionary).

As we have also seen, Laclau's political onto-logic, as expressed *inter alia* in his theory of populism, offers not only an explanation of social sedimentation, but, first and foremost, a theory of the passage from the micro-political level of sedimented social routines to the macro-political of politics proper. This is the moment of political reactivation when 'unpolitical' subcultures turn into politicised counter-cultures, or when, to name another field where the study of micro-politics was blooming for many years, Media Studies, presumably always already 'active audiences' become macro-politically active eventually, thus starting to function as citizens rather than purportedly active consumers. This moment, the moment when the political in the strict sense enters the scene, is clearly visible in the conversion of what Laclau and Mouffe call *relations of subordination* (which are socio-cultural) into *relations of oppression* (which are political in the strict sense):

> We shall understand by a *relation of subordination* that in which an agent is subjected to the decisions of another – an employee with respect to an employer, for example, or in certain forms of family organization the woman with respect to the man, and so on. We shall call *relations of oppression*, in contrast, those relations of subordination which have transformed themselves into sites of antagonisms. (*HSS* 153–4)

It is important to understand that the representation of relations of subordination within the social field as well as within popular culture – for example, stereotypes of women in subordinated gender positions in TV programmes – can only be studied as an indicator of *latent* antagonisation, that is to say, *sedimented* antagonisms. While they do have political roots, it would not be correct to describe such relations as antagonistic in the strict sense. For:

> [A] relation of subordination establishes, simply, a set of differential positions between social agents, and we already know that a system of differences which constructs each social identity as *positivity* not only cannot be antagonistic, but would bring about the ideal conditions for the elimination of all antagonisms – we would be faced with a sutured social space, from which every equivalence would be excluded. (*HSS* 154)

In other words, a social system which could be described as a 'sutured', closed and self-contained system of differences would not be able to establish any antagonistic, that is, macro-political relation in which differences will be united against a common enemy into a chain of equivalence. Under these conditions – without any politics proper – one actually would encounter the social or cultural in a 'pure' state: sedimented forms of traditions, rites, stereotypes, clichés in a purely repetitive and differential form. It is worth quoting Laclau and Mouffe at length on this point:

> It is only to the extent that the positive differential character of the subordinated subject position is subverted that the antagonism can emerge. 'Serf', 'slave', and so on, do not designate in themselves antagonistic positions; it is only in terms of a different discursive formation, such as 'the rights inherent to every human being', that the differential positivity of these categories can be subverted and the subordination constructed as oppression. This means that there is no relation of oppression without the presence of a discursive 'exterior' from which the discourse of subordination can be interrupted. (*HSS* 154)

Let us take the example of racist constructions of cultural identity. Nothing in these racist representations automatically triggers a civic rights movement, nothing automatically leads to the politicisation of sedimented micro-frontiers within popular culture into political protest. What has to be assumed is an additional category if we want to account for the moment of reactivation where the sedimented racist practices suddenly come to be perceived as relations of oppression that have to be confronted. The role of such an additional category can be played, for instance, by human rights discourses which might turn out to be the universalising means to effectively establish a chain of equivalence around certain relations of subordination. But in a more radical sense it is, of course, antagonism itself which comes from the outside – since it is not itself an element of a differential system of subordination but, rather, the event by which this very system is restructured into an equivalential chain. And it is through this struggle – the event of the political breaking into the field of the socio-cultural – that cultural relations of subordination are retroactively revealed *as* political relations of oppression. So if we are prepared to follow Laclau and Mouffe, we have to conclude that the passage from relations of subordination to relations of oppression is a passage from the social (the field of micro-politics) to politics (the field of macro-politics) 'mediated' by the emergence of a third term: the political in the form of antagonism. Insofar as the political can emerge in any social and cultural area – that is, insofar as *all* relations of subordination can potentially be experienced as relations of oppression – it must be distinguished from politics in the narrow sense; hence the constitutive difference between the political and the field of politics, a difference which for most practitioners of micro-sociology or Cultural Studies does not play a major role.[8] Let us for a moment return to the Cultural Studies approach.

The distance between Laclau and Mouffe's hegemony theory and Cultural Studies can be measured precisely with the yard-stick of the political difference. By focusing on micro-politics and by leaving to political scientists the study of the moment of politicisation, Cultural Studies became – to a large degree – the study of political frontiers in their *sedimented form* and not in their *reactivated form*. This point is sometimes conceded by Cultural Studies practitioners, for instance in the recognition by John Fiske that Laclau's 'concern is primarily with the radical and the macropolitical, whereas I believe popular culture to be most effective in the progressive and the micropolitical' (Fiske 1991: 159). Fiske assumes that one must not expect the links between popular culture and politics, or between the tactic and the strategic, 'to be direct or immediate – rather, we must expect them to be diffuse, deferred, and not necessarily entailed at all' (165). While this might be correct from the viewpoint of a student of micro-political forms of resistance, and while Fiske agrees that the 'forging of productive links between the resistant tactics of the everyday and action at the strategic level is one of the most important and neglected tasks of the left' (162), it does not really explain how the popular gets linked to macro-politics, how indirect forms of action turn into direct forms. What is missing is a clear determination of the nature of the link between the 'micropolitics of everyday life and the macropolitics of organized action' (161).

On the Road to Political Subjectivation

In this chapter, we have presented antagonism as an answer to the question as to what links the micro-politics of everyday life to the macro-politics of organised action. Antagonism serves as the missing link through which micro-political tactics (a form of 'pre-political politics' which, without doubt, happens all the time at the level of everyday practices even though one should resist the temptation to call it 'politics') develop into macro-political strategies. However, this answer is not yet entirely satisfactory. Not because, presented in terms of the Laclauian logic of difference and equivalence, it was too abstract, but simply because antagonism, as we said, comes from the ontological outside as an event in the radical sense, that is to say, as a disturbance and dislocation of sedimented socio-cultural patterns. This outside, though, is only an outside when looked at from within the spheres of culture, the social or politics. Nonetheless, an antagonistic chain of equivalence – for example, in the form of an alliance between differential positions – is something which has to be actively constructed and organised within the 'ontic' sphere of politics. Therefore, the ontological account, precisely because it must be valid for *all* societies, does not *per se* explain particular instances of political mobilisation within concrete historico-political contexts. A certain grievance, a particular social need will be experienced on the basis of a dislocatory event that can have multiple sources (from local sources like the construction of a motorway to more general sources, for instance the effects ascribed to economic globalisation). As long as those social needs will be negotiated differentially – as long as they can be mapped onto traditional meaning patterns of a certain cultural formation – nothing happens in terms of macropolitical mobilisation. Only when those needs are turned into requests directed at an outside instance, and only when these requests will be frustrated and reaggregate into an equivalential series of demands, does a process of 'going macro' set in. Let us, in few words, recapitulate and specify the argument.

Antagonism, from the ontic perspective of politics, is the name for the passage – a passage through negativity and equivalence – through which social needs and isolated requests turn into political demands in a moment of protest. To the extent to which such a category of antagonism has to be distinguished from conflicts in the field of macro-politics in the conventional sense, it can emerge within *any* social system, not only the political system, and every social practice can thus be turned into a political practice. This is the reason why it is advisable to conceptually distinguish, as we consistently do, politics in the sense of macro-politics from the political as the category designating the experience and logic of antagonism.[9] To take into account, pace Laclau, the necessary passage through antagonism will finally also put us in a better position to explain the process of political subjectivation. Identities in the field of culture will as such be constituted by *subject positions* (*HSS* 114–22), that is to say, they will be constructed through their relational positioning within a field of differences. In other words, their socio-cultural forms of subjectivation will – partly at least – be stabilised through repetitive, or iterative, ritualistic practices (Butler 1997). *Political subjectivation*, however, will be premised on the emergence of the radically different register of equivalence. It is in the moment of antagonism, articulated by way of the equivalential linking of previously dispersed demands and practices, that socio-cultural subject positions turn into *political agents*.

If these aspects are taken into account in their entirety, we must conclude that there is no unbridgeable ontological chasm between macro-political discourses, as studied by the Essex School of discourse analysis, and cultural practices as studied, for instance, in a Cultural Studies tradition. The difference between macro- and micro-politics is, ontologically speaking, a difference in the *mode* of being: a difference between the sedimented and the activated mode of the political. While the focus within the Essex School paradigm so far was on the construction of larger hegemonic formations, many analyses in the Cultural Studies trajectory were mostly concerned with micro-political forms of resistance. However, what was missing so far was a clear and distinct account of how 'the popular' in the cultural sense gets linked to populism in a political sense, how, to put it differently once again, indirect forms of action turn into forms of direct action. What was missing was a clear theoretical determination of the nature of the link between the 'micropolitics of everyday life and the macropolitics of organized action'. In this chapter I have presented the concept of antagonism as an answer to this problem. It was identified as the key category indicating the moment at which cultural practices, in their process of 'going macro', *pass* through the experience of negativity. Protest, from this perspective, is nothing other than a name for the moment when subject positions assume agency as they experience negativity and antagonisation. By themselves, without this passage through negativity, the tactics of everyday life will never add up to a broader strategy, nor will social needs and requests ever be turned into political demands.[10]

Not all roads lead to Rome, and not all paths lead to politics. A notion of antagonism is indispensable if we wish to account for this process. The moment in which our social or cultural identities are – potentially – politicised is the moment in which we run up against antagonism. This moment was framed most succinctly by Jerry Rubin's famous definition of the yippie (the political version of the hippie): a yippie was a hippie, Rubin said, who had been hit on the head by a policeman. I am tempted to think that, at an ontological level, this encounter is precisely what creates a political epiphany, a moment in which unconscious subject positions are converted to politically self-conscious subjects. It is the moment when the experience of antagonism is given voice in the language of protest. And yet, shifting back to the ontic side of the political difference, we must not forget that in politics, more than anywhere else, the principle counts: *ex nihilo nihil fit*. A 'collective will', as Gramsci would have insisted, *has to be organised*. A newly emerging political force and project does not come from nowhere (even if an *event* in some sense does). Thus, one question remains to be answered regarding the nature of the line between the micro- and the macro-political. Does this line, we have to ask, belong to the side of micro-politics of everyday life or do we have to think of it as part of macro-politics? In other words, can the link between the micro- and the macro-sphere be forged by micro-political tactics or is it to be forged by macro-political strategy? Without denying the political importance of culture or social location, from the perspective of hegemony theory it seems obvious where the emphasis must lie: if we do not believe in the revolutionary spontaneity of the masses, we have to assume that the link between the micro-political and the macro-political is primarily to be established *macro-politically*, that is, through protestation. This is what I will call Minimal Politics.

6   On Minimal Politics: Conditions of Acting Politically

Minima Politica

What happens, as Jerry Rubin quipped, when a Hippie, hit by a policeman's truncheon, turns into a Yippie? A transubstantiation of a particular kind can be witnessed: the emergence of a political agent from the sedimented routines of the social in a moment of protestation. In Laclau's theory of populism, this was characterised as the moment when a social request transforms into a political demand. While, for Laclau, populism serves as the quintessential case of political mobilisation, I have tried to substantiate a more general claim: that the transition from request to demand involves a moment of protestation to be found in all political mobilisation. Politics, when traced back to its 'degree zero' of reactivation, is always *protest politics*. Whatever else might be called politics – in everyday language or in political science – is merely a sedimented social practice (a practice of governance, for instance) that remains untouched by the reactivating moment of the political. Spaces for politics, in a strict sense, only open when the instituting ground of social sedimentations is reactivated by antagonism and the social world is suddenly perceived as contingent and conflictual. In such a moment of dislocation, dispersed social differences become available for political articulation, but only if they are turned against *what they are not*: against an instance of radical negativity that is presented as the ultimate source of their frustration.[1] Laclau was right in claiming that, politically, this involves the transformation of a frustrated request into a more widespread political demand:

129

into an empty signifier that holds together an equivalential chain. And because politics, in the moment of reactivation, turns against – and is activated by – a radical outside, all politics is protest.

Let us attempt, on this premise, to establish some further *conditions* of political action – in the very prosaic sense of politics. Keeping our previous critique of micro-politics in mind, we will ask: What does a process of 'going macro' in actual fact imply on the ontic level of ordinary politics? We must proceed with care, however; it would not do to simply make a checklist of an arbitrary choice of conditions, similar to an Aristotelian catalogue of categories. There is a problem facing the establishment of a plausible notion of politics – a problem which follows from the very nature of the political difference *as* difference. On the one hand, the sought-after criteria must be appropriate to the 'ontic' domain of politics: they must draw a realistic image of politics. They must be firmly rooted in the Machiavellian Moment, which is also the Gramscian Moment. On the other hand, however, they must cohere to a certain degree with the ontological dimension of the political: they must be compatible with the ontology of antagonism. Therefore, the conditions of political action can be envisaged from an ontic as well as an ontological point of view. On the one hand, all political acting is ontically limited by historical conditions, institutional constraints and the opacity and power-ridden unevenness of the social. On the other hand, there are conditions of possibility of politics that issue from the ontology of antagonism. These, now, must be systematised and calibrated with the empirical conditions that are faced by political action. Only then will there emerge a notion of politics that is both empirically meaningful and ontologically plausible.

The following will thus inquire after these *minimal conditions* of politics. It is our aim in this chapter to establish a criteriology of *political minima*. Doing so will require the mind game of 'minimising' politics to the point where it stops being politics and starts disappearing into the micro-social, into the trembling world, in Laclau's sense, of differences (see our discussion in Chapter 4). Our guiding questions will be: What might politics look like just before it disappears beyond the horizon and is no longer describable as politics? What are those forms of action that we would describe as *just about still* political? Or, more briefly: What is *minimal politics*? In the course of this experiment, some categories that were only touched upon at the end of the previous chapter, but are central to any discussion of politics, including action, agency and the subject of politics, will be further elucidated.

Beyond 'Grand Politics' and 'Micro-Politics'

Let me state at the outset that there are political stakes riding on the reformulation of the problem in terms of minimal politics. Our intention is to rehabilitate those forms of political actions that are too often denied a political status, and which are frequently said to be too inefficient (because they did not have an effect), or too small (because they did not cross the mass media's horizon of perception), or too corrupt (because part of them rests in the institutions of the state, or indeed because they entered into deals with 'the enemy'). Although the truth of such accusations can only be assessed *in concreto* for each individual case, we can nevertheless state that these accusations largely adhere to a historically outmoded notion of politics. They hardly do justice to modern-day social movements, which act on the basis of mobile and growing associations and in doing so do not measure the success of their efforts at political mobilisation in the mere number of demonstration participants or the simple breadth of mass media reports. They look for and create different kinds of public presence. They have recourse to highly diverse forms of political action that usually take place on a small scale, quite like the more traditional forms such as vigils or neighbourhood councils, but which are also not centrally concerned with issues of size anyway. In a way, they fly underneath the radar of traditional perspectives on politics (see Marchart 2013b).

In the traditional perspective, the fantasy of 'grand politics' dominates, whether that is taken to mean the politics of grand collective actors (parties, trade unions, state institutions) or those of 'grand' individuals. On the Marxist Left, the grandness of the agent was a result of the global, historical mission of a universal class. All action was guided by a political act that itself had to be of sufficient magnitude to guarantee a total breach with the past. The classical left-wing idea of grand politics culminates in the notion of the revolution. The revolution of the whole of society, however, is only possible when (a) society is imagined as a totality and (b) the universal subject is equipped with a metaphysical guarantee of omnipotence in order to achieve the total breach with the past. The phantasmatic character of this notion is obvious. Yet, the notion of the 'grand' individual that is apparent in particular on the political Right is no less phantasmatic, assuming, as it does, that the mere deeds of an individual – from Bismarck to Trump – can elicit political upheaval. Social movements are rarely bothered by such fantasies, even as they are regularly charged with producing no palpable or lasting effects. However, political mobilisation cannot so easily be judged with regard to efficiency and inefficiency, effect or lack thereof. Protests can, for instance, assume the function of exemplarity (see, for example, Ferrara 2008), even when they themselves have next to no effect and tend to gravitate towards the *zero degree* of politics. A political activity's impact as an example is not affected by the criterion of 'size' by numbers. A given action serves as an example as soon as it is interpreted in the public eye as a reference to more far-reaching political front lines.

The same cannot be said for those practices that are usually subsumed under the somewhat misleading term of 'micro-politics'. I have already touched on these in the previous chapter at the hands of my critique of Cultural Studies. Such micro-political practices – having been lauded, among others, by Michel de Certeau (1988) – have to be clearly differentiated from practices of *minimal politics*. That does not make it entirely wrong to speak of micro-politics on some occasions. When feminism issued the battle cry that the personal is political, it quite rightly spotlighted the sphere of daily life and the balance of power and subordination that is negotiated therein. We cannot deny what Antonio Gramsci has pointed out: that consent and consensus, meaning hegemony, need to be organised in the realm of everyday culture and common sense (Gramsci's *senso comune*), that the validity of social identity patterns are in fact negotiated in that very realm (Gramsci 1971). It may therefore have made sense in the 1970s and 1980s to oppose a foreshortened notion of macro-politics and emphasise the subversive dimension of apparently a-political social practices. However, there was a tendency to over-stretch the argument. Félix Guattari, who, together with Gilles Deleuze, is possibly the main philosopher of micropolitics, presumed to claim that even a two-year-old child participated in practices of resistance. Describing a toddler's behaviour with the term 'micropolitics' (Guattari and Rolnik 2007: 78) empties this notion of political meaning. Although the theories of micropolitics therefore set an important impulse, they did tend to for their part displace the macro-political dimension from their point of view. In the absence of a convincing set of criteria, everything eventually becomes politics.

Laclau's differentiation between the social and the political, on the other hand, leads to other conclusions. The idea that social practices originate in an original founding moment that has later been forgotten – the moment of *the political* – does not necessarily imply that they mount up to *politics*. In Chapter 4, Laclau's categories were interpreted to mean that the social – the field of sedimented, unquestioned rituals and institutions – is nothing but the political in the sleeping mode, ready to be reactivated at any moment. Those social practices that are usually considered 'politics', because they are ritualised, rule-guided and institutionalised in the shape of the political system, belong to the register of the social. But what about those political practices that break with the well-rehearsed rules of conventional politics, which do not merge into the institutional shell of the political system, reactivating as they do the contingent nature of the social by reactivating antagonism? They should not strictly speaking be considered part of the register of the social, but are in fact participating in the moment of the political. They can be subsumed neither by the 'politics' of the political system nor by micro-politics.[2]

Let us juxtapose Guattari's example of an infant's 'micropolitics' with an activity that, minimal as it may be, very much can be regarded as political.[3] During the Paris May of 1968, it would often happen, as reported by Claude Lefort, 'that a professor was confronted by his students in the lecture hall. It was demanded of him that he justify his teachings, the rules in place, the form of the lectures and the examinations; or an unknown person would interrupt in order to ask the attendees to join an assembly or an improvised demonstration' (Lefort 2008b: 273). Immediately, the differences between this behaviour and the 'micro-politics' of toddlers are apparent. The students did not act individually nor, in contrast to their own self-description, spontaneously: they acted collectively, in concert and with a particular purpose. It was their aim to convince those assembled in the lecture hall to join a political demonstration, to bring the street into the university and the university onto the street. They were looking for an articulation with a wider, collective project; they activated a political antagonism, which emanated right through the lecture hall. Finally, they demanded that the sedimented institutional routines ('teaching', 'rules', 'form') be justified, thereby revealing the contingency of the institution and shifting the social into the mode of the political. Lefort stressed that such situations were *minor* events, but that May 1968 was in fact an assembly from such minor events: 'It is such minor facts in great numbers that denote the essential character of May 1968 and that are in danger of being forgotten over the memory of the great, explicitly political discussion and the street fighting' (Lefort 2008b: 273).

How are we able to define the political character of these and similar moments, thereby to delineate them from micro-politics on the one hand and systemic politics on the other? Which criteria can we use to establish which practices can still sensibly be described as politics and which cannot? It is apparent that these criteria cannot simply be inferred from the nominal definition of the political: we must set off from the phenomenic domain of real politics. It is equally clear that criteria cannot simply be read off empirical practices; that would merely result in a list of impressions, unguided by any conception of the political. Therefore I suggest carving out the *minimal conditions* of political action, as limited as this action may be in its scope and aims. For this purpose, let the boundary point of politics be a guide: that point that marks the least possible extent of politics, its *just-about* – or *presque rien* – the point of *minimal politics*.

Becoming-Major

Let us begin with a very simple aspect, nicely illustrated by Lefort's account, that cannot be subtracted from political action: politics tends to maximise the number of participants. Assemblies of pro-testers representing a demand that can be universalised entail within them the tendency to *become more*. In the Paris May of 1968, the final goal of this trend was the general strike. The politi-cal demonstrations of students and workers, in contrast to sectar-ian manifestations, were not organised with the aim of keeping to oneself. However, it was established above that numerical size is not a relevant criterion, since a small demonstration can also serve as a political example. We must therefore go beyond a merely numerical understanding of *becoming more*. Ultimately, such poli-tics are about the construction of a majority, encapsulating not the numerical majority of the population, but the symbolic one: it is about *becoming-major*. This needs to be stressed not least because the tendency of becoming-major is certainly controversial within social movements as well as in theories that are in close proximity to movements. Deleuze, together with Guattari, even formulated an influential micro-political concept that suggests the opposite: *becoming-minor* (Deleuze and Guattari 1986). For Deleuze, a minority – women, people of colour, Jews, etc. – is not in itself a *minority*, it needs to *become* minor. This, he says, will affect in turn the members of the majority, who are now also exposed to becoming-minor. For Deleuze, any becoming, regardless of the number of people affected by it, can therefore always occur only in the direction of the minoritarian.

The Deleuzian concept of becoming-minor speaks for a con-stant process of degrounding, instead of one of grounding. This is an anti-foundationalist perspective on politics. From our post-foundational perspective, a process of grounding would require an attempt at self-majorisation, which Deleuze had declared to be impossible. Therefore, Deleuze's concept of becoming-minor draws near to a politics without politics. The genuine political movement, given the background of the Machiavellian Moment, where Laclau still positions himself as well, runs in the oppo-site direction. It aims for the establishment of a 'collective will'

(Gramsci) – which is of course never achievable in its entirety – i.e. an alliance of social powers. Agents who want to live up to this demand will have to expose themselves to a process not of becoming-minor, but of *becoming hegemonic.*

Laclau (*E* 20–35) rephrased this aspect of Gramsci's theory of hegemony into his own dialectic of universality and particularity: every particular demand must, if it wants to become politically effective, present itself as being 'more universal' than its actual contents imply. Any given particularism can hegemonise the social field only on the basis of an excess of universality. At the same time, if there is no ultimate ground for society, the universality that is aspired to cannot in fact have a content in its own right. This, from a post-foundational perspective, does not, however, make the dimension of universality gratuitous quite yet: if it were, we would live in a world of diverging monads or in a state of war of all against all. The place of universality can only be incarnated passingly by a particularism; but no particularism is equal to the task, as it would otherwise turn into a foundation of universality. Nevertheless, every political project is condemned to take up this impossible challenge if it wants to enforce its demands. Remember Laclau's standard example of the Polish trade union movement Solidarność (*PR* 81). While it initially articulated the particularistic demands of the Gdansk dock workers on the one hand, all sorts of further oppositional demands were then, on the other hand, bundled into it. It therefore eventually acquired the universal function of incarnating opposition against the regime as such.

Political action has to assume the mutual entanglement of particularity and universality. This argument supports our first minimal condition of politics: in order to be reasonably describable as political, a particular project has to possess the tendency to *becoming-major*, even if it will never be able to achieve the status of full universality (i.e. of absolute sovereignty), nor possibly even of comprehensive majority and dominance. Political movement only exists when it is directed towards expansion of its own project. An agent who aims for the opposite, meaning a particularistic project of self-minorisation, and eventually of self-ghettoisation, would effect a standstill in the movement towards universality and thereby induce the project's resignation from politics.

There is no implication here about the extent or size of a hegemonic project. The only condition that was named was that minimal politics must achieve a movement towards the majoritarian. This should also do away with one potential misunderstanding. Minimal does *not* mean: as little politics as possible. In fact, it means the exact opposite: as much politics as possible, *even if it is little* (given the circumstances). Practices of minimal politics do not aim for minimisation but maximisation of politics. It may, from the perspective of 'grand politics', appear to be minimal and ineffective. Indeed, a demonstration, for example, of a handful of people in front of a deportation prison will rarely have an immediate effect on the state's deportation practices. Yet such a demonstration is *no less* politics – that is to say, *not less* politics – than are protests of a national or even global dimension. If we apply the criterion of universalisation, then no practice is too poor, no action too ineffective, no small gaggle of demonstrators too few for politics, since nothing can be attained without those minimal, everyday actions, from which molecules the hegemonic struggles are assembled.

Acting and the Act

Having resolved this minimal criterion, we must turn to establishing a more precise definition of two terms that have until now been used quite innocently. What do we categorially take political *action* to mean, and what kind of *agent* is behind this action? In other words, how can we establish the minimal conditions of action and agency? These questions impose themselves out of the circumstance that, obviously, the post-foundational approach initially implies the obsolescence of the categories of agent or subject and of action. Following Heidegger, we no longer assume the presence of a subject of volition to be *at the basis* of certain political actions. That would constitute a case of subject metaphysics. Sociological objectivism, which grants the status of agents to social groups, also offers no alternative to metaphysics (it is only a variant of metaphysics), as long as it claims that the existence of these groups precedes their political formation. Post-structuralists typically propose as a solution that political agents (groups, parties, movements, etc.) ought to be considered not a ground but a retroactive effect of political action. Action thereby gains primacy over the agent. Even as I tend to accept this view, several questions remain to be answered: if the agent is subordinate to the action, how can the very occurrence at all of political action be explained, since the metaphysical subject of volition must be discounted as the source of action? There is a direct political component to this question: Why does it appear in the course of political action to still be necessary for the actors to imagine themselves as subjects of their action? Obviously, nobody would engage in politics whilst lacking any trust at all in their own agency. Would this post-structuralist thesis of the agent as a mere effect of a-subjective actions not, then, turn out to be extremely quixotic? Finally: Which ontic as well as ontological conditions have to be met by political action for an 'agency effect' to emerge at all? Let us first sound out this final question, before we then return to the relationship of the categories of subject and agent.

In some post-foundational theories, we can discern a difference that is analogous to the political difference between politics and the political, but is rarely systematised: the difference between acting and act (see Marchart 2007b). It is particularly apparent where the act is summoned at the cost of activity, i.e. as a repression of profane political action. Slavoj Žižek, for example, submitted an ontology of the political act (inspired by Badiou's concept of the event), which gives a striking demonstration of the dangerous consequences of purified politics. According to Žižek, an act in the radical sense aims for an 'impossible' intervention, which changes the reality principle of a given situation, meaning the parameters of what is possible. While we can follow Žižek up to this point, his conclusions appear quite implausible against the backdrop of ordinary politics. Indeed, they are even highly problematic. A 'true' act, finds Žižek, has no support in the symbolic order that precedes it. It touches on the unsymbolisable Real and is of utterly groundless nature. Žižek's ideal type of such an act is exemplified by Lenin's allegedly lone decision to risk a second, Bolshevik revolution:

With Lenin, as with Lacan, the revolution *ne s'autorise que d' elle-même*: we should venture the revolutionary *act* not covered by the big Other – the fear of taking power 'prematurely', the search for the guarantee, is the fear of the abyss of the act. (Žižek 2002: 8)

This adventurist model of leaping into an abyss is unacceptable from a post-foundational point of view. The abyss can no more be approached directly than the ground. What is called for is the development of tools for a theory of action that do consider the ontological register of the act, but do not imagine it as if it were to be realised in a vacuum. This hits upon the very boundary between a Gramscian approach and an approach in line with Žižek. For we always act on a terrain criss-crossed by antagonisms and unevenly formed by sedimented institutions. For this sort of action Gramsci found the metaphor of a 'war of position'. With this metaphor, he recalls the convoluted trench systems on the battlefields of the First World War. Like these, the civil societies of the developed states in the West are made up of a very complex, yet resistant structure of interlaced institutions that are being contested. By introducing this notion, Gramsci let go of the classical idea of sovereign power long before Foucault did. Gramsci saw power in the developed societies not located in a given state apparatus (such as the government), nor in any place of society: he recognised that it is distributed throughout the entire civil society. Accordingly, it is not enough to storm the Winter Palace and take over power, as in the model of the revolutionary 'war of movement'; the achievement of hegemony must be preceded by a long 'war of position'. As in the trenches of the First World War, the shifts that are achieved along the front line are but minimal and slow. The precise location of the front line is perhaps not even always apparent. In a trench war, Gramsci reminds us:

[I]t would sometimes happen that a fierce artillery attack seemed to have destroyed the enemy's entire defensive system, whereas in fact it had only destroyed the outer perimeter; and at the moment of their advance and attack the assailants would find themselves confronted by a line of defence which was still effective. (Gramsci 1971: 235)

In that same way, hegemonic territorial gains are always embattled, potentially short-lived, and in danger of being reversed by inimical forces. Politics takes place in such an obfuscated trench system. Hegemony, in Gramsci's eyes, is a molecular process, in which ideological molecules are successively combined into larger formations.

The molecular nature of politics undermines every revolutionary Manichaeanism. The ontological level of the act and the ontic level of acting remain interlocked. It is precisely because of this necessary link between the ontic and the ontological, politics and the political, action and act, that a pure act – as a 'leap' from the realm of the conditioned – is simply not performable. It is only due to the inextricable relationship that exists between the politico-historical situation within which we act and the ontological condition of the political, that action is at all possible. Otherwise we would find ourselves in a rational choice universe of pure calculability, or in Žižek's vacuous universe of 'the act'. In either case, potential action – the strategic play with the unforeseen under hegemonically limited conditions – is no longer possible. Political action therefore means: calculation with that which cannot be calculated – the groundless – but still never without premise, and always under the conditions of a concrete, as political scientists would put it, 'opportunity structure', i.e. in the presence of partial grounds.

Strategy, Organisation, Collectivity

These same considerations suggest at least three further minimal conditions of political action: *strategy*, *organisation* and *collectivity*. There can be no politics without strategy, because the option of a pure act of decision, relieving us of strategic considerations, is precluded by a realistic model of politics. Every act, it was said, no matter how radical, can only be realised in the form of concrete political actions. It thus can only be realised under particular social as well as historical conditions and in direct competition with other political projects. To think otherwise would amount to political megalomania. However, that also implies that action can only sensibly be considered political if it is not limited to *ad hoc* piecemeal activities. Political action proceeds, to pick up on Michel de Certeau's differentiation, not so much tactically as strategically. More precisely: a micro-political tactic of everyday life, if it is to meet the criteria of minimal politics, must be embedded in broader or more long-term strategies. It must be connectible with a hegemonic project. Otherwise it would go up in smoke without a trace.

The development of more long-term strategies will only work out for a political project to the extent to which it is organised. Political action therefore unfolds in the form of at least a *minimal organisation*. Machiavelli ascribed this function to the Prince, who was to organise the unity of Italian states. Gramsci considered this figure of the Prince to be a creation of concrete imagination with the purpose of organising the collective will of the people (Gramsci 1971: 125–33). It was therefore, he said, the task of a *modern* Prince – for Gramsci this was the Communist Party of Italy, whose co-founder he was – to organise the unity of the working class and eventually the construction of a new hegemonic alliance. Our claim that the link between micro-politics and macro-politics can only be constructed from a macro-political standpoint might become less controversial if we consider for a moment Gramsci's own conception of politics. The point is simply that any counter-hegemony, any new political will, has to be incorporated and organised by a modern Prince that takes up the task of founding a new social order by way of constructing a popular will. Gramsci himself explains the function of the modern Prince – the party – as follows:

> The modern Prince must be and cannot but be the proclaimer and organiser of an intellectual and moral reform, which also means creating the terrain for a subsequent development of the national-popular collective will towards the realisation of a superior, total form of modern civilisation. (Gramsci 1971: 132–3)

Both tasks of the modern Prince turn out to be two aspects of the same operation: the party's task is both moral and intellectual reform and the construction of a collective will. One does not fully understand the Gramscian notion of hegemony as long as one restricts hegemony to micro-political questions of culture rather than taking into account the macro-political function of cultural *reorganisation* ('intellectual and moral reform') and the construction of what today we would call a political project (the 'collective will'). Nowadays, of course, the party form is not the only form of political organisation available; but in order to organise, synthesise and give a direction to otherwise entirely dispersed micro-political struggles, there must be *some* formational agent, some institutional nodal-point on the macro-political level. In the post-foundational variant of hegemony theory, as developed by Laclau and Mouffe, organisation – and therefore political action – in the end means nothing but the articulation of heterogeneous elements into a chain of equivalence. Only once this condition is at least rudimentarily fulfilled can we speak of politics.

This does not yet say anything about the size or power of a given political organisation. The minimal condition of being organised is fulfilled even by the smallest links, the most modest forms of political organisation, not only by mass parties. This obviously touches on fundamental questions regarding the status of the agent. Post-foundationally, it was said, the agent can no longer be defined as the ground or source of political action, because that would imply a metaphysical subject of volition. How, then, do actions come into being? Or, to paraphrase Heidegger who paraphrased Aristotle: Why is there action rather than no action? This question can only be answered after first pointing out a further minimal criterion of political action: politics always and exclusively brings forth *collective* agents, even if the impression may arise that it is supported by individuals (such as individual activists). The agent emerges from the action as *collectivity*. This is the reason why Gramsci spoke of hegemonic politics as the construction of a 'collective will'. Already the 'Condottiere' conjured up by Machiavelli, in his *Il Principe*, as the unifier of Italy must not be confused with the real prince Lorenzo de' Medici, who is invoked by Machiavelli in the epilogue and the dedication of *Il Principe*. Lorenzo is but the 'anthropomorphous' symbol of the collective will (Gramsci 1971: 125). That which Laclau calls 'the name of the leader' (*PR* 100) in his theory of populism is simply such an anthropomorphous symbol. We can conclude, therefore, that the collectivity of the agent, quite like the desired majority of a political project, is in the end of symbolic and not empiric-social nature. Collectivity as a unifying symbol is a product of a political process of organisation, not its source. And it could not be otherwise. To the extent to which every politics must be concerned with the problem of inclusion/exclusion and with the question of 'where to draw the line' (Marchart 2002), to which it must undergo the experience of antagonism, every politics is collective. Not because, as Lenin was convinced, there is no politics without the masses (by which he actually understood class politics), but because there is no politics within a pure field of differences, that is, without some degree of antagonisation. Which also explains why, contrary to the liberal view, a politics of the individual does not exist. The elementary unit of political agency is not the individual, it is the collective agent.

We have thus arrived at a definition of political action as the strategic organisation of a collective agent. Having excluded, on a more general philosophical level, this agent as a primordial *source* of action, there remains the question of what does in fact set off political action. The political ontology of antagonism is hard put to make do without psychoanalytical support at this point. Referring to Lacan, Laclau, in his work after *HSS*, also assumes a constitutive lack at the heart of each identity and therefore the Freudian notion of *Ichspaltung*. In Lacan's notion of the subject, the subject is understood – in juxtaposition to the metaphysical notion of a self-sustaining subject of volition – as the very constitutive lack of substance: as a *subject-of-lack*. Phrased in the terminology of political post-foundationalism, this category of the subject is but a metaphor of the absent ground, which, by virtue of being absent, is experienced *as lack*.

The Subject of the *As If*

As was already indicated in Chapter 2 in our short historical outline of social negativity, Lacan's own model of the subject was based on an ontology of negativity. For Lacan, it is on the premise of the subject's lack-of-being – and 'subject' in Lacan is just the very name for that lack – that a dialectics of desire is set in motion. This dialectics is itself indebted not only to Sartre's notion of a *lack-of-being*, but also to Alexandre Kojève's dialectics of recognition. For Kojève, man's desire (*Begierde* in Hegel) is always another desire: it is the desire for recognition by the other and, hence, for the *desire of a desire* (i.e. the desire *of the other*) around which the struggle for recognition turns. In short: the motor of history is fuelled by nothing else than desire for an other desire. However, for Kojève, this other desire is a purely negative term since the desire one desires does not really 'exist', at least not in the way objects of the natural world can be said to exist, nor does it have any specific content. If it existed, and if we could be certain of it, we would not need to desire it. Desire is therefore defined by Kojève as the '"manifest" presence of the *absence* of a reality' (Kojève 1980: 225).[4] Lacan, for his part, radicalises these insights by speaking about desire as being *le désir de l'Autre*, the symbolic desire of the Other.[5] Here, 'the Other' designates the symbolic order – language or society – as the instance by which the subject (and the subject's desire) is addressed. Depending on the context, this Lacanian phrase can be read in a variety of ways: it can mean that man's desire is desire *for* the Other – starting with the (m)other – or, that man desires what the Other desires, or, that man always desires something other (always something else). In any case man's desire is not to be found within the subject – which is lack – but originates from the outside world of language and society. The subject remains *eccentric vis-à-vis* itself. On the imaginary level, desire is positivised within an object promising to fill up the subject's lack-of-being. This *objet petit a* serves as a positive incarnation of what is absent. And, since the subject of desire is pure lack, what is absent can only be *pure* presence: *jouissance*, a presymbolic, real enjoyment that was lost when the subject entered into the symbolic order. With his formula of fantasy – designating the attempt at re-establishing an imaginary fullness – Lacan places the divided subject of the symbolic order (the subject of lack) in a relation to the *objet petit a* as an element that necessarily escapes the grasp of the subject and still serves as the (absent) *cause* of his or her desire for being.

It is already discernible how this psychoanalytical model can be translated into the ontology of the political and eventually will explain the *why* of action. According to Laclau (1994), political identity can only exist because identifications have occurred; and identifications take place because of the need to fill an original lack. The *ontological* nature of this claim should not be missed: 'An important consequence of this distinction between identity and identification is that it introduces a constitutive split in *all* social identity' (Laclau 1994: 3). The psychoanalytical notion of the subject therefore turns out to be fundamental to the development of Laclau's political ontology. In his book dedicated to the category of the subject, Slavoj Žižek even went as far as declaring the subject in his subtitle to be the 'absent centre of political ontology' (Žižek 1999). There, Žižek identified the subject with the two aspects of grounding and degrounding: the gap within the positive ontological order (the subject of lack) and, once again, the *act*, which fills this gap and founds the ontological order (subject of decision). Any ontology that is founded on such an act, he stated, is political. Basically, this depiction is not incompatible with the arguments proposed here so far, but the aspect of ordinary politics is entirely ignored by Žižek. As we have seen, there is a basic issue with Žižek's notion of the act, which once again appears here in the guise of the subject. The subject-of-the-act lacks an 'ontic' counterpart – an agent – provided that every form of ontological institution must be ontically mediated via action and agency.

In order to bring back the ontic level of the agent, this ontology of the subject needs to be modified. How do agents imagine themselves in the moment of their action? It should be evident that they do not perceive themselves as a subject-of-lack, but rather understand themselves as autonomous subjects of their own will. They act as if they were the source and ground of their own action, as if they had instigated their action themselves. In our political everyday imagination, we appear unable to consider anything other than ourselves to be the source of our ability to act. We therefore act in an *as if* mode – a mode that has received attention from thinkers spanning from Kant via Sartre to Derrida and Rancière, but the theoretical history of which is yet to be written. In fact, a minimal degree of such self-misperception is required in order for us to act at all in the first place. From the perspective of politics, it is therefore not the irremovable lack that motivates the agent into action, but the imaginary notion that we can *overcome* the lack (without this fantasy, the result would not be political activity but passive nihilism). That means, simply, that a metaphysical moment in the stricter sense cannot be removed from the notion of politics. Political action presupposes the 'will-to-will' – Gramsci's collective will of a political project – which Heidegger quite rightly criticised in Nietzsche as a remnant of metaphysics. However, politics, even in a post-foundational mode, cannot make do without such a remnant of a certain will-to-*foundation*. The subject of the *as if* can only act on the basis of the transcendental illusion that it does have foundational power, and is therefore able to will its own will – and, as Heidegger put it, this 'will-to-will, i.e. willing is: to will yourself' (Heidegger 1961: 33).

To be clear, it does not make much difference whether, philosophically speaking, human actors are in actual fact equipped with a faculty of volition, or whether this is just a counter-factual assumption. We are not into brain research. The capacity to act (and be activated) is simply a working assumption without which it would make little sense to speak about political acting in the first place. Yet, this assumption should not be hypostasised into a voluntarist ideology. The political cannot be brought to life by an act of pure will. It would be a mistake to assume that we can construct a political situation in the same way in which a car or a house can be constructed. It is a well-known fact of experience that the successful organisation of, for instance, a street manifestation is far from being a matter of pure will. Those who believe in pure voluntarism will most likely end up standing alone at a street corner. Something additional has to happen. A political situation cannot simply be constructed, it must also be encountered: *there is* a political situation – *there is* in the very sense of Heidegger's *es gibt*, or the *il y a* of the French Heideggerians, understood as shorthand for an a-subjective event or *Ereignis*. A political situation emerges from the event of the political – an event which, by virtue of being one, cannot be constructed through an act of will. If a political situation is encountered, then because it is brought about not 'by us', it is brought about by the a-subjective force of the political, the most appropriate name for which is antagonism.

Where we originally rejected the fantasies of the omnipotence of 'grand politics', it now turns out that this fantasy is essential, in reduced form, even for minimal politics.[6] Every form of agency – and therefore every politics – is based inescapably on a minimum of megalomania; in the best of all cases on regulated megalomania. Translated into Lacanian terminology: political action demands some form of fantasy, where a subject – by way of a metaphysical, and thus illusory, act of willing – turns itself into the object of its own desire. Or, in Nietzschean terms: political subjectivisation aims to overcome the lack in the will-to-will. In this way, the subject assumes an agency which is not its due but without which political action would be impossible. In this regard, political action is an entirely circular affair: a dialectic between a constitutive lack and the illusory will to overcome it. Hence, ironically, Melville's literary figure Bartleby is the incarnation of anti-politics *per se*. I say ironically, because Bartleby, who rejects all calls to action with the famous sentence 'I would prefer not to' until he starves to death in jail, has become an icon to theoreticians like, among others, Giorgio Agamben, Maurizio Lazzarato, Michael Hardt and Antonio Negri because of this very attitude of refusal. But, with his figure, Melville had in fact created the very counterpart to Machiavelli's and Gramsci's figures of the Prince as the organiser of a collective will. Bartleby is the incarnation of anti-politics because he prefers not to affirm his will. After all, 'the growth of a nothingness of the will', as Deleuze (1997: 70) would put it, is the very opposite of the political *will-to-will*. Bartleby embodies the anti-political side of politics: he incorporates the self-dissolution in the minoritarian, the abandonment of every strategic option, the absence of all organisation and, eventually, regressive individualisation in the form of passive nihilism. He has abandoned the will to become majoritarian, to act strategically, to organise and to construct a collectivity.

Splitting the Objective: Antagonism

Becoming-major, strategy, organisation and collectivity are minimal criteria of politics that have so far been discussed. A recourse to psychoanalysis demonstrated that we act as agents as if we were the ground for our actions, while in fact our actions are only possible because of the lack of a Ground (a lack named, in the field of acting, 'subject'). In order to explain, then, why action takes place at all and not rather not, we had to resort to shifting from the ontic examination of the domain of politics to the ontological level and to recur on an ontology of lack. The category of the subject is located on this ontological level, not that of politics. This explains why the subject of lack can never appear as such in the world of agents: nobody has ever seen such a 'subject' other than in those very moments when political agents break apart and political actions go amiss. In such instances, the subject starts to be voiced by way of Freudian slips – indeed, every attempt to overcome the lack will in the end be spoiled by blunders.

This is wonderfully illustrated in one of the most infamous instances of self-outfoxing in recent history, which resulted in the immediate fall of the Berlin wall. On 9 November 1989, the SED politburo member Günter Schabowski read out a note in the course of a live transmission: it would in future be possible to apply for visas for the purpose of private travel abroad without fulfilling the conditions that had hitherto been in place. Schabowski was obviously not quite aware of what he was announcing, and, having lost track entirely – in fact, having lost all purchase in any form of higher authority – he found himself in a position where he was forced to more specifically explain the note. Eventually, he stuttered in response to the question when this directive was to come into power: 'In my knowledge, that will . . . that is now, immediately.' This became the news item 'GDR opens its borders', which was taken literally by the citizens who rushed to the border posts and began to tear down the wall. While the adjustment of the travel conditions had been a last-ditch attempt by the politburo to keep a handle on the dynamic of the situation, Schabowski's slip of the tongue achieved the opposite: the dam had broken and proof had been delivered that it was not possible to steer the dynamic of the situation. Although Schabowski's blunder appears to have been entirely individual, it was in fact entirely collective in its causes and effects. It was the 'objective situation', namely the weakness of the state and managing elite of the GDR vis-à-vis an increasingly antagonistic population that prevailed in this instance and began to speak itself through the mouth of a high official of the state who no longer knew how to keep to established rules of engagement and normal political processes. More generally put: the antagonism that split the country constituted the 'objective condition' of a situation in which *the subject* was able to grab a brief appearance among the agents of politics – in the shape of blunders. Schabowski allowed the subject use his name for a brief moment, but it was not Schabowski speaking. What spoke through Schabowski was the lack of a foundation in the 'objective conditions', a lack that had been reactivated by the emergence of antagonism, i.e. the political.

Two consequences can be drawn from this example. The first concerns the ontological register. The example seems to suggest that there is a correlation on the ontological level between the category of the subject and that of antagonism. The contingent and antagonistic nature of social objectivity somehow correlates with the absence of a subjective ground (with the subject of lack). Put in Lacanian terms: it is not only the subject that is split, but also the great Other, i.e. society (Stavrakakis 1999). But are these two categories – the subject and antagonism – co-original? Or can one term claim ontological priority? Laclau seems to suggest the subject (as lack) is in fact primordial. As he puts it in an interview:

> But antagonism is only possible because the subject *already* is that 'lack of being' you refer to. As you know, the incorporation of the individual into the symbolic order occurs through *identifications*. The individual is not simply an identity within the structure but is transformed by it into a subject, and this requires acts of identification. It is because the subject is that 'lack of being', which demands and prevents suture, that antagonism is possible. (*NR* 211)

In this passage, antagonism becomes an *effect* of a primordial lack (and we have already criticised Laclau for granting ontological priority to the a-political category of dislocation rather than antagonism). This, however, would compel us to formulate a psychoanalytic ontology – an ontology of the subject rather than antagonism. An ontology of *the political*, on the other side, would suggest that it is the subject that results from the antagonistic structure of all identity and all social meaning.

This is not an exalted chicken-or-egg question. It makes a practical difference, in terms of what we look for in empirical analysis, whether one starts with an ontology of the political or with anthropology or psychoanalysis. But also, if we want to be consistent in our ontological approach, antagonism must be considered prior to the subject. It can be conceded that we can only achieve identity qua identification because the subject is lack; yet this lack of subject simply results from the incompleteness of the symbolic order. Lack, another word for dislocation, exists because society is blocked by a fundamental antagonism. Perceived from this angle of an ontology of the political (rather than from the point of view of psychoanalysis), antagonism logically precedes the subject. There is a lack in the structure – a lack we call subject – because of the labour of the negative. If antagonism describes on the one hand the logic of politics, which consists of the articulation of differences into a chain of equivalence against a negating outside, it refers on the other hand to that instance of radical negativity which hinders the social to close itself into the totality of society. In the first sense I proposed to speak of Laclau's political ontology (his *onto-logic* of politics in an enlarged sense), in the second sense we have to develop the implications of a more radical ontology of the political.

But what are the consequences, in the ontic register, for our theory of minimal politics? The notion of antagonism, more fittingly than any other, can direct our attention to two further, indispensable minimal conditions of politics: *conflictuality*, of course, and implied therein: *partisanship*. The social is laden with conflict on the ontic plane, because society cannot be concluded into a totality – the ontological name for which is antagonism. Any political activity that is aimed at maximisation is eventually bound to fail, since it will never be able to gain power over the whole. And for this reason, every activity in an open field is always but one of many. A political project is likely to collide with other projects at any time, and these in turn are also facing a plethora of obstacles. This implies, beyond the need for strategy discussed above, the positionedness of each agent: an agent will always be located at a determined – and yet changeable – position within the 'war of position' among conflictually intersecting projects. An agent therein necessarily comes to be placed on one or the other side of a concrete antagonism. This aspect of always being positioned implies partisanship. Even in a plural field of antagonisms, there is – from the perspective of the antagonists – no neutral position: *tertium non datur*. Whether we accept it or not, as agents we are party to many struggles.

Politics on Doves' Feet

It was stated at the outset that this exploration of the minimal conditions of political action was not intended to result in an arbitrary list in the style of an Aristotelian catalogue of categories. The ontic criteria of politics must remain theoretically compatible with the notion of the political employed. Even further: without wanting to claim that it is possible to logically and necessarily deduce a given notion of the political from a given notion of politics (or vice versa), ontic and ontological categories must enter a game of reciprocal definition that has an inner conclusiveness against the background of the respective other level.[7] In the Machiavellian moment of the political, which Laclau is a part of, political action takes place within a confusing terrain of relations of conflict, power and exclusion. The hypostasising of political action into an *actus purus* – a leap into the ultimate vortex of 'the act' – would lead away from the Machiavellian moment (as much as the monadological or pointillist dissolution of politics into an endless multitude of singularities would lead us astray).

Further, I pleaded for the support of a notion of the political that counteracts any potential depoliticisation and befits the understanding of politics in the Machiavellian mode. In a nutshell, the post-foundational model of politics, guided by Laclau and by the left-Heideggerian principle of political difference – as difference between ontic politics and the ontology of the political – emerges as follows: the social world is, according to the ontological definition, prevented from closure by a fundamental antagonism (in turn creating a subjective lack). Because of this openness, it brings forth ontic conflicts and struggles – meaning a plurality of antagonisms – which demand a partial closure of the social into a totality, which

151

cannot, however, be finally achieved. The absence of an ultimate ground identified by the notion of antagonism produces attempts at partial foundation: *antagonisms*.[8]

What form might those social struggles for a temporary foundation of the social take? Let us recapitulate the 'ontic' implications of our ontology of antagonism. The condition of *conflictuality* already referred to the fact that any practice under the auspices of the political – antagonism – will involve taking a position and therein showing *partisanship*. It will always have to place an *us* against a *them* (see Mouffe 2000). Now it is possible to demonstrate that the other minimal conditions – becoming-major, strategy, organisation and collectivity – can also be referenced to each other as well as to the category of antagonism: a political project must, in order to achieve partial regrounding of the social, have a tendency to generalise and *majoritise* its own position. In order to do so, it will have to overcome obstacles. These obstacles are on the one hand the institutionalised conditions of power and exclusion that will certainly be encountered within the social, and on the other hand a multiplicity of competing projects of regrounding. The different layers of sedimented foundations on the one hand and the 'war of position' of hegemonic struggles on the other create obstacles that have to be dealt with *strategically*. For strategy not to degenerate into an individual tactic of micro-politics, which would in the end not be sufficient to achieve the majorisation of a political project, a minimal form of *organisation* must be found. This organisation does not at all need to take the form of a traditional party, although it does presuppose a certain degree of partisanship: without a negatory outside – without an antagonistic opposite – there would be no motivation for an organised unity. Eventually, a political project that is to be organised in a strategic-antagonistic manner will result in a *collective will* as described by Gramsci. Political conflicts not only are collective, they first of all *produce* collectives. That closes the circle with the first minimal condition of becoming-major.

The categories mentioned above are minimal conditions also in the sense that they only need to be fulfilled in minimal doses – which is, of course, mostly the case when one speaks of necessary conditions. In this case, however, there is a purpose to underlining the minimal character. The fantasy of grand politics as well as the reduction of politics into systemic macro-politics are to be juxta-posed by a notion of politics that allows the political nature of even the smallest and apparently most ineffective actions to be illumi-nated. Even the most minor forms of acting, the most minute collec-tive, the most vanishing demonstrations, the most paltry strategies, the worst organisation, even the apparently most individual activi-ties may be called politics as long as they appear in conjunction with somewhat wider movements and alliances, as long as they dislodge the embedded rituals of a hegemonic formation and as long as they recall the original political moment of foundation, and thereby the contingency of the social.

Acting, in other words, becomes political as soon as it is mobil-ised by antagonism. If this is the case, actions articulate, that is, organise themselves into a political collective will of whatever kind. Every political activism is preceded by an encounter with the political, with the activating force of antagonism. That is why political agents are not the metaphysical subjects of their activ-ism (even as they necessarily mistake themselves as the Ground of their own actions) but themselves *are activated* by the political. No social conflict can be voluntaristically enforced. And yet: we acti-vate the political in our activism to the same degree to which we are activated by the political by acting *as if* we were subjects of our own will. The name for this paradoxical undertaking is politics. As little as it is possible to enforce an antagonism, we still create the potential for its appearance as soon as we actively intervene in the play of the world – which certainly is not a rare occurrence, nor does it always happen on a scale of grandiosity.

Therefore, anti-hegemonic shifts even of the smallest order are never pointless, as long as they cause the dominant forma-tion to have to work on tightening its hegemony. Beyond that, nobody can predict where minor shifts might accumulate to become greater faults in the hegemonic order and, in the words of Lefort, create a 'breach' in the dominant structure of institutions and cause cracks in the order of legitimacy: 'Only a breach?', Lefort said with reference to May 1968 in France, 'maybe . . . . But the trace of the breach will remain, even once the veil has been rewoven' (Lefort 2008a: 52). These traces remain not least because of the exemplarity of political action. While the general strike and the occupations did not smash the structure of society, they have shown, Lefort holds, the contingency of a political model otherwise considered invulnerable. The political, even in its smallest possible dosage, is therefore everywhere. However, this everywhere, it must be pointed out, is a very strange place that nobody has ever seen. The presence of the political as the ontological moment of the foundation of society can, as I have tried to demonstrate, only be accessed from the experience of the absence of a firm ground, meaning from our experience of the incompleteness of the social. Nobody has ever come across 'the political' in all its purity at any other place than in the breaches, gaps and cracks of the social, which are filled, stretched or closed by – *politics*. Insofar as this happens constantly, it also happens on the smallest scale. Taking up a metaphor by Nietzsche, who was not only the philosopher of megalomania, but also the philosopher of dance and effortless facility: it is the minimal actions that bring on the storm, for 'Thoughts that come on doves' feet guide the world' (Nietzsche 1999: 189).

Part III
Politicising Thought

7 The Final Name of Being: Thinking as Reflective Intervention

Taking Laclau beyond Laclau

In Parts I and II of our investigation I have consistently distinguished between two versions of political ontology. In the case of the 'onto-logics' of politics – which, in Laclau, is called hegemony and comprises a general theory of signification – the concept of antagonism has a particular function in any process of signification: it allows for the articulation of differences into a chain of equivalence by providing them with a common negative outside. While Laclau describes, with great intellectual clarity and elegance, the *laws* of discourse and hegemony, he was hesitant to draw the ontological consequences. But these consequences are quite obvious. If his discourse theory amounts to a political theory of signification, rather than just a theory of political signification, then antagonism is involved, to some degree, in the stabilisation (and dislocation) of *any* meaning – no matter whether political or social. And if, as Laclau presumes (*NR* 100–3), all social being is discursively structured, then, given his theory of signification, antagonism must assume ontological status with regard to *all* social being. But we do not need to engage with Laclau's theory of discourse in order to arrive at this conclusion. Analogous consequences can be drawn from Laclau's theory of sedimentation and reactivation as presented in Chapter 4. If all things social are instituted politically (i.e. by *the political*), and if the moments of institution continue reverberating throughout the instituted – by making social institutions 'tremble' – no social being will remain untouched by antagonism.[1] As soon as this point is accepted, we are forced to move beyond Laclau's political 'onto-logic'. We have to turn our view towards an *ontology of the political*. The latter exceeds any theory concerned with the symbolic laws of discourse or political articulation. What will be at stake is the political nature of social being *eo ipso*. We have thus to approach, as far as it is possible, antagonism *as* antagonism, the ground *as* ground. But is that a feasible undertaking? In order to answer this question we need to reflect on the status of ontology *as* ontology – that is to say, we have to determine the very status of *thinking*.

Laclau will be of little help in addressing such meta-theoretical questions. He rarely expressed concern over the status of his theory or the methodology of his approach. Like many other left Heideggerians, he shared Heidegger's aversion to anything that smacks of epistemology. In the two remaining chapters of our investigation, I would like to demonstrate that it is possible to account for the status of our theoretical endeavour *without* having to engage in any kind of epistemological reasoning. We will not plant a new head onto the multi-headed Hydra of epistemology. Instead, I will propose an alternative form of self-reflection that is firmly located *in the ontological register*. Such a political form of self-reflection has little in common with the kind of reasoning taken for granted in traditions of scientific and philosophical rationalism. Rather, it means to accept the wager of *thinking*, that is, of 'reasoning' in a non-epistemological mode: a mode of political ontology. Contrary to what can be expected in the Western metaphysical tradition, this kind of 'thinking' is not predominantly a matter of cognition, nor is it concerned with what can be 'known' with certainty. Thinking is something we *do*. But, what exactly are we doing when we think? My response – which will also give me the opportunity of weaving together many of the threads delineated in previous chapters – will bring us back, full circle, to ontic politics. For, to determine the role and status of *political thought* – as a practice of thinking 'the political' politically – we have to pass through politics. In other words, we have to politicise thought.

So, how to move beyond the dominant horizon of epistemology? As stated in Chapter 1, Heidegger's great lesson was to shift the terrain of interrogation from questions regarding being-qua-understanding to those regarding being-qua-being. In the earlier Heidegger, this meant that we had to accept that whatever we know will arise from our being-in-the-world. This does not preclude theoretical reflection, but we have to be very clear about the meaning of reflection in an ontological sense: to *reflect* means to implicate ourselves in our being-in-the-world, thereby accepting that we are always already fully implicated. Herein lies the Heideggerian significance of Foucault's enigmatic phrase of an 'ontology of ourselves'. It should not only be understood in the trivial sense of *Zeitkritik*. What Foucault calls a critical 'ontology of actuality', an ontological account of our present condition, has to pass through 'ourselves'. Thinking, I contend, is reflective in the sense of creating a flection, of folding ourselves back into the matter of our thought and of unfolding thought into an 'ontology of ourselves'. Thinking is a *material* practice. It is part of, and concerned with, the matter of our social world.

As soon as we pass Heidegger by granting primary status to the political, the above claim requires two specifications. First, the world in which we implicate ourselves is a world formed and deformed by antagonism. We implicate ourselves in an embattled place. Thinking, for this reason, is far from being a purely meditative practice, a vacuous activity presented by the later Heidegger as 'passivity'. By way of thinking we actualise the political rather than merely meditating on its concept. Nor can there be thinking 'pure and simple', self-sufficient and without any object matter. We always think *something*; even though, in the case of an ontology of the political, this something is not an ontic object among other objects of potential research, but something that escapes empirical measurement: a radical negativity that becomes tangible only in a play of difference-as-difference. We have called this instance of differential negativity antagonism. And second, we can implicate ourselves in this embattled world because it is a place we *already* occupy.[2] We are always already thrown into a conflict zone, struck by exclusion, power and unevenness, a zone that very much resembles Gramsci's description of civil society as 'a powerful system of fortresses and earthworks' (Gramsci 1971: 238). And it is by way of thinking the inescapable facticity of this politically instituted space that we learn to *embrace* the political. Embracing not in the sense of *amor fati*, but in the sense of *amor facti*: of accepting antagonism as a *factum politicum*. It might be asked: Why should one learn to embrace something inescapable? The answer is simple: Because everyone believes it to be escapable. Most of the time people tend to deny, repress or disavow the antagonistic nature of the world they live in. But as we start thinking antagonism we begin to actively occupy what, up to that point, we had passively inhabited. In this regard, thinking is a practice of affirming, and thereby enacting the political.[3] More than a cognitive reflection, it is a reflective intervention.

A Political Theory of Naming

A reflective intervention, by arousing dormant conflicts, will produce effects of reactivation. Thinking, as defined here, reactivates the sedimented routines in which ideas are conventionally embedded. These routines are institutionalised into scientific disciplines, academic habits and accepted rules of reasoning, and they reproduce and certify the sedimented layers of canonical knowledge. With regard to its potential to dislocate and reassemble these routines and sedimented layers, a reflective intervention into the realm of discipline and *doxa* is a form of acting, rather than mere reasoning or meditating. A variety of strategies might be applied. The most powerful form of acting, as we will see, is *naming*. To understand this, we have to first take note of the fact that 'antagonism', from the point of thinking, is not, or not predominantly, a concept. Antagonism is a name. In the political ontology that I tried to develop in previous chapters, antagonism served as our *name* for being, that is, for the never-ending play between institution and dislocation, ground and abyss of the social. This claim is not as far-fetched as it may sound. As Alain Badiou, *à propos* Deleuze's suggestion of 'life' as a name of being, argued: 'assigning the name of being is a crucial decision' for it 'expresses the very nature of thought' (Badiou 2000: 193). I agree, but would add that assigning the name of being is not a purely intellectual and intra-philosophical affair. To name being, rather, involves an investment which, in turn, cannot rely on any ultimate ground of justification.[4] But it is precisely because such justificatory ground is not available that it has to be supplemented in a political move. In this political sense, it is the name that provides a supplementary ground; the name becomes, as Laclau put it, the *ground* of the thing. Therefore, Badiou is only partially right: assigning the name of being is a crucial decision indeed, but it is a political decision. It does express the very nature of thought – but not only its philosophical nature: it attests to the *political* nature of thought as a practice of naming. Contrary to what Badiou believes, the nature of thought is political.

Laclau's theory of naming, especially his distinction between concept and name, will help to elucidate this claim. In his book on populism, he turned to the debate between descriptivists and anti-descriptivists in analytic philosophy. Descriptivists (like Bertrand Russell) argue that proper names are related to their objects by way of descriptive features. Laclau gives the example of 'George W. Bush' as an abbreviated description of 'the US President who invaded Iraq' (*PR* 101). The anti-descriptivists, spearheaded by Saul Kripke, argue against this idea, since even if in another world Bush had not invaded Iraq, the name 'Bush' would still apply to him. Kripke famously argued in *Naming and Necessity* that names (and this holds not only for proper names but also for common names such as 'gold') are *rigid designators* that refer to one and the same object in all possible worlds (Kripke 1980). They designate their object not through descriptions but through an initial and founding act of 'primal baptism'. While this solution is more convincing than the descriptivist solution, it encounters problems of its own. According to Žižek (1989: 89–97), anti-descriptivists cannot provide an answer to the problem of what makes the object of rigid designation identical to itself in all possible worlds and beyond all descriptive changes. The Lacanian solution, proposed by Žižek, is that this 'X' which guarantees the identity of the object in all counterfactual situations is nothing else than '*the retroactive effect of naming itself*: it is the name itself, the signifier, which supports the identity of the object' (95). Laclau basically concurs: the identity of any object is not 'expressed' by a given name, but is the retroactive result of the very process of naming. Naming, hence, becomes productive in a new sense because it is not restricted any more to the moment of pure designation, as in Kripke's primal baptism, but it must be performed.

The practice of naming, and this is why Laclau's theory is helpful, consists in the emptying of a concept. Naming is conceptualised best along the lines of the logic of the empty signifier, elaborated by Laclau in an earlier paper (*E* 36–46). The emptying of the signifier is a direct result of the equivalential extension of demands for which the empty signifier functions as a nodal point that represents the chain in its entirety. To reiterate one of Laclau's preferred examples, the name 'Solidarność' initially functioned as a signifier for particular demands in the particular situation of dockers in Gdansk. Had it signified a certain demand of these workers only, this demand could have been accommodated by the institutional setting of the Polish system, it could have been integrated into a system of *differences*. To the extent that it connected with other demands by other discontented sectors of society, however, a chain of equivalence was built which the system could not handle any more in a differential manner. From the perspective of this chain of equivalence the communist system functioned as the antagonistic other which, in purely negative terms, served as the ground for the equivalential linking of the most diverse anti-systemic demands. 'Solidarność' then turned from the slogan of a local group of workers into a name for opposition *as such*. At the same time, though, it had to be emptied of its specific content in order to function as a name for a much wider counter-hegemonic equivalential chain. It turned into an empty signifier increasingly devoid of particular signifieds.

The logic of the empty signifier, as it evolved in Laclau's work into a general theory of naming, bears radical implications for the way we envisage political action. While for objectivists the 'group' is an entity that pre-exists the process of naming, in Laclau's post-foundational approach a social agent only exists to the extent that it is named: 'the identity and unity of the object results from the very operation of naming' (*PR* 104). Politics does not give expression to pre-given interests or pre-established identities, but is to be understood as the very process by which a group assumes its name.

Hegemony theory is thus reformulated by Laclau as a theory of naming: if the identity of a given social group cannot be derived from a stable ground (from the position within the relations of production, for instance), it can only be the result of a process of hegemonic articulation. The group will be held together by the name that emerged from this process. The name, consequently, 'does not express the unity of the group, but becomes its ground' (*PR* 231). One can see how, compared with the Lacanian logic of the signifier as presented by Žižek, a political twist is given to the operation of naming. Politics is all about the hegemonic struggle over the expansion of a chain of equivalence at the expense of the field of 'positive' differences, and concomitantly over the emptying of the signifier. The primal baptism of a political agent (such as Solidarność), by which this agent comes into existence, results from a hegemonic intervention. Naming, in this regard, is the quintessential political activity. Naming is grounding.

Naming Being

There is no reason why Laclau's argument should exclusively apply to names in the field of politics. If our assumption is correct that Laclau's theory of signification is to be granted the status of a general theory that provides us with the laws of meaning production *tout court*, then the operation of naming may occur in meaning formations other than political discourse – scientific and philosophical discourses included. The latter discourses, however, pride themselves on their *conceptual* nature. And here the distinction between name and concept is key. Any conceptual order is predominantly structured according to the logic of difference: a particular content is assigned to a concept by way of the differential positioning of the latter vis-à-vis other concepts. Take, for example, a system of definitions: ideally, every single defined item has to be sufficiently differentiated vis-à-vis all other items of the system. An item whose content overlaps with the content of another item would be poorly defined because the entire order functions according to the logic of difference and not equivalence. Theories tend to be in general constructed along the differential axis of signification. A philosophical system is considered well built when every single concept is assigned an exclusive content, so that conceptual confusion and redundancy can be avoided. Similarly, a scientific approach to 'politics' will either proceed nominalistically and via definitions, as typically in Max Weber, or by presenting a cluster of empirically derived descriptive features and locating these features within a classificatory system. Applied to the study of politics, this means that a social science approach would always seek to insert the phenomenon of politics into a conceptual order of differences. Both philosophy and the social sciences, even where the latter conceive of themselves as 'empirical', are predominantly located on the conceptual axis.[5]

Moving on to political ontology, we have to ask whether or not the same holds for an ontology of the political. Is it a conceptual system? Is 'the political' a *concept*? Certainly, a conventional notion of 'politics', as distinguishable from other social practices, falls into the order of the conceptual. This remains the case even if we enlarge the concept of politics in the direction of *minimal politics*: a set of criteria, applicable to any moment of political protestation, allow politics, in even its minimal form, to be distinguished from other social practices (and in particular from what is deceivably called 'micro-politics', which, in our view, has nothing to do with politics). But 'the political'? In many accounts, most famously in Carl Schmitt's *The Concept of the Political* (Schmitt 1963), it operates as a concept, as is to be expected from the book title. For Schmitt, the term is meant to provide a distinctive criterion, the friend/enemy distinction, that allows discriminating between, on the one side, the political and, on the other, the economic, the religious, the artistic, and so on, each of which is defined by its own distinctive criterion. With Laclau, however, the political can be given a more radical interpretation. If Laclau's thesis of the primacy of the political is accepted, the term comes to denote the instituting moment of the social and, therefore, is nothing less than the foundation of all other social distinctions, criteria or categories. It is not delimitable, it does not refer to a particular region within the social topography or to a criterion that could be distinguished from other social criteria – not on the same ontological plane, by all means. From an ontological perspective, even its counterpart, the social, overlaps with the political. As was argued in Chapter 5 on the basis of Laclau's primacy of the political thesis, the social is nothing other than the political itself in a sedimented mode. Hence, 'the political' cannot be of the order of positive conceptual differences.

A similar mistake would be to assume that the political could be clearly distinguished from politics. As I have repeatedly insisted, the political difference should not be mistaken for a particular ontic distinction. Rather, an interminable play makes the political appear (in moments of politics) and disappear (by way of sedimentation) within the field of positive social differences; and this play cannot be conceptually grasped. The analogy, if it is an analogy, with Heidegger's onto-ontological difference is striking. Heidegger's 'beyng' – the evental play of difference-as-difference – does not amount to a concept that could be nailed down by a definition or a host of descriptive features. As a self-unfolding process it escapes conceptualisation so that Heidegger, again and again, attempts to approach the play of difference through many avenues: as *aletheia*, as ab-ground, as the event of enowning, as clearing, as presencing, as the fourfold, the giving (*Es gibt*) or simply as being, which all are, at best, variations on the same theme. These are equivalent ways of encircling something which escapes conceptualisation and, therefore, can only be approached by way of thinking. I have criticised the later Heidegger for the Zen-like vacuity of his notion of being as well as for the amorphous shape of what he calls 'thinking'. In political ontology, if it is truly political, thinking must not be envisaged as the meditation of something ineffable. One has to avoid the trap of total vacuity, without falling into the converse trap of reifying being into an ontic entity. In the first case we would leave the realm of thinking in the direction of mysticism, in the second we abandon thinking for the sake of empiricism. What we are looking for is a *political* kind of vacuity that avoids the symmetric traps of the mystical and the empirical – which is why a political theory of naming proves to be essential. While the play of grounding and degrounding cannot be, in the strict sense, conceptualised, it can nevertheless be named.

The reason is evident, given Laclau's theory of naming. If the conceptual order functions differentially, the nominal order works on the basis of equivalence: a name emerges as a nodal point around which differences are structured into an equivalential chain. A name takes over the task of representing the totality of this chain *without* expressing 'any conceptual unity that precedes it' (*PR* 108). No conceptual correlate exists to which the name could refer. There is *no particular* signified that would be attached to the signifier.[6] This may sound like a rather Heideggerian kind of vacuity, but in political ontology, equivalence is based on *antagonism*: on a radical negativity against which the unity of the chain can be established. That a name does not signify anything particular does not imply, therefore, that it signifies an indifferent Zenish 'nothing'. What it does signify is the *unity* of all differences that are brought into a relation of equivalence. And if this unity is signifiable only in opposition to an outside that is experienced as threatening and dislocating, a name will always bear the mark of negativity. 'Solidarność', to take up the previous example, signifies unity only to the extent to which it signifies opposition to a hostile political system. Without radical negativity no equivalential unity could be established to begin with. A name, by signifying equivalence, will at the same time signify antagonism. *Any* true name, to be precise, will – by implication – be a name of antagonism. It will not only serve as an empty signifier for a given chain of equivalence, it will also point us, if only implicitly, to the instance of antagonism as the very source of institution/dislocation of that chain.[7]

What I want to propose now may seem like a rather simple operation: to make explicit, to turn inside out, what is the implicit nature of all names. If antagonism is the ultimate referent of any name, political ontology needs to name antagonism. If, as demonstrated, any act of primal baptism points to an ontological instance of radical negativity, then the act of primal baptism peculiar to an ontology of the political consists in naming this instance. This task might not be as easy to achieve as it seems, for it obviously involves a *non*-theoretical, yet reflective intervention into theory. It cannot be purely theoretical, scientific or philosophical, given that theories are predominantly ordered conceptually, that is, along the differential axis. Since naming always involves equivalence, the conceptual character of theory will thus be disturbed, and it will be all the more disturbed as, for an ontology of the political, 'antagonism' is supposed to name the very ground and abyss of *all* ontic being. As repeatedly argued, antagonism names the being of all social beings both in their sedimented and their reactivated state, both in spatial and in temporal form. As a name for social being *eo ipso*, it of course creates an extremely expanded chain of equivalence.[8] And yet, the name 'antagonism' is not just a simple 'X', an entirely emptied signifier. It bears traces of a concept (a signified) that can be followed back to a school of thought and a network of intellectual debate; it is even applied as an analytical tool in many studies in the framework of post-foundational discourse theory. Selecting 'antagonism', rather than any other term, is therefore not an arbitrary choice, as it results from a naming operation rooted in a social and political context. What is more, the term 'antagonism' suggests itself for its historical dimension: it is within a particular tradition of left-Hegelianism and Marxism that our move assumes verisimilitude. Assigning the name of antagonism, thus, does not come down to an act of decisionism, for the name may, or may not, assume plausibility within a particular politico-theoretical context and tradition. For someone working in an entirely different paradigm – say, a rational choice theorist – it does not make sense at all. But then again, 'rational choice' does not fare any better from the perspective of political ontology.

Laclau: Populism as a Name for Politics

Thinking, we have seen, does not unfold within a transparent medium of cognition, as 'ideas' presumably do; instead, it intervenes from a place *outside* the cognitional order of an isolated mind. We now have to discuss the implications such a kind of intervention may produce for the field of philosophy. To recapitulate: while political theories, as a rule, content themselves with proposing a concept of politics (mostly a depoliticised concept of politics), political ontology has to propose a name for the political. This involves an operation of naming which, in turn, can only be political by nature. But can it be *purely* political? The answer is certainly 'no'. If fully politicised, a given political ontology would turn into a party manifesto, with its philosophical or theoretical value close to zero. In the Soviet Union, cohorts of academic ideologists worked relentlessly to achieve the ideal of a fully politicised philosophy called dialectical materialism. I have no intention of recommending the model. I am not proposing that antagonism is a name and a name only. Undeniably, it is also a concept, and we have tried to retrace the conceptual evolution of this concept from the Kantian antinomies via Hegel and Marx to Laclau. Concurrently, political ontologies do not only belong to the nominal order; to the extent to which they are theories with some degree of conceptual consistency and internal differentiation they also belong to the conceptual order. For this reason, I have proposed to envisage the practice of thinking in terms of intervention, and not of imperialism. While being a political intervention into the conceptual order, thinking should not deteriorate into mere sloganeering (which would be even worse than being reduced to a purely intellectual pastime). Thinking has, as we will see in the next chapter, political attributes (the attributes of minimal politics), but is not exhausted by politics.

What I want to defend is the following: it is because of its political force that thinking can intervene in the field of theory, the latter being understood as an intrinsically uneven and partially opaque terrain of differences. By the creation of a name, a conceptual order is both disturbed and reassembled. Naming reactivates the sedimented order of definitions, classifications and conceptual hierarchies specific to a given philosophy, a philosophical paradigm, an intellectual tradition or an accepted canon of ideas. Naming brings conflict to concepts. It rouses dormant antagonisms and brings to light the forgotten partisanship of certain theories, their exclusion of alternatives and the lines of conflict that cut across the borders between the world of theory and the world of politics. Only by creating a flection, by inflecting ourselves as political agents into the, supposedly, depoliticised fields of science and philosophy, can we begin to accept that we are already implicated, that the borders between the theoretical and the political field are already criss-crossed by multifarious antagonisms, and that there is no politically neutral point of observation (the great fantasy of the epistemologists). This can be exemplified with Laclau's own reflective intervention in mainstream political science theories of populism. *On Populist Reason*, the book where he presents his theory of naming, is based on a scandalous claim that has troubled many reviewers: populism, for Laclau, is not a particular form of politics among others. Rather, by encapsulating political rationality *tout court*, it should be identified as the quintessential form of politics.

It did not go unnoticed that, with this claim, the very distinction between politics and populism was abolished (Stavrakakis 2004). Laclau himself anticipated the critique in the preface to his book: 'One consequence of this intervention is that the referent of "populism" becomes blurred, because many phenomena which were not traditionally considered populist come under that umbrella in our analysis' (*PR* xi). Interestingly, Laclau uses the term 'intervention' and, given what was said before, it is clear that he is engaged in an equivalential operation of naming. Populism becomes the Laclauian name for politics because the latter, for Laclau, is about constructing a frontier between us and them, which also is the essence of the former: articulating a chain of equivalence among the people *versus* the elite. What he does not say, because he does not bother reflecting on the status of his theory, is that his own operation proceeds along the same lines of equivalence by proposing populism as a name that comprehends all other forms of politics. He justifies the curious move by pointing out 'that the referent of "populism" in social analysis has always been ambiguous and vague', and that his attempt 'has not been to find the *true* referent of populism, but to do the opposite: to show that populism has no referential unity because it is ascribed not to a delimitable phenomenon but to a social logic whose effects cut across many phenomena' (*PR* xi). What this explanation lacks, even as the equivalential nature of the term is asserted, is the recognition of the fact that Laclau himself engages in a naming operation. But this is exactly, I would argue, where the political edge of Laclau's intervention has to be located: by way of rebaptising politics, Laclau moves populism, a formerly denigrated phenomenon of political mobilisation, from a marginal place into the limelight. He inverts the terms of debate by transposing a concept from the register of difference (the conceptual order) to the register of equivalence (the nominal order), in that way contributing not only to the theorisation of politics but also to the politicisation of theory.[9]

Laclau's theory of populism, by elevating a concept that – just as the corresponding concept of 'the people' – used to be marginal and denigrated, to the status of a name, contributes to the effective politicisation of mainstream political theory and science. It brings into view the customary disavowal of *the political* in mainstream political science. Laclau's operation is an example of what I call a reflective intervention, or simply *inflection*: a practice of thinking by which actual politics is folded into theory. The political motivation of Laclau's intervention is patently obvious. Who else would dare to make populism the centre of political thought if not a lifelong Peronist who, apart from being an academic theorist of populism, was at the same time a public advocate of Kirchnerism and other variants of progressive populism? Not surprisingly, *On Populist Reason*, a supposedly highly 'abstract' work of theory, was hailed in Latin America as a timely comment – and a philosophical endorsement – of the 'pink tide' of left-leaning populist governments. If thinking, as a practice of inflection, means to redirect political antagonisms towards the conceptual order, thus making them cut through the sedimented layers of what Thomas Kuhn called 'normal science', then Laclau's inflection resulted in nothing less than a political reversal of the fundamental terms of the academic debate on populism.

Why Ontology?

The preceding discussion may help explain why we hold onto the name 'ontology'. Let me clarify why an apparently overcome philosophical discipline should be retained. As explained in Chapter 1, modern philosophy has turned into a quest for the conditions of *understanding*, bypassing all questions concerning the nature of *being*.[10] Why, then, hold onto such an apparently outdated enterprise? Not for reasons of philosophical nostalgia, to be sure, but in order to maintain its radical potential. 'Ontology' is a name for the nominal order – the order of equivalence – in philosophy. For what is of interest from an ontological point of view is not this or that sub-species of beings, but the being of *all* beings. This remains true even for a post-foundational ontology in which the ultimately abyssal nature of all grounds is affirmed, and by which traditional ontology is both transformed and politicised.

In the first place, it is transformed because ontology is not to be conceived any more as the quest for a stable ground of being; instead, it is turned into what Derrida has so appropriately called 'hauntology': the spectral presence of a ground that remains absent, but exerts an uncanny presence in moments of conflict and contingency. The name 'ontology' can thus be retained as a post-foundational name for the science of the foundation, not of one ontic region of social being or another, but of the instituting ground, and destructive abyss, of being as such. What is still 'ontological' about this science is its universal scope: the reference to being-qua-being. And it could not be otherwise. If we were to grant merely regional validity to a post-foundational ontology, we would leave the possibility of *at least one* foundation somewhere that could quite rightly lay a claim to ultimate grounding. But this would bring us back to the foundationalist stance we had excluded *ex hypothesi*. A post-foundational ontology will thus retain the traditional status of a *metaphysica generalis* or *first philosophy*, except that its metaphysical claims with regard to an ultimate foundation are seriously weakened.

Secondly, it is politicised because ontology, if retained, will only make sense as *political ontology* – or, to be more precise, as an ontology of *the political*. And again it is easy to see why. If an ultimate ground is not available, and if on the other hand a universe devoid of all grounds would be an unliveable, psychotic place, then the absent ground has to be substituted. Evidently, metaphysical replacements – be they God, Reason, the laws of the Market, or the human Genome – are unpersuasive from a post-foundational perspective. But persuasive or not, whatever comes to serve as a substitute for the absent ground will emerge from a political struggle. In the last instance, all these fraudulent grounds result from a *political* act of institution: no God without the hegemonic

power of the church; no Reason without the struggle of bourgeois enlightenment; no blind Market forces without the forces
of their blind ideologists; and no believe in the determining role
of the human Genome without the life sciences being made the
authoritative model of social explanation. Grounds emerge from
hegemonic paradigm shifts. For instance: while social phenomena
were authoritatively explained, for the most part of the twentieth
century, by sociologists, they are now explained by economists,
biologists and brain researchers. This would not have been possible without large-scale shifts within the hegemonic formation. So,
to lay a ground means to exclude equally available alternatives,
which in turn requires the power to do so. On the other hand, we
cannot not invest in the grounding game. Ignoring the necessity
of at least *some* foundation would catapult us out of the realm of
the political, leaving behind the illusory image of an entirely pacified and harmonious society – a dream world for fundamentalists.
Grounding is necessary as a political activity. And what comes to
replace the Ground, from the viewpoint of a post-foundational
ontology, is *the political* as the grounding/degrounding moment of
all social grounds. Ontology, for this reason, can only be retained
as an ontology of *the political*.

How, then, to determine the philosophical status of this
ontology? On the basis of the previous points, I see only one
possibility: by way of self-implication, which also means self-
application. To be congruent, ontology, if it is to retain its universal scope, must be self-applicable. After the outer-worldly
standpoint of epistemology has been abandoned, ontological
claims do not issue any longer from a place located beyond the
realm of their application. Whatever is ontologically claimed
about the entirety of ontic beings must also apply to ontology
itself. Think again of Laclau's theory of signification. By virtue
of describing (like any other theory of language) the laws of
meaning production *in general*, his theory must also be applicable to itself – provided that it is meaningful. Similarly, a theory
of hegemony *à la Laclau*, in which hegemony is seen as perme-
ating the entire field of the social, should itself be understood
as constituting a hegemonic move within the social field of

theory. And, consequently, to develop an ontology of *the political* necessitates a *political* move within ontology. What may sound scandalous for epistemologists is only consequential for political ontologists. Provided the latter cannot – and do not want to – arrogate a God's-eye view, political ontology must be considered a social discourse like any other and therefore has to be founded, like any other, on a political act of institution. It must therefore also be possible to, as it were, self-apply political ontology to the field where it is formulated, philosophy, by reactivating the latter's political grounds of institution and by undermining its sedimented structures.[11]

However, caution is advisable, for 'undermining' does not amount to 'overthrowing'. From what was said one could be tempted to draw the conclusion, as Laclau seems to do, that transferring the primacy to politics simultaneously evokes the very end of philosophy: 'Once undecidability has reached the ground itself [. . .] the realm of philosophy comes to an end and the realm of politics begins' (*E* 123). But is the disappearance of philosophy the only logical alternative? Not necessarily. The quote could also be read as implying that the realm of philosophy, once grounds have turned shaky, will become *politicised* without simply disappearing. I thus consider it hardly constructive to frame 'the end of philosophy' and 'the beginning of politics' as two successive, mutually exclusive historical stages. From a post-foundational perspective, that idea of leaving behind the terrain of metaphysics is but the last fantasy of metaphysics. The aim should not be to overcome metaphysical philosophy – for 'overcoming' is, as Heidegger showed, but another trope of metaphysical foundation – but rather to politically subvert the metaphysical terrain on which we all stand. Instead of dealing with two successive phases – previously philosophy, now politics – we are faced with a contested political front line that cuts across the borders of philosophy. This front line needs to be retraced. My argument, for the remaining parts of this chapter, is that the task of thinking – as a reflective intervention – consists in twisting front lines, so that political antagonisms bend into the field of philosophy. Where this succeeds, philosophical grounds will be reactivated, and it will become apparent that they have always been political.

The Political History of Ontology: Negri's Descartes

Such a practice of reflective intervention may appear ambitious; yet, and perhaps surprisingly, it is not without precedence. In the materialist tradition of intellectual history a number of treatments have been able to highlight the manifold intersections of philosophy and politics (Goldmann 2013; Macpherson 1962; Meiksins Wood 2012; Wood 1983). Let us briefly consult two of the most important studies. We turn to them because they can provide proof of the fact that ontology, in the traditional metaphysical sense of the term, was always already deeply political – perhaps, it *was* political ontology without ontologists conceding it.

In his books on Descartes and Spinoza, Antonio Negri showed that the historical crisis of traditional metaphysical ontologies – a crisis that would lead to the dominance of epistemology – was ultimately a *political* crisis, a crisis of the hegemonic formation (Negri 1991, 2004, 2007). Negri provides a largely convincing description of how Descartes' philosophy was inscribed into the political battles of its time. The ingenuity of Descartes' strategic move consisted in the idea of reinventing an ontological *prima philosophia* on epistemological terms. As is well known, Descartes' attempt was to grant the *ego cogito* the status of an ultimate grounding or *fundamentum inconcussum*. But this was, already in Descartes' time, a 'metaphysical accident'. It was not compatible, in its own time, with the dominant academic understanding, which was the scientific philosophy of mechanism. And yet this apparent step backwards into metaphysics proved to be an important point of departure for the further development of philosophy. How is this to be explained? Negri submits that Descartes advanced his metaphysics at a moment in history when the 'original defeat' of the early bourgeoisie had to be processed. Following the defeat of the sixteenth-century humanist revolution, the bourgeoisie was in isolation, separated from the sphere of political power that it had sought to attain. In an unstable alliance with absolutism it remained caught between feudal nobility on the one side and the revolts of the multitude on the other. While accepting the impossibility of a political alternative to absolutism, the bourgeoisie insisted on at least having *social* hegemony (Negri 2007: 199).

So, according to Negri, Cartesian metaphysics is still far removed from the triumphalist sense of victory that imbues the bourgeois rationalism of later centuries. It is shaped by an awareness of the defeat suffered by Renaissance humanism as well as the isolation of the early bourgeoisie. The separation of the ego from the world, as is autobiographically laid bare in the first part of the *Discours* as well as the first *Meditation*, sums up the inner erosion of humanism. However, in the course of the second meditation, the anti-foundationalist temptation of radical scepticism is transformed into a positive demand for reconstructing the relationship with the world. In order to ensure that not all foundations are undermined in this process, at least one firm principle is required. The solution is well known: the notion of a regrounding of man himself – in the shape of a thinking ego – makes it possible even for an isolated subject to reattain objective being via *self-grounding*. In metaphysical terms that is: the being (the essence) needs only itself in order to attain existence.[12]

According to Negri, the historical condition for Cartesian metaphysics lies in the separation between the sphere of bourgeois autonomy (civil society) and the repressive apparatus of the state which thwarts the political rise of the bourgeoisie. Descartes' solution within the field of philosophy: the (bourgeois) subject's isolation from the world is turned into a positive and becomes a source of its autonomy, which in turn forms the basis for a future reconstruction of the world and hence the retroactive overcoming of isolation. Yet this does not suffice for Descartes. He alters the perception of the crisis by developing what could be described as the *hegemonic project* of Cartesianism. For this purpose, he must – that is the essence of the politics of Cartesian ontology – intervene in the complex array of alternatives at his disposal. He must go beyond the positions of the subversive *libertins*, the long-established Aristotelians and the mechanists and their alliance with absolutism. Although Descartes' alternative project subscribes to a mechanist demand for a methodically founded 'new physics', it does not fully merge with mechanism. Where it is based in the ontological foundation of a self-aware, autonomous subject, it exhibits a politico-metaphysical surplus that turns out to be the only explanation for its enormous historico-political significance until the time of the French Revolution. Hence, Cartesianism amounts to a *political ontology*, even as Descartes has not written a political theory, and quite independently of his rather conventional moral-theoretical emissions.

Important, from our perspective, is the conclusion drawn by Negri in the current postface to the English edition. He argues that every author's ontology includes the seeds of such an '*implicit political dispositif*' (318), which defines its historical efficiencies and also its connectivity for future generations. Negri explicitly notes 'that every metaphysics is in some way a political ontology – as has been clearly demonstrated by Machiavelli, Spinoza and Marx (and, subsequently, has been the basis for the broad philosophical consensus that runs from Nietzsche to Foucault and Derrida)' (317). This insight goes beyond the findings of, for instance, the Cambridge School of intellectual history, which considers political theories to be polemical interventions into the ideological conflicts of their time. While this is certainly the case, it must be stated that it does not hold true only for works of political theory, but indeed also for the apparently a-political works of metaphysics.

Unfolding Philosophy: Balibar's Spinoza and beyond

Next to Antonio Negri (1991, 2004), Étienne Balibar also elaborated on the indivisible relationship of political battles and philosophical ontology. In a study on Spinoza's philosophy, Balibar went one step further than Negri by no longer exclusively tying the political battles of an era to the category of class. This allows him to be historically more specific. In his study on *Spinoza and Politics*, Balibar is able to root Spinoza's philosophy in the immediate political battles and structures of alliance in which it had intervened on the side of the Republican party.[13] But also on the side of philosophy, Balibar argues, it is necessary to expand the investigation beyond Spinoza's works of political theory in order to understand his intervention. Only once the fundamental separation between the *Ethics*, meaning Spinoza's ontology, the *Tractatus Politicus* and the *Tractatus Theologico-Politicus* is removed, would it be possible to recognise Spinoza's understanding of 'ethics' as a name for the reciprocal relationship between philosophy and politics. Although there are manifold differences between the three œuvres, they do have one thing in common: they are all *simultaneously* philosophical and political investigations:

> [Spinoza's] work is not divided into a metaphysics (or an ontology) on the one hand and a politics or an ethics, which are seen as 'secondary' applications of 'first' philosophy, on the other. From the very beginning, his metaphysics is a philosophy of praxis, of activity; and his politics is a philosophy, for it constitutes the field of experience in which human nature acts and strives to achieve liberation. (Balibar 2008a: 102)

In Spinoza's work, philosophy and politics are in a relationship of mutual implication. This is why his philosophical study of political problems never constituted a distraction from his metaphysical examinations. Quite the opposite: these problems enabled Spinoza to trace the true interests and problems of philosophy, and vice versa:

> By posing specifically philosophical problems, Spinoza is not choosing to approach his political concerns by an indirect route, he is not transposing them from their proper place and recasting them in a 'metapolitical' medium. He deals in philosophical terms because only philosophy can give him means to know exactly [. . .] the power relations and the particular interests that are at stake in politics. For only thus can he know them *by their causes*. (Balibar 2008a: 4)

Balibar and Negri agree that even the most abstract metaphysics in Spinoza's works is inseparably related to politics. Negri's studies have shown that any metaphysics, at least implicitly, becomes a political ontology to the extent to which it is moulded by a given 'hegemonic dispositif'. The question to be aimed at Balibar, however, is whether this reciprocal relationship between ontology and politics describes only the works of Spinoza or whether we ought in fact to suspect that it is inherent in the production of philosophy itself. If the thesis remains limited to Spinoza, there is a danger that Spinoza will be celebrated as an exception among thinkers (a quite traditional tendency that can still be found in Negri, Deleuze and others). What might happen, however, if we remove this limitation? It will turn out that the most abstract works of ontology are always already implicated in a hegemonic formation (as political instruments, not by merely reflecting political developments), and that they might have been *political* ontologies all along. The entire history of philosophy would then have to be researched with regard to its onto-political implications. This, of course, would be beyond the scope of our project.[14] Our short digression into the history of philosophy was simply intended to illustrate the unbreakable relationship between (a) ontology as a metaphysical science of foundation, and (b) political battles in the context of a hegemonic struggle, a Gramscian 'war of position', i.e. integral politics. Intellectual history in the materialist tradition has confirmed our suspicion that the ontological, in actual fact, is none other than the political in a metaphysically recoded form, even where metaphysical categories do not necessarily follow the semantics of politics. The Cartesian *ego* as the metaphysical *fundamentum inconcussum*, for instance, is a deeply political category, or rather: a *name* formulated in the context of a hegemonic project.

With regard to historiography we can conclude that an examination of any ontology must take into account the strategic positioning of this ontology within the hegemonic formation of its time. How, in a given historical conjuncture, metaphysical signifiers were articulated with political struggles can only be examined historically. The 'history of Being' must be unfolded historically; but not, to be sure, in Heideggerian fashion by pronouncing *urbi et orbi* an 'epochal' history of Being.[15] It has to be closely studied how apparently static metaphysical points of reference (i.e. philosophical 'grounds' that appear transhistorical), through their insertion into a constantly shifting terrain of hegemonic power struggles, receive a certain political *spin*, how they will always assume historico-political meaning. What is at stake is the reconnaissance of that 'trench system' of political fronts which transverses the field of philosophy at all points. While the materialist tradition of Antonio Negri or, from a different perspective, Ellen Meiksins Wood remains a valuable source of inspiration, their analyses are nonetheless hampered by their focus on class as the exclusive category of reference. On the other side, analyses in the Cambridge School tradition have focused on philosophers' connection to political discourse in a narrow sense, without developing a broader Gramscian view on politics. It would take a historically oriented discourse analysis along the lines of an Essex School approach in order to develop a non-deterministic and multi-dimensional perspective on politico-philosophical formations.

Such an approach has not been developed yet, but should it be considered a worthwhile research programme for the future, it cannot be envisaged as an exclusively historiographic project. It would have to be compatible with the political ontology elaborated so far. Observing philosophical discourses with the detached gaze of a historian afraid of committing the worst crime possible, the crime of prolepsis, i.e. anachronism, will not allow for a political attitude of self-implication. Being-in-the-world means being-in-history – a place, and time, we always already inhabit. But in order to implicate ourselves in history (through a process that we have called thinking), history must be reactivated. As Laclau once remarked about the 'radical historicity' of social sediments:

> [T]he being of objects is . . . historical in that it is socially constructed and structured by systems of meaning. To understand something historically is to refer it back to its contingent conditions of emergence. Far from seeking an objective meaning in history, it is a question of deconstructing all meaning and tracing it back to its original facticity. (*NR* 36)

Taking into account what has been elaborated so far in this book – is it at all conceivable that such a goal could ever be achieved by way of a purely intellectual activity? The original facticity of which Laclau speaks was identified by us as the instance of antagonism. And, as I have argued, a dormant antagonism can only be reactivated *by antagonism*. What is needed, thus, is a political activity of folding antagonism back into philosophy, of reactivating the historical instance of the political, and of unfolding the political substrate of the philosophical. Politicising philosophy – in both its diachronic and synchronic dimensions – proves possible because philosophy is and has always been political. But, to make a Nietzschean point, in order to 'become who we are' we have to make an effort to occupy the place we already inhabit. With a view to philosophy, what will get us to this place (where we are) is thinking, understood as a practice of reflective intervention – of inflecting antagonism and reactivating the political. Such a practice is not quite philosophical in itself. It is 'more' than philosophy because it involves the thinking of radical negativity and difference-as-difference; and it is 'less' than philosophy because it involves politics. We will now turn to the political conditions of this practice: the *politics* of thinking.

8   Being as Acting: The Primacy of Politics and the Politics of Thought

Being – Thinking – Acting

Our detour into the history of philosophy yielded the following conclusion: the line between philosophy and politics is drawn politically. For this reason, it will never be possible to clearly separate the former from the latter. Philosophy remains manifoldly traversed by political struggles. At this point of the argument, the two Heideggerian questions that have guided us converge and transform themselves into an utterly un-Heideggerian one.

Heidegger's 'question of being' – in Vattimo's profanised rendering: 'What's going on with Being?' – initiated our inquiry; and from the beginning our intuition was that something political – *the political*, to be precise – is going on. As soon as it is decided to approach the being question via the instance of the political, i.e. antagonism, instruments and methods of empirical research will prove insufficient. For what is under investigation is an ontological notion, and ontological notions cannot be measured by empirical means. When confronting the instance of antagonism, which points us to the abyss and ground of the social, audacity is needed in order to 'think' where 'science does not think'. Yet 'thinking' must not be confused with intra-philosophical procedures of concept formation. By virtue of being a *name*, antagonism – our name for being – must not be squeezed in the Procrustean bed of the institutional discipline of philosophy. Antagonism is to be *thought*.

Therefore, a further question ensued: 'What is called thinking?' Once more, Heidegger loomed large in our response. Thinking, provided it is not – or not merely – envisaged in terms of cognition, is a way of actively occupying what is given to us, of refounding the place where we find ourselves. In other words, thinking, as finding, is founding. This is not without consequences. For what is given to us is, in the last resort, the political. And founding, i.e. the activity of laying penultimate grounds in the absence of an ultimate one, is a matter of politics in an enlarged sense of the term. Hence, if we want to inhabit the social world *as a political world*, that is to say: if we are to affirm the essential politicality of our world, we are required to engage in the practice of politics. Not in the narrow sense of 'party politics', of course, but in the sense of what I have called *minimal politics*. The political can only be affirmed by way of an organised, collective, strategic, partisan and majority-oriented conflictual practice.

It is in this latter sense that the two Heideggerian questions converge in an entirely un-Heideggerian one. To approach the 'being question' as a political one means posing the perennial question of politics: 'What is to be done?' The matter has to be considered carefully, though. Political ontology cannot tell us *what* to do in a particular politico-historical situation; it cannot provide us with concrete political recipes. It would be a non sequitur to derive a particular political injunction from what is ontologically given. For this reason, as was explained in the Introduction, the question to be posed within the framework of an ontological investigation is not 'What to do?', but 'How to act?', or, more generally, 'What does it mean to act?' Thinking, it will be argued in this chapter, is a form of acting, as much as being is a form of acting. In order to understand the, at one and the same time, affirmative *and* critical edge of thinking, we first have to come to terms with the fact that, by way of thinking, we occupy the world in the mode of politics. Thinking is an active effort towards affirming the politicality of the world.

The Anarchy Principle

To assert that being, as much as thinking, *is acting* is to reverse the order of priority between the ontic and the ontological, politics and the political. So far I have insisted on the primacy of the ontological side of the political, while ordinary political actions were located on the ontic side of the political difference. However, if the political difference is envisaged *as* difference, the play between the ontic and the ontological cannot be stopped and the two instances may very well change places. What, then, if we decided to revert our perspective? What if we were to think politics not as a derivative function of the political, but, rather, as a practical *a priori* of the latter? What, to be more precise, if the political did not exist as such (other than in its aggregate state of sedimented social routines), except when brought to life *by politics*? The order of priority between politics and the political would be reversed. Primacy would have to be granted to politics rather than the political.[1] Perceived from this angle, it is not the ontological instance of antagonism that takes on the function of ground – it is the ontic practice of politics in its *grounding* capacity.

The claim is not so far removed from our Heideggerian starting point. Heidegger, as Reiner Schürmann observed, transformed the metaphysical quest for grounds by understanding 'any ground as grounding – as a verb –, not a noun' (Schürmann 1990: 90). Rather than imagining 'ground' in terms of a solid base we have to think of it as an activity. It was Schürmann's enormous achievement in his landmark study on *Being and Acting* to point out Heidegger's inversion of the age-old hierarchy between Being and acting.[2] Such an inversion, of course, only makes sense in a post-foundational framework where 'ground' has become questionable. When Schürmann – who, together with Miguel Abensour, Bernard Stiegler and Jacques Rancière, belongs to the *an-archic* current in contemporary post-foundational thought – advocated a paradoxical 'anarchy principle' (his book was originally entitled *Le Principe d'anarchie*), he did not refer to an anarchistic programme of action. He referred to the quasi-transcendental structure of being. An-archy designates the withering away of 'the rule always to seek a first from which the world becomes intelligible and masterable, the rule of *scire per causas*, of establishing "principles" for thinking and doing' (Schürmann 1990: 6). Schürmann's important point was that the withering away of first principles will in turn assume the paradoxical function of a principle: the principle of the withering away of principles. The paradox of an 'anarchy principle', as Schürmann continues, is dazzling, 'because in two words it points within and beyond the closure of metaphysics, thus exhibiting the boundary line of that closure itself' (6). At this boundary line, which marks the end of metaphysical foundationalism, the perennial question of politics re-emerges: 'What happens to the question, What is to be done? at the end of metaphysics?' (231).

Schürmann's answer is clear. As the age of metaphysics draws to a close, action is set free from ultimate principles and, thus, proves to be an-archic on principle (4). Yet, there is a corresponding implication that remains to be carved out: if all principles are, as it was claimed, action-based, it follows that action in turn becomes the new principle of the withering away of principles. On the grounds of the absence of ultimate grounds, acting becomes the grounding instance of social being. And we can now begin to see why being may in itself be of 'active' nature.[3] Once having lost its status as a solid foundation, all being is grounded on acting, i.e. on the primordial activity of grounding which, in turn, cannot be grounded. Translated into our theory of political difference: the hauntological ground/abyss of social being has to actualise itself in the practical form of ontic politics. And at this point we must part company with Schürmann and Heidegger, who shy away from a truly political notion of acting. What they defend is a form of acting bereft of all activism. Indeed, what they defend is nothing other than a higher form of passivism, of an utterly *passive* activity. In the pastoral scenery sketched by the later Heidegger, man, the guardian of Being, is supposed to remain passively active; that is to say, man acts by retaining a passive attitude towards the unfolding play of being.

It hardly needs to be pointed out that such a notion of passive activity comes at a heavy price: the depoliticisation of acting. The political nature of being is repudiated in the very moment in which it is affirmed. Schürmann's search for an 'other politics' (243) is a search for a politics bereft of politics: a way of acting 'other than "being effective"' or strategic (84). Any kind of strategic and effective action would be dismissed by Heidegger as well as Schürmann as metaphysical. And if, for Schürmann, actions are supposed to turn into 'a groundless play without why' (243), this might be an apt portrayal of the hauntological nature of the political, but it does not capture the ontic nature of politics. Is there any kind of politics, other than an entirely depoliticised one, that would ever amount to a 'play without why'? A politics that does not involve strategic reasoning or seek to achieve particular goals would be hardly imaginable *as politics*.

If we now move to the Heideggerian notion of thinking, what has been said about acting must also apply to thinking. While the latter is convincingly portrayed by Heidegger as a practical activity embedded 'in-the-world', the kind of action attributed to thinking is described in rather peculiar terms 'of "authentic temporality", of "releasement", of "dwelling" in language, or of "letting things come to presence in their world"' (7). These are the Heideggerian tropes of passive activity. Thinking, from this perspective, involves a strong inclination towards passivism so typical for a metaphysical tradition where thinking has always been associated with meditative contemplation as far as possible detached from political involvement.[4] A characteristically Heideggerian attitude towards acting, as well as thinking, would thus be to 'wait and see' what is going to unfold as the 'happening' of being. The Heideggerian rendering of the event of being is reminiscent of Allan Kaprow's Zen-inspired definition of (artistic) happenings as 'events that, put simply, happen' (Kaprow 2003: 16); and a similarly tautological definition of thinking is provided in Heidegger's famous 'Letter on "Humanism"':

> Thinking does not become action only because some effect issues from it or because it is applied. Thinking acts insofar as it thinks. Such action is presumably the simplest and at the same time the highest because it concerns the relation of being to humans. But all working or effecting lies in being and is directed towards beings. Thinking, in contrast, lets itself be claimed by being so that it can say the truth of being. Thinking accomplishes this letting. (Heidegger 1999: 239)

It is easy to once more detect an anti-political sentiment behind these lines. As the event of being simply 'happens', thinking has to 'let itself be claimed by being'. Any kind of intervention, any attempt at activating antagonism would be detrimental to thinking. In an earlier book I have criticised the Heideggerian notion that 'thinking acts insofar as it thinks' for constituting a typical case of philosophism detached from the world of political action (Marchart 2007a: 170–1). One should thus be prepared to reverse the terms: thinking acts only insofar as it acts. Rather than depoliticising thought by presenting it as 'active' *eo ipso* (while at the same time claiming that true activity consists in remaining passive), our notion of thinking should be forthrightly politicised.

Acting as the Negation of the Given

Because of their elevated ontological pre-assumptions Heidegger and Schürmann are ill-equipped to develop a truly political notion of thinking. They are confined to a 'higher-order' passivism because they adhere to an equally 'higher-order' idea of thinking. Yet, as I suggested by taking Laclau as an *exemplum*, thinking occurs both above *and below* the philosophical: it is both more *and less* than philosophy. If I have concentrated in Chapter 2 on what in the Heideggerian tradition of thinking escapes the disciplinary grasp of philosophical procedures (the thinking of difference-as-difference, which amounts to 'more' than disciplinary philosophy), in the present chapter we concentrate on what is 'less' than purely philosophical: thinking as a way of doing politics. As is well known, practical politics did not belong to Heidegger's agenda as a thinker. The deplorable episode of his Freiburg rectorate attests to his rather quixotic ideas about practical politics. And while his later retreat from any kind of political engagement is sometimes interpreted as a sign of frustration, in my view the reasons for this retreat go deeper. There is an anti-political bias in Heidegger's thinking that may derive from his philosophical, rather than political, pre-assumptions. With Heidegger's insistence on an ontology of difference-as-difference at the expense of an ontology of negativity the world of politics is removed from view. It is true, Heidegger knows about the terror before the 'nothing' and annihilation, but the negative is not given any productive function in a conception of 'ontic' action. He criticised Hegel for retaining a notion of negativity that was not sufficiently radical (which is the case indeed, given Hegel's logicism), but did not provide us with a better alternative. Instead, he reverted to a Zen-like passivism devoid of all negativity.[5]

To develop a more realistic picture of political acting the Hegelian tradition has to be taken on board. As explained in Chapter 2, today's radical notion of antagonism has its historical roots in Hegel's 'labour of the negative'. A post-foundational ontology of difference has to be supplemented by an ontology of radical negativity, the latter of which must inform our notion of ontic politics. A form of acting that exhausts itself in the Derridean play of *différance*, in an endless postponement of its political goals, could hardly be called political. Politics begins with negation. From an *ontological* perspective, this would of course imply the 'evental' emergence of an antagonism; yet, from the perspective of *ontic* practices, which is at the centre of this chapter, negation has to be brought about. Negativity, in other words, is not simply 'out there' as a cosmic principle or an objective feature of the world. Negativity is to be produced by our actions. Therefore, when trying to invert the order of priority between the ontological and the ontic, one has to insist on negativity as an ontic practice – for the ontological instance of antagonism will only emerge when activated by our worldly actions. There is antagonism because politics – as much as political thinking – proceeds through negation. In order to fully account for this reversible, or circular, relation between politics and the political, Heidegger should be supplemented with Hegel and the left-Hegelian tradition. In fact, the intuition that 'being is acting' is inherent to the whole tradition of radical negativity that runs from Hegel via Marx to Laclau. Nobody had a clearer idea of the activist nature of being than Alexandre Kojève who inaugurated an entire series of twentieth-century ontologies of negativity. In his celebrated lectures on Hegel's *Phenomenology of Spirit*, Kojève – certainly inspired by Heidegger (and Marx), but long before Schürmann – insisted on a conception of being-as-acting *through negation*:

> Man is not a Being that *is*: he is a Nothingness that *nihilates* through the negation of Being. Now, the negation of Being is Action. That is why Hegel says 'the *true* being of man is his *action*.' Not to *act*, therefore, is not to be as a truly *human* being; it is to be as *Sein*, as given, natural being. Hence, it is to fall into decay, to become brutish;

and this metaphysical truth is revealed to Man through the phenomenon of boredom: the Man who – like a thing, like an animal, like an
angel – remains identical to himself, does not negate, does not negate
himself – i.e. does not act, is *bored*. And only Man can be bored.
(Kojève 1980: 54)

This is one of the key passages in Kojève's lecture series and, in my
view, of twentieth-century philosophy. Unfortunately, there is no
space to develop an in-depth interpretation here. But let me indicate some of the most important aspects. Kojève has been charged
with 'anthropologising' Hegel and Heidegger, yet what is called
'Man' in this passage is devoid of any positive human essence. The
human being is non-identical with herself. If any kind of being is to
emerge from this non-identity, it can only be grounded on human
actions. And all action, in turn, is devoid of a positive essence too,
as to act simply means to negate being (which includes the being of
man who, otherwise, would remain self-identical and reduced to
a thing or animal). As Kojève continues explaining: 'In fact, Man
can be satisfied only by *action*. Now, to act is to transform what
is real. And to transform what is real is to *negate* the given' (54).
The end of action, if achievable, would mean the end of negation,
which would lead to the end of politics – and, for Kojève, the end
of history – and, from there, right into a post-political world of
boredom and self-identical animality. In two steps Kojève presents
us with an activist anthropology – or rather: an ontology of active
Being. First, antagonism – especially the Hegelian antagonism
between lord and bondsman – is brought down to the worldly
ground of action. And second, action – the negative essence of
human being – is defined by Kojève as the negation of the given.

What does this short excursus into twentieth-century Hegelianism tell us about the nature of thinking? It would be a mistake
to assume, with Heidegger, that thinking acts insofar as it thinks.
As our excursus has shown: thinking acts insofar as it negates the
given. To think is to provoke the academic powers that be (and,
perhaps, many other powers). Not in an individualistic, childish
way of self-indulgent provocation; but in a more coherently political manner which, by itself, is 'less' than academic. Disciplinary
philosophy, as one of many layers of 'the given', is thus negated

from below. This place below the sedimented institutional layers of the academy differs from the one portrayed in an extraordinary essay by Stefano Harney and Fred Moten as the 'undercommons', i.e. the underground maroon communities of underpaid adjunct lecturers, mentorless graduate students, isolated Marxist academics, students whose visas expired, and so on – who nonetheless continue working academically in unregulated and seemingly unprofessional ways (see Harney and Moten 2013). They are not simply academic drop-outs. According to Harney and Moten, these maroons refuse refusal and resist resistance to academic professionalisation; i.e. their aim is not to negate the given, but to continue working below the radar of the given. In this sense, however, they do not 'act'. While I would not wish to ignore the subversive and potentially productive dimension of such an 'undercommon' academic practice of what they call 'study' – reading and discussing together as a persistent yet 'fugitive' practice – I very much doubt that a micro-political practice in the academic catacombs will, as such, achieve much politically. The 'undercommons' remain, from a Laclauian perspective, in a stage of eternally frustrated request, rather than moving on to the stage of demand. By avoiding direct politicisation, they, in Harney and Moten's terminology, 'study', but they do not necessarily 'think' in the sense of negating the given.

It was already determined what 'to negate the given' implies for the field of politics. In Chapter 5 it was claimed that true politics, which according to Laclau consists in reactivating the sedimented routines of the social, is essentially *protest politics*. If a particular request can be easily integrated into a (differentially structured) institutional arrangement, there will be no need for politics. Only if the request is frustrated by its institutional addressee, may it turn into what Laclau defines as a demand. Only then, in a moment of protestation (when a chain of equivalence is built in opposition to the forces of bureaucracy, for instance), can we speak of political action in the strict sense of the term. To be sure, the step from request to demand can be a very small one. Thinking-as-acting, it was said, activates antagonism through negation. But this can occur, if it occurs, on a minor scale and to a barely visible degree of politicisation. Instead of putting our political cards on a micro-politics of study – which, it is agreed, might be important in preparing for a future event of politicisation – I would propose to better engage in a minimal politics of thinking.

The Minimal Politics of Thinking

Thinking, if it is to be political, must accord to the minimal conditions of politics. What are these minimal conditions? In Chapter 6, it was argued (a) that all politics is a collective enterprise; (b) that a political collectivity – in contrast to a multitude dispersing in all directions – has to be organised; (c) that in aiming at a particular goal one has to proceed strategically in order to overcome obstacles; (d) that there are obstacles because there are adversaries, i.e. because all politics is conflictual; (e) that conflict implies partisanship; and (f) that, in order not to dissolve itself in mere sectarianism, any collective, organised, conflictual and partisan strategy has to be geared to becoming majoritarian, that is, hegemonic. I have spoken about minimal conditions because it is perfectly possible that these conditions, in a given situation, are met to only the most minimal degree. Nothing is said, thereby, about the size or nature of a collective or an organisation (it could be a tightly organised party, it could also be a social movement with a rather low degree of organisation). Nothing is said about the way in which conflicts and partisanship are enacted (peacefully or violently, agonistically or revolutionarily). And nothing is said about the effectiveness of a particular strategy or the actual chances of gaining hegemony. Even if confronted with the tiniest collective, the poorest organisation, the worst strategy, the most insignificant conflict, the most hesitant partisanship and the bleakest chances of becoming-major – we can rightly speak about political action as long as these conditions are met. Politics is not a matter of scale, it is a matter of kind. And, for the same reason, it is not restricted to a particular locus in the social topography (such as the political system) but can emerge wherever these minimal conditions are met – even in philosophy.

How, then, does thinking 'act', that is, how does the practice of thinking transform into a political practice? In the same way in which any other practice mutates into politics – by turning collective, organised, strategic, conflictual, partisan and majority-oriented. Thinking is political if it coheres with the minimal conditions of politics – not necessarily to a spectacular extent, but to *some* extent. Hence, thinking must be practised collectively, has to overcome obstacles, must involve itself in conflicts, take sides and organise with a strategic view to achieving politico-intellectual hegemony. Again, a politics of thinking does not require the organisational form of a party politburo; in most cases it is organised in the form of a loosely connected network of scholars, in some cases in the form of a more tightly connected academic school. It will have to proceed strategically, as obstacles must be overcome: an outdated canon has to be reshuffled, the gatekeepers of 'normal science' have to be outmanoeuvred, institutional procedures and policies have to be attacked, reformed or put to different use. This, in turn, will necessarily encounter hostility, produce resentment, and, if successful, redraw the lines of exclusion and subordination. Note that in a hidden, sanctimonious way, this is what goes on all the time anyway, as everyone knows who has ever experienced life in academia. Yet, one has to understand that philosophy – or any other academic discipline for that matter – is inscribed into broader hegemonic formations and traversed by larger lines of conflict. Even the small-minded machinations typical for intra-academic petty politics are inscribed into extra-academic power relations (thus relying on extra-academic resources which can be mobilised when it appears promising). The difference between this kind of petty politics and what I have proposed in terms of 'thinking-as-acting' is simply the following: thinking, as a reflective intervention, consists in an effort to *affirm* the politicality of a world – including the academic world – which, of course, is always already political. Thinking is an effort to actively occupy what, otherwise, we would merely inhabit.

No doubt, such an effort implies a massive paradigm shift regarding the way intellectual work is envisaged. One has to move from a conception of the traditional intellectual to what Gramsci called the 'organic intellectual'. The latter term, for Gramsci, does not so much refer to a particular social group, but, rather, defines a certain function: the function of *organising* a collective will. For Gramsci, labour union activists or the militants of a political party are, in this regard, organic intellectuals. What they organise is, in the final instance, the collective subject that is supposed to bring about a new hegemonic formation (or, if they are organic intellectuals of the ruling classes, they seek to foster an existing hegemonic formation). Most academics located in the discipline of philosophy will certainly conceive of themselves as traditional intellectuals. However, in the eyes of Gramsci, everyone is an intellectual, for everyone is equipped with intellectual capacities, even if only a few people have the social function of a traditional intellectual. Concordantly, all of us in our daily actions either stabilise or subvert a given hegemonic formation – but not all of us have the function of organic intellectuals. A reflective intervention in the field of philosophy will thus result in a change within our forms of subjectivation. Traditional intellectuals, who tend to cultivate their self-image of the isolated mind, turn into organisers of a new collective will. And they will do so by way of *self*-implication: of implicating themselves into their being-in-the-world in terms of their being-in-the-political, i.e. by inflecting, or folding back, an external antagonism into the field of theory. The task, as was argued in the previous chapter, of a reflective intervention consists of bending political lines of conflict into the field of theory in order to reactivate what is taken for granted: the canon, the procedures, the rules of reasoning, the terms of publication, the institutional hierarchies, etc.

It may be helpful to briefly compare our proposition of thinking as reflective intervention with Althusser's more orthodox claim 'that philosophy is, in the last instance, class struggle in the field of theory' (Althusser 1976: 27). Class struggle, for Althusser, can take three forms: an economic, a political and a theoretical form, the latter being the most concentrated one. With a view to Lenin's depiction of politics as a concentrated form of economics, Althusser describes philosophy as 'the theoretical concentrate of politics' (38) – which includes seemingly apolitical variants of philosophical speculation:

> Even speculative ideologies, even philosophies which content themselves with 'interpreting the world', are in fact active and practical: their (hidden) goal is to act on the world, on all the social practices,

on their domains and their 'hierarchy' – even if only in order to 'place them under a spell', to sanctify or modify them, in order to preserve or reform 'the existing state of things' against social, political and ideological revolutions or the ideological repercussions of the great scientific discoveries. 'Speculative' philosophies have a political interest in making believe that they are disinterested or that they are only 'moral', and not really practical and political: this in order to gain their practical ends, in the shadow of the ruling power which they support with their arguments. (Althusser 1976: 57)

Philosophy works like a burning-glass through which the 'light rays' of politics are bundled and condensed into theoretical forms and shapes. Conversely, by virtue of being a form of class struggle in itself, philosophy produces political effects. The rays of politics are reflected back onto the world of social and political practice. We are furthest away from the idea of the thinker as a 'guardian' of the happening of being, but neither can philosophy be reduced to a scientific sub-discipline. In contradistinction to the sciences, it is not the practical goal of philosophy to produce knowledge, nor is philosophy organised around particular objects. Instead of having scientific objects, philosophy has political *stakes* in a 'strategical and tactical war' to be waged 'against the adversary's theoretical forces' (Althusser 2017: 160). Althusser does not hesitate to describe the terrain of philosophies given in a particular historical period as a theoretical battlefield – Kant's famous *Kampfplatz* of metaphysics – on which an eternal struggle is fought out and where philosophical concepts serve as 'weapons in the class struggle in the field of theory' (Althusser 1976: 38). Althusser's idea is Leninist, yet it is also inspired by the Gramscian conception of a 'war of position' that silently rages within the institutional trench system of civil society. This becomes evident from the lines where the terrain of philosophy is described by Althusser:

> [A]n irregular, uneven battlefield, scarred with the trenches of old combats, bristling with abandoned fortifications that have been occupied and reoccupied time and again, studded with the names of places where the fighting was particularly fierce, and forever exposed to the resurgence of fresh battalions that can loom up out of the past and join the new forces on the march. (Althusser 2017: 160)

The main difference with regard to our own approach to thinking as a way of activating antagonism should be obvious: antagonism must not be confused with, or reduced to, class struggle. Antagonism is not rooted in the firm base of the economy, nor are there two, and only two, fundamental classes. This means that the proletariat cannot possibly be the privileged political (or philosophical) agent that – 'always under the leadership of its party' (Althusser 1976: 38) – struggles in the field of theory. When Althusser speaks of politics, he always refers to *class* politics. Such an understanding – because of its dualistic nature – is prone to a polemological ontology and potentially captivated by the fantasy of grand politics. Consequently, philosophy, for Althusser, turns into an eternal battle between the two grand paradigms of idealism and materialism, i.e. the philosophy of the bourgeoisie and the philosophy of the proletariat.[6] Consider, on the other side, the ontology of antagonism as proposed here: if, on the ontological level, antagonism has little to do with a dualistic friend/enemy distinction but, instead, refers to a fundamental blockade that issues from an incommensurably negative instance, then a plethora of highly diverse concrete antagonisms will be unleashed. Conflicts will multiply, as will agents, strategies, organisations and parties. The Gramscian metaphor of a 'war of position' is helpful in pointing us to the complex and uneven nature of the social – or philosophical – terrain shaped by political action. But, when employed by Althusser, it is hardly congruent with the Manichaean design of his theory. The philosophical terrain is complex because it is always already criss-crossed by a multiplicity of antagonisms. Thinking is the practice of bending one or more of these antagonisms – which on the face of it appear external to philosophy – into the field of thought, thus contributing to perhaps only minute shifts within a given hegemonic formation.

Acting and Antagonism: The Circular Nature of Agency

Philosophy, for Althusser, is the condensate of politics – which, conversely, is the condensate of economics. What may initially appear as a politicising move turns out to be rooted in an economism of 'the last instance'. But what if the idea of economic determination in the last instance – or any other ultimate foundation – is abolished? Evidently, a *hauntology* of the political would necessitate a different, post-foundational conception of action and agency – one by which action is not reduced to class struggle but remains 'an-archic'. For the last parts of this chapter, the task will be to reconnect this ontic view on action with our general ontology of antagonism. This is not a trivial task, given the reversible, if not circular, nature of the ontic and the ontological, of politics and the political. We cannot avoid moving back and forth between these two registers if we are to escape the symmetrical impasses of Heideggerian passivism on the one hand and an activism for activism's sake on the other. Adhering to the former would result in political paralysis; following the latter, by exclusively focusing on the ontic register of political action and agency, would lead us right into the trap of political voluntarism. The dilemma is obvious. Acting, it was said, proceeds by activating antagonism. However, antagonism, as an outside instance of radical negation, cannot be activated by sheer will.

Instead of bypassing the dilemma, I propose to hold onto these two apparently contradictory claims: (a) In order to act politically, antagonism must be activated. Politics, in other words, is the ontic business of activating the political. (b) From an ontological perspective, however, antagonism – a constitutive blockade that is experienced as an event – cannot be activated. It may emerge at any point in the social fabric, yet cannot be 'forced' into the open. Moreover, no self-identical source of action exists as a 'ground of the ground' from where antagonism could be forced to emerge. In other words, there is no willing subject that could serve as the foundation for our actions. But, how to activate what cannot be activated? And who is the 'subject' supposed to activate what escapes activation? Facing this conundrum, the only answer congruent with the post-foundational framework of political difference is the following: political agents act *as if* they could activate antagonism.

In Chapter 6 I have described the idea of the volitional subject of politics as an impossible, yet necessary metaphysical fiction. Political actors cannot but think of themselves as the 'subject' of their actions, for otherwise they would not start acting in the first place. While we are not the source of our actions, we must attribute to ourselves the capacity to act unless we want to remain passive bystanders.[7] What is more, political agency results from an encounter with antagonism while, at the same time, an agent is supposed to act antagonistically, i.e. to negate the given. So, rather than being the source of their actions, political agents emerge from this circular process. In a manner not entirely dissimilar to Kojèvian dialectics, a given social identity (a social group, for instance, defined by its differential location in the social topography), is activated into becoming a political agent by a purely negative instance of dislocation, and, by starting to negate the given in turn, comes to emerge as a political actor –an actor who may very well pronounce: I am because I negate – and I negate because my being is negated.[8]

Politics, therefore, is a truly circular affair. As political agents we are activated by antagonism in the very moment we encounter conflict and contingency; and yet, our task as political agents is to activate antagonism in the first place. From this follows a political imperative: *act as if you could activate what activates you*. Rather than 'acting' in the mode of Heidegger's passive activity, one has to shift to a mode of *active passivity*. Acting amounts to no more than putting a wager on the emergence of antagonism within the field of ontic social practices. By virtue of being an attempt, and no more than that, it may easily fail. And yet, antagonism – as the truly activating force – *must be activated*. There is no other possibility for antagonism to emerge as it does not, in any substantial sense, pre-exist its activation by ontic practice (to be precise, antagonism does not exist other than in its aggregate state of social sedimentation; see Chapter 4). As was explained earlier, antagonism as an instance of radical negativity, far from constituting something of the order of a natural force somewhere out there, detached from our practice, is always politically produced. What from an ontological perspective is the name for an insurmountable blockade of society – a mere incommensurability that *cannot* be constructed – *is* constructed, from an ontic perspective, through a particular practice: the negation of the given. No doubt, there could always emerge the problem that, put trivially, 'the given' does not bother very much. The dominant powers may be too strong, hegemony too deeply entrenched for a particular politics to succeed in reactivating sedimented antagonisms. Be that as it may, a dormant antagonism does not awake from its slumber by itself. Its awakening must be provoked – without any guarantee of success. Politics, by way of protestation, is about provoking antagonism. With regard to the latter, the political agent acts as *agent provocateur*. This *agent provocateur* is Kojève's 'Man' – that 'Nothingness that *nihilates* through the negation of Being'.

We have now arrived at the point where the identical argument can be applied to our conception of thinking. As a way of acting politically, thinking must be conceived along the same lines as acting. While it is not, or not necessarily, a condensed form of class struggle, as Althusser would have it, it certainly compels us to engage in an open effort towards repoliticising sedimented conflicts in the field of theory – which obviously implies that thinking accords to exactly the same minimal criteria as any other kind of politics (it must be envisaged as a collective, organised, strategic, partisan and conflictual endeavour aimed at attaining intellectual and, in the last instance, political hegemony). Furthermore, thinking, I have insisted, should be seen as a mode of political agency that begins to unfold by way of activating antagonism. It is thus drawn into the same virtuous circle as any other kind of politics. Thinking needs to be activated by antagonism, which, in turn, needs to be activated by thinking. This reversible relation between thinking and antagonism – tentatively expressed by the title of this book: *Thinking Antagonism* – bears radical consequences with regard to the subject of thinking. It is certainly not an individual. What we call a 'thinker' is, in its essence, a group or collective that is partially working in the field of philosophy (or, above and below the field of philosophy). This assumption runs counter to received opinion with regard to thinking. It nonetheless follows from what was previously established: it is the agent (in the form of an organised collectivity) that results from acting – rather than acting emanating from an agent. Similarly, what is called a 'thinker' by convention, far from being an individual, emerges from hegemonic struggles by way of tendentially organised, collective strategic and partisan activities.

To provide an example (others could be added *ad libitum*): the philosopher known under the proper name Spinoza did not work in solitude, as is regularly insinuated by those propagating the romantic image of the secluded genius. As mentioned in the previous chapter, Spinoza was politically allied with the Republican party of his time. In the philosophical field he did not act in isolation either. He was part of a European-wide republic of letters, and, what is even more important, belonged to a clandestine politico-philosophical local network whose members espoused views that could appear even more politically radical than Spinoza's. His philosophy teacher Franciscus van den Enden – sometimes described as a proto-Spinoza – developed, under the influence of Machiavelli's *Discorsi*, the idea of a free and egalitarian democratic republic which he sought to realise in Normandy by stirring up revolt with the help of French émigrés. He was captured by the French and executed in the Bastille (Israel 2002: 180–4). In the Netherlands, Spinoza's close intellectual circle – the first clandestine 'sect' of Radical Enlightenment – had been led by Van den Enden and his brightest pupil Spinoza. With regard to the members of this group, and those closely affiliated, it is nearly impossible to disentangle the political aim of a free and democratic republic from philosophical innovation (atheism, substance monism and rationalism). As even a superficial glance at this case proves, the prevalent tendency to focus on the individual thinker in both left- and right-wing accounts of Spinoza is entirely misplaced historically. There is no such thing as solitary thinking. It is impossible to disentangle, in a process of thinking, the political and the collective from the cognitive and the individual. And this implies that cognition, or what is commonly understood by it, is actually inscribed into strategic attempts towards constructing a hegemonic project.

Affirming Affirmation

Let us summarise what has been established in the course of this final chapter. Political thinking has little to do with what is typically understood by cognition, nor should it be approached from the viewpoint of epistemology. The practice of thinking does not primarily turn around problems of correct understanding or the apprehension of truth. As a *political* practice the final aim of thinking is to activate antagonism, to bend lines of conflict into the field of the philosophical, thereby dislocating and reactivating philosophical *doxa* and procedures – an aim that can only be achieved by way of contributing to the hegemonic construction of what Gramsci called a 'collective will'. Let us draw the conclusions. If, indeed, the aim of political thinking is to construct a collective will, we find ourselves compelled to once more change perspective. To act politically, i.e. to negate the given, requires the capacity to act – a capacity an agent does not possess *a priori* (to assume otherwise would mean adhering to the metaphysics of the Subject). The passage from passivity to activism is premised upon an experience of dislocation and frustration, but more is needed for a demand to be raised and the given to be negated. The capacity to act has to be asserted by the agent – even as no such capacity exists or precedes the action. Consequently, an agent, we saw, has to act *as if* it were equipped with the capacity to act. Let me expand on the metaphysical implications of such a mode of action.

As was argued in Chapter 6, political action presupposes a *quasi*-metaphysical 'will-to-will' as a will-to-foundation. The agent acts as if it were a volitional Subject in command of its will, and, in order to do so, must will its own will, for 'willing is: to will yourself' (Heidegger 1961: 33). The circularity is unavoidable if we are to move from a foundationalist to a post-foundational theory of acting. When ultimate grounds dissipate, political subjects must pull themselves up their bootstraps. But the point does require two specifications. First, from a political perspective, this 'will' that has to be willed does not pertain to an individual. It can only belong to a collective agent – which is why Gramsci speaks of a 'collective will'. Therefore, the capacity-to-will flows from the collective nature of the agent; it results from the force of politically being-in-common, and of organising with a view to attaining hegemony. If individuals or aggregate members of a hegemonic project are also equipped with a capacity to will, this is only because they participate in a collective faculty of volition. They are *capacitated* to act by the power radiating from a hegemonic project. Should this power wane, their capacity to act will also be debilitated. And, secondly, we should not make the mistake of imagining this will-to-will to be a destructive force. In order to negate the given, I said, an agent has to affirm capacities that it does not possess. In a moment of self-assertion one's will-to-act has to be *affirmed*, for otherwise we would remain in a state of coach-potato 'passive nihilism'. Becoming active, in other words, is premised upon the affirmation of our capacity to act, that is, our will-to-will. To act – and, therefore, to negate – means to affirm affirmation.

The latter insight, counter-intuitive as it appears, finds support in what arguably was one of Gilles Deleuze's greatest achievements, his early interpretation of Nietzsche's philosophy (Deleuze 1986). Deleuze points out that in Nietzsche '[b]ecoming-active is affirming and affirmative' (68). This might seem to blatantly contradict our definition of acting as the negation of the given. And Deleuze himself rejects any compromise between Nietzsche and Hegel (195). However, pure affirmation, as presented in Nietzsche, does involve negation. Only in simple affirmation – in the 'Ye-a' of the ass, the pack animal that bears the burden of the given – is the given accepted as it is:

> Nietzsche's argument can be summarised as follows: the yes which does not know how to say no (the yes of the ass) is a caricature of affirmation. This is precisely because it says yes to everything which is no, because it puts up with nihilism it continues to serve the power of denying – which is like a demon whose every burden it carries. The Dionysian yes, on the contrary, knows how to say no: it is pure affirmation, it has conquered nihilism and divested negation of all autonomous power. But it has done this because it has placed the negative at the service of the powers of affirming. To affirm is to create, not to bear, put up with or accept. (Deleuze 1986: 185–6)

To affirm the given with the simple 'yes' of the ass is to affirm the nihilistic condition of the world. It is to make peace with those relations of exclusion, oppression and subordination that to a large extent define the given. The ass is a burden-carrying creature devoid of political agency. A single 'yes' is therefore not sufficient: 'two affirmations are necessary to turn the whole of negation into a mode of affirming' (Deleuze 1986: 180). Acting means to affirm affirmation. Political agency, therefore, must not be confused with either passivism (what Nietzsche called 'passive nihilism') or destruction for destruction's sake (as in cases of adventurism or blind insurrectionism). True political activity begins when, in Deleuze's words, 'the will to nothingness is converted and crosses over to the side of *affirmation*', when it begins to relate 'to *a power of affirming*' (174), when it becomes a will-to-will. Affirmation is needed because, as it was argued, an agent must assert itself as the Subject of its actions – that is to say, it has to metaphysically affirm its capacity to negate as a capacity to will (if only in the *as if* mode). But, what is more, affirmation is necessary because 'to negate the given' only makes sense when put in the service of the creation of a positive project – a project that has the potential for recruiting widespread consent and for 'becoming-major'. In this latter sense, 'to affirm is to create' would mean that we must bring to life, as Gramsci put it with reference to Machiavelli, a 'Modern Prince', or perhaps, as Stephen Gill added, a 'Postmodern Prince' (Gill 2000). By affirming our own will-to-act we also affirm this project of collective will formation.

There are good reasons for turning towards a theory of double affirmation. In recent years, especially in the an-archic current of post-foundational political thought, adventurist and insurrection-ist theories – best exemplified by the manifesto entitled *The Coming Insurrection* (The Invisible Committee 2009) – have gained attraction. The insurrectionary paradigm is premised upon a rather one-dimensional notion of attacking 'the State' or 'the police order' – as if the State existed as homogeneous bloc that could be frontally attacked by maverick grouplets. Miguel Abensour's more sophisti-cated notion of a 'wild democracy' pitted 'against the State' bears traces of the same misconception (Abensour 2011); and even the Rancièrean famous 'disagreement' of a 'part of no part' appears to be modelled upon a binary logic of insurrection: 'Whoever has no part – the poor of ancient times, the third estate, the modern proletariat – cannot in fact have any part other than all or nothing' (Rancière 1999: 9). Subjecting politics to a logic of 'all or nothing' means to relegate political action – which, in reality, unfolds on a complex terrain criss-crossed by a multiplicity of antagonisms – to the realm of the imaginary. We are given a blunt choice by these authors: passivity or insurrection. No space is left, in this framework, for any positive political programme that could provide us with a starting point for constructing a new hegemony. Yet, the creation of a new collective will is precisely what is needed today, at a historical conjuncture when neoliberal hegemony crumbles and the political vacuum grows. We are not living through a revolutionary situation, though, that would warrant a politics of 'all or nothing'; what we experience, rather, is the increasing dislocation of the hegemonic formation in most Western countries. In a historical situation like this, the political task consists in bringing to life a 'New Prince', that is, in affirming affirmation.

Such a project is not furthered by insurrectionary fantasies, nor is it furthered by the empty phraseology of a metaphysical 'idea of communism' (Badiou 2010) or the invocation of a pseudo-Leninist avant-garde party (Dean 2012). Approaches like these have exhausted themselves – for practical reasons, because a new hegemon can only result from what the militants of Nuit Debout in France called 'la convergence des luttes': the convergence of actually existing struggles; as well as for theoretical reasons, as in politics the given cannot be negated *in toto*. In order to attack the totality of what is given one would have to find an Archimedean point beyond this totality. Without a point that could provide us with an ultimate foundation for our actions it is impossible to negate abstract totalities such as 'the system', 'the State', 'capitalism', 'patriarchy', and so on. The very idea of a monolithic system of oppression is phantasmatic, as is the attempt at attacking that system head-on. Negation, therefore, can only mean *determinate* negation, i.e. the negation of something concretely given rather than merely imagined as all-powerful totality.[9] The same is to be said about affirmation. It only makes sense as *determinate* affirmation: the creation of an actually existing project and collective will.

Thinking Democracy

One of the main tasks of political thinking is to recognise the seeds of such a hegemonic project and identify a toehold in social reality from where it could evolve. Therein lies the practical meaning of

affirmation. Whoever seeks to engage in counter-hegemonic politics will have to say 'yes' to saying 'yes', and political thought must
contribute to organising a new hegemon that will take up the task
of reconstructing social reality. The moment of political negation,
which is a moment of protestation against the given, should thus
be envisaged, not as a nihilistic refusal of totalities such as 'the
State', 'the police', or 'the system', but as an *affirmative refusal*
by which something determinate is negated in the name of a project worth affirmation. By negating the given through affirmation,
the possibilities inherent in the given are revealed in a way not
unrelated to what Niklas Kompridis calls 'critique as a possibility-
disclosing practice' (Kompridis 2011). To be sure, a moment of
negation is unavoidable if we are to develop a 'sense of possibility' (the *Möglichkeitssinn* described by the Austrian writer Robert
Musil in *The Man Without Qualities*). The ultimately groundless,
that is, contingent and contested nature of what appears to be
given must be demonstrated, and can only be demonstrated by
weakening, challenging and undermining the fortifications of a
given hegemonic formation. It has to be demonstrated through
negation that sedimented social routines are, by nature, possi-
bility-*foreclosing*-practices. By leading us back to the moment of
their institution, when some possibilities were foreclosed and others actualised, political action blows a breach into unquestioned
actuality. But it does not proceed from an Archimedean point
beyond, or any ground deep underneath, the actual. It makes new
possibilities emerge, not by proposing abstract utopias, but by
throwing *the actual against the actual*, hoping that an antagonism
may emerge and the contingency of what is given will be demonstrated – together with the potentiality of what could be given. In
fact, there is no option other than throwing the actual against the
actual, for nothing else exists. In politics, as everywhere else, one
always finds oneself in a given situation: a world of actuality – and
if no ground exists that would transcend the actual world, the only
option is to turn the actual against itself.

So, where to find the toehold for a future hegemonic project?
The answer, of course, can only be given by a concrete analysis
of present circumstances – by what Foucault called an 'ontology
of actuality'. This is not the place to advance such an analysis

(see, instead, Marchart 2013b). Yet, on a more general level of political theorising the following hypothesis can be advanced: in a situation where nominal 'democracy' has turned into an unsurpassable horizon for most regimes on the planet, with the notable exception of Arab theocracies, an outright attack against democracy (in the name, for instance, of a purely hypothetical communism) would be ill-advised. Democracy, while employed in mainstream political discourse as an empty signifier, is not a self-sufficient entity. The range of meaning of the term is not exhausted by mainstream discourse, no more than the range of democratic practices is exhausted by institutions of liberal democracy. The democratic horizon constantly undergoes internal shifts and rearticulations. In recent years, 'actually existing' liberal democracy came under pressure from neo-authoritarian political parties with, in most cases, a hidden neoliberal agenda, but formally located within the democratic horizon. On the other end of the ideological scale, social movements and, sporadically, left-wing populist parties have emerged with an agenda of defending, if not deepening, democratic rights. These actors can be defined as radically democratic in a double sense: internally, they tend to experiment with democratic procedures, rather than adhering to a hierarchical and quasi-military model of party organisation; with regard to their political demands, they show characteristics of democratisation movements: they aim at the 'democratisation of democracy', described by Étienne Balibar as 'the name of a struggle, a convergence of struggles' for democratisation. And, as Balibar insists, '[i]n a crucial sense, democracy is never something that you *have*, that you can claim to possess (therefore "bring" or "confer"); it is only something that you collectively *create* or *recreate*' (Balibar 2008b: 526).

These radical movements understood that 'democracy' is not simply the cover-up for a bourgeois conspiracy. Democracy, rather, is 'a permanent struggle for its own democratisation and against its own reversal into oligarchy and monopoly of power' (528). Precisely because it is not a homogeneous and self-sufficient entity, democracy can be turned against itself with the aim of deepening the democratic revolution. This task involves the construction of a democratic will-to-democracy which, in turn, can only be founded in democratic action. Democracy, as an ontic regime, does not follow with necessity from any ontology of the political, but it can be affirmed, created, and recreated by way of politics. To do so, one has to throw democracy against democracy. The democratic horizon has to be expanded and democratic principles rejuvenated. The theoretical contours of such a project of radical democracy are presented in an accompanying volume entitled *Post-Foundational Theories of Democracy: Reclaiming Freedom, Equality, Solidarity* (Marchart, forthcoming) and cannot be delineated here – for reasons of space, but mainly because they do not fall under the jurisdiction of political ontology. It would be a non sequitur to make the project of radical democracy the subject matter of an ontology of the political; and yet, a theory of radical democracy can in fact become a matter of reflective intervention. For, to inflect ourselves into the matter of our thought is to enter the realm of the actual by allying theory with politics – which can, and should, be done in the name of 'democratising democracy'. Cracking points will be produced in the liberal-democratic façade when democracy is brought to collide with itself. Possibilities might be disclosed that are latently present, but effectively foreclosed by the institutional routines of liberal-democratic regimes and liberal-democratic thought. To engage liberal democracy by way of *affirmative refusal* is to assert a democratic will. It means saying 'no' – by saying 'yes' to saying 'yes'.

Conclusion: *Ostinato Rigore*, or, the Ethics of Intellectual Engagement

The ontology of the political, as proposed in this book, has brought us to the following conclusion: being-in-the-world is, in fact, equivalent to being-in-the-political. The world we inhabit is formed by antagonism. The hegemonic structures of this world are as contingent as they are contested – and antagonism is the name that was proposed for the co-original condition of conflict and contingency. There is no need to engage in a detailed description of the phenomenic forms of the 'play between ground and abyss': the evental play through which antagonism shows itself in the reactivating moments of (micro-) rupture, in the myriad forms in which the uneven nature of social relations becomes apparent and micro-conflicts of everyday life emerge. These moments in which we experience, most of the time pre-consciously, subordination and oppression, rage and indignation, humiliation and pride, are ubiquitous. To phenomenologically describe these moments was not our aim in this book. Political ontology must pass from the descriptive level to a quasi-transcendental stage of developing the 'logic' of political conflict and social sedimentation. This passage led us, in a Laclauian vein, to the symbolic laws of difference and equivalence – or metonymy and metaphor – and their relation towards an instance of radical negativity: it led us, hence, to Laclau's description of the 'onto-logics' of antagonism. And yet, our aim was to advance the argument beyond this stage of explaining the symbolic functioning of antagonism. In Laclau's model, antagonism is a precondition for establishing frontiers within political discourses. But, as I have demonstrated, antagonism is indispensable for the production of *any* kind of meaning and, ontologically speaking, of any kind of social being. Everything social assumes its 'being' – i.e. a determinable identity – by way of delimitation vis-à-vis what it is not: a radically negative outside by which the identity of any kind of social being is, at one and the same time, stabilised and dislocated. Antagonism, therefore, points us to the ground of being.

We intuitively know this from the force-field of micro-conflicts and micro-contingencies that is our daily life. Being-in-the-world means being caught in a limbo, in the inter-play between ground and abyss, which announces itself through the pre-conscious experience of what I tried to describe, pace Hegel and Nancy, as the 'absolute restlessness' of the social. Antagonism is experienced, in its social mode, as the 'trembling' of social sediments, of institutionalised routines, of cultural, sexual or class identities. We all are immersed in the micro-conflictual turbulences that do and undo social sedimentations. One has to understand that the source of these turbulences is nothing other than the labour of the negative, antagonism, resulting in constant, but jolty, oscillations between its instituting and its dislocating side.[1] Not only is it repressed by hegemonic forces; we, as social beings formed and deformed by hegemony, are complicit in repressing the experience of the political. In Part III we have seen that there are two diametrically opposed ways of engaging with the politicality of the world.

The first option, to the extent to which it is an option, consists in neglecting, actively denying or unconsciously disavowing the antagonistic character of social life. No doubt, life would be impossible to lead if we were to constantly focus on its antagonistic nature. This, however, does not absolve us from *thinking* antagonism. Political theory and political philosophy, in their liberal mainstream variants, can best be described as an elaborate attempt at evading the traumatising fact of ultimate groundlessness and, hence, the grounding role of the political. Given the academic hegemony of liberal approaches, any theory underlining the fundamental dimension of social conflictuality (without reducing the latter to some sort of liberal 'competition') will immediately face the charge of ignoring 'consensus', 'rational deliberation', 'functional imperatives' or 'institutional path-dependencies'. Agreed, all this may have regional validity, and it can be legitimate in some instances to focus on consensus, deliberation, function or institutionalisation. At the same time, it should be made clear: these are only multifarious ways of coping – consensually, rationally, functionally, institutionally – with the abyssal character of the social and the necessity of its political refoundation. Otherwise, the liberal approach would merely attest to what in psychoanalysis is called a 'defence reaction' – which is not only intellectually dishonest; it could also be politically dangerous. Ignoring the struggles that form our social world will not prevent them from raging on. More than that, those who ignore a conflict of which they are part have already been defeated. A victorious force tends to retrospectively obliterate all traces of its struggle for hegemony. And yet, no victory is ever total, no oblivion definitive. Struggles will continue drawing a trace through social order, as peaceful as the latter may appear on the surface. The social will remain subjected to the labour of the negative whose effects are constantly suppressed and relegated to the political unconscious while, from time to time, re-emerging unexpectedly. As a consequence, society experiences moments when repressed conflicts, rendered unthinkable within a given hegemonic formation, make themselves felt in whatever displaced way. Every society, in other words, undergoes the experience of the uncanny. To grant ontological status to antagonism means to remain attentive to the memory traces of past and present struggles that continue haunting the hegemonic narratives of order and tranquillity. Thinking antagonism, therefore, has little to do with abstract speculation. It is about facing a brute *factum politicum*.

Which brings us to the second option. Instead of taking refuge in denial and resistance, the ontological nature of antagonism must be affirmed, and, as we have seen, can only be affirmed politically, i.e. by way of political action (the mode of which, in the intellectual field, is 'thinking'). I have therefore proposed in the previous chapter a political imperative: *act as if you could activate what activates you!* In order to act politically we have to 'activate ourselves' (we have to affirm a hypothetical will-to-will that, in actuality, we do not possess). But, political acting is only conceivable because we are always already activated, if only – most of the time – on a microscopic level, by antagonism. So we are caught in a virtuous circle: that which brings us to life as political actors, antagonism, will have to be brought to life by our actions. It has to be provoked, by way of politics, if the contingent as well as conflictual nature of the social, otherwise hidden under social routines and institutions, is to be made apparent. To *think* antagonism, in the political sense of thinking, is to provoke antagonism – and, in turn, to allow oneself to be provoked *by* antagonism. I have used the term 'reflective intervention' for such a – collective, organised, strategic, contentious and partisan – practice of thinking by which actual politics is folded into theory. From this follows what one could call an imperative of thinking as a political, rather than individual or cognitive practice: *think as if your thinking could activate that by which it is activated!* It is not in our hands, as individuals who mistake themselves as subjects of volition, to activate thinking. And yet, only by mistaking ourselves as subjects of volition and affirming our will-to-will can we even hope to provoke antagonisms to emerge.

However, I would like to add a word of warning against any adventurist interpretation of political thinking. What must be affirmed in a process of reflective intervention is volition, not voluntarism. Let us remember the famous Gramscian motto: 'pessimism of the intellect, optimism of the will', which is often given an all too trivial interpretation. The quote is mostly taken to mean that, no matter how depressing the political situation, one still has to act against the odds. Yet, the meaning of the Gramscian motto is not exhausted by this standard interpretation. It is certainly true that no political action will be successful without a certain 'optimism of the will', or, pace Nietzsche, a 'will-to-will'. But, on the other side, without a clear and disillusioned analysis of the political conjuncture, that optimism will remain unguided. It will degenerate into pure voluntarism or decisionism without any strategic direction. Therefore, the 'pessimism of the intellect', far from expressing a version of leftist melancholia in the face of overwhelming forces of reaction, has a very precise function. The phrase accentuates the need for intellectual realism in politics. An 'intellectual pessimist' is not a leftist academic who suffers from depression, but someone engaged in a sober analysis, someone resisting the temptation of wishful self-deception. Intellectual work, in this respect, is oriented towards what Machiavelli called *la verità effettuale della cosa*; and only a good dose of 'pessimism of the intellect' can prevent us from falling prey to wishful thinking, naïve voluntarism or dogmatic self-righteousness.

If we are to avoid these dangers, it is important to recognise the ethical injunction hidden in the Gramscian motto. In order to abstain, as much as it is possible, from wishful or dogmatic thinking one has to cultivate an ethics of intellectual engagement. This is the reason that what we have termed 'reflective intervention' must not be confounded with political adventurism in the field of philosophy. And, in order to resist the temptation of either adventurism or dogmatism, a rather outdated virtue is required: intellectual rigour. As Laclau and Mouffe made clear when replying to an orthodox Marxist shortly after the publication of *Hegemony and Socialist Strategy*: dogmatism constitutes an obstacle to developing the socialist project. It is impossible to reconceive a hegemonic project without sober analysis and theoretical rigour:

> As participating actors in the history of our time, if we are actually to assume an interventionist role and not to do so blindly, we must attempt to wrest as much light as possible from the struggles in which we participate and from the changes which are taking place before our eyes. Thus, it is again necessary to temper 'the arms of critique'. The historical reality whereof the socialist project is reformulated today is very different from the one of only a few decades ago, and we will carry out our obligations as socialists and intellectuals only if we are fully conscious of the changes and persist in the effort of extracting their consequences at the level of theory. (*NR* 97)

Laclau and Mouffe then continue by proposing as a rule for intellectual work the personal motto ascribed to Leonardo: 'obstinate rigour'. This kind of intellectual tenacity 'leaves no space for complacent sleights of hand that seek only to safeguard an obsolete orthodoxy' (*NR* 97). Interestingly, Laclau returns to Leonardo and the motive of 'obstinate rigour' twenty years later in the concluding pages of *On Populist Reason*:

> There is an ethical imperative in intellectual work, which Leonardo called 'obstinate rigour'. It means, in practical terms – and especially when one is dealing with political matters, which are always highly charged with emotion – that one has to resist several temptations. They can be condensed into a single formula: never succumb to the terrorism of words. (*PR* 249)

This 'terrorism of words' makes itself felt whenever analysis is replaced by moral condemnation (as in the case of a moralistic critique of fascism devoid of explanatory value), or, conversely, by dogmatic fetishisation:

> On the Left, terms such as 'class struggle', 'determination in the last instance by the economy' or 'centrality of the working class' function – or functioned until recently – as emotionally charged fetishes, the meanings of which were increasingly less clear, although their discursive appeal could not be diminished. (*PR* 250)

For Laclau, the 'politico-intellectual task' is therefore to think through, as consistently as possible, today's conditions of political action, including the phenomenon of populism; and in order to live up to this task – which, for Laclau, 'is necessarily collective' (*PR* 250) – we will have to abandon all moralistic or dogmatic attitudes.

Let us draw the lessons from Laclau's attack against orthodoxy. Intellectual rigour is the opposite of dogmatism. Indeed, dogmatism is a sign of intellectual sloppiness – only those are in need of a dogma, who do not dare to engage in thinking. In a process of thinking – and precisely when thinking, affected by antagonism, is geared towards political effectivity – one must not let oneself be carried away by faulty reasoning, dogmatic slumbers, age-old wisdom, commonsensical banalities, taken-for-granted ideological assumptions, incontestable 'positive facts', pseudo-political

delusions or moralistic indignation. There is an ethics of intellectual work which, for political rather than moral reasons, consists in the relentless questioning of whatever may offer itself as
an ultimate foundation – no matter whether the latter appears in
the guise of a moral, traditional, ideological, commonsensical or
'positive' ground. To paraphrase Laclau: never succumb to the
terrorism of Grounds. And the only thing that will keep us alert
and, hopefully, prevent us from giving in to such terrorism, is
'obstinate rigour'.

One more thing needs to be stressed, though: the same rigour
involved in intellectual work must also serve as a principle guiding political action. To clarify this point it may be worthwhile
to revisit Leonardo's motto. As a matter of fact, it is not entirely
clear whether, for Leonardo, the phrase merely referred to his
own 'work ethics' as a meticulous artist and pioneering natural
scientist. The motto, written as *'hostinato rigore'* in characteristic
mirror writing, belongs to an emblem designed by Leonardo in
1508 or 1509, the pictorial part of which presents a plough drawing a furrow. Renaissance and Baroque emblems are meant to
remain deliberately complex, if not partially obscure, in order to
leave ample room for contemplation. The meaning of Leonardo's
emblem becomes clearer when compared with another emblem
on the same sheet. This second emblem shows a compass directed
at a star (while being placed on a revolving water wheel) and
accompanied by the motto *'destinato rigore'*. Leonardo apparently means to transmit the message that, in focusing on a particular destination, we must not revolve or deviate from our course.
This message, however, has little to do with artistic or scientific
rigour. A clear *political* meaning is hidden in the drawing, for
three miniscule fleurs-de-lis are placed within the star, thus turning the latter into a symbol of the French king, Louis XII, for
whom Leonardo was working as a court artist at the time of the
drawings. No doubt, it would be easy to detect a message of sub-
servience in line with the opportunism of a court artist hired to
glorify the king. Taking into account the polysemic dimension of
Renaissance emblems, however, the drawing may also be understood as an emblematic representation of political virtue. The

motto '*destinato rigore*' would then imply that a political cause must be followed unwaveringly – no less than any intellectual cause. When ploughing a furrow in the intellectual landscape, or when pursuing a political goal, we must not waver in our course, no matter how furiously the wheel of fortune is turning.

So, the same kind of rigour is requested, Leonardo seems to imply, by intellectual and by political work: the virtue of not deviating from one's course, in other words, of not abandoning the very *cause* of one's actions. Obviously, an ethical imperative is involved in such a kind of tenacity. Thinking is to remain faithful – or act *as if* one could remain faithful – to the political source of activation: antagonism. To affirm the politicality of the world is to remain faithful to the experience of conflict and contingency by which one was activated. Why insist on this? Because there are always, as mentioned, other options: neglect, denial, disavowal. But, as political actors, we are activated by antagonism, and we only retain our status as actors as long as we reactivate antagonism – which, in politics, manifests itself in the ontic form of a particular cause and struggle. This is rarely a matter of ideological dogmatism or party discipline. On the contrary, political steadiness can easily lead oneself to *oppose* party discipline, as much as intellectual stringency can lead oneself to *counter* ideological dogmatism. In their response to their orthodox critics, Laclau and Mouffe, by claiming for themselves the ethical principle of obstinate rigour, refuted the charge of having abandoned the intellectual tradition of Marxism or the political project of socialism. The charge was laughable anyway. Their orthodox critics, while portraying Laclau and Mouffe as traitors and renegades, were unable to recognise the utter absurdity of their own position. To defend sclerotic dogmas and sectarian projects is, in fact, the opposite of politico-intellectual rigour. It is as sign of intellectual sloppiness and political faintheartedness.

Perhaps it is exactly his ethics of obstinate rigour that lies at the core of Laclau's work and life as academic intellectual and political militant. Rather than fusing the political with the philosophical in a lukewarm compromise (which could easily result, for instance, in some kind of engaged journalism without theoretical value), he was unwavering on both fronts. And, perhaps, there is no feasible alternative. Whoever seeks to inflect politics into theory, *and* to remain rigorous politically as well as academically, must accomplish the coincidence of opposites. To explain the point, I should be allowed a few concluding remarks on a personal note.

When I co-edited with Simon Critchley *Laclau: A Critical Reader* (Critchley and Marchart 2004), we ventured the idea of using for the cover a photograph of the bombed editorial office of *Lucha Obrera*. Laclau, in his youth, was chief editor of *Lucha Obrera*, and putting the bombed office on the cover would have emphasised that an apparently abstract theory, sometimes charged with formalism, emerged from rather material struggles. To our surprise Laclau was strictly against it. Instead, he opted for his *alma mater*, that is, for the beautiful façade of Buenos Aires University as a cover photograph. We agreed but I remember that I found it awkward to have a baroque façade on the reader. Not because this was the exact opposite to an image of violent political struggle, but his choice, I gathered, set a riddle for most readers. The deeper meaning of a baroque façade on the cover must have appeared as mysterious to them as it appeared to me.

Reflecting on this episode, I came to understand why Laclau chose this photo. It seems that, for him, Buenos Aires University must have been a place of a peculiar *coincidentia oppositorum* between academic learning and political militancy. Let me put it this way: to everyone who knew him, there were two sides of Laclau, two personae. On the one side, there was the persona of the militant, the singer of revolutionary songs who had dozens of Italian partisan songs in his repertoire and would ask his multinational crowd of University of Essex PhD students in our regular gatherings at a local pizzeria to collectively sing the 'Internationale' in our native tongue. This persona stood in obvious contrast, if not opposition, to academic customs, yet it was entirely congruent with his self-image as a life-long partisan of the left wing of Peronism and his support, in more recent years, for the Kirchner governments. As he said in one of his last television interviews, he had never been an academic intellectual in a conventional sense as he had never stopped being a militant.

However, notwithstanding the persona of the militant, and in contradiction to what he claimed in the interview, there *was* the persona of the scholar, someone predominantly interested in the development of a coherently argued system of political thought. This was where readers of Laclau could, in fact, experience a contradiction. Consider the apparent paradox that the most ardent defender of populism was, in his theoretical and pedagogical work, as remote from any populistic attitude as is possible. There was no sophistry to his lectures, nor was there anything self-congratulatory, as is typical for 'famous' academics. It would not have crossed his mind for a second to compromise on the rigour of the argument for the sake of presenting it with more bravado or to produce artificial effects in order to get the message across. No rhetorical device would distract from the course of reasoning. Although he theorised the 'rhetorical foundations of society', as the title of his last and posthumous book goes, his goal was to *reduce*, as much as possible, the rhetorical foundations of his theory.

Of course, he knew that ultimately this goal was impossible to reach. In *New Reflections on the Revolution of Our Time*, the book where he presents his theory *à l'ordre de raison*, he confesses that a *more geometrico* presentation of his arguments runs counter to everything he believes about language (*NR* 5). Yet, by presenting his thought in the clearest possible way, rather than garnishing it with a plethora of stories and jokes, he made his theory all the more intelligible to his audiences. No obscurantism, no unnecessary detours, no distractions, no trickery allowed. This intellectual attitude was driven by a deep desire for consistency, and was scholarly in almost a medieval sense. His crystal-clear and 'logical' style gave the impression of a deconstructive version of negative dialectics, brought into the argumentative form of scholastic reasoning. No wonder, given this medieval style of reasoning – and I mean this as a compliment – that his preferred theoretical instrument was Occam's razor. Cutting away everything arbitrary, he achieved an unheard-of degree of theoretical condensation. One of his key articles, 'The Impossibility of Society' (*NR* 89–92), is four pages long.

To return to my observation concerning the two personae of Ernesto Laclau, it is worth insisting that the philosophical advances achieved by 'Laclau the scholar' were not disconnected from the political interests of 'Laclau the militant'. Laclau was uncompromising on both fronts. Part of his charisma as a teacher and lecturer came from the paradox that within one and the same person the two personae of the militant and the scholar were clearly distinct, but at the same time were identical. Not that he had to bring them into balance or to compromise; both were total, and he was both of them in one. He was totally immersed in politics, and totally immersed in theory. There was nothing 'hegemonic' to the relation between these two sides, no unstable equilibrium to be established between partiality and universality. He was at once totally partial and totally universal, at once a 'political animal', as they say, and a scholar of quasi-medieval stature. Maybe this was not only a personal attitude. Maybe it was characteristic of Laclau's generation of radical intellectuals on the Left, even though he brought it to its apogee. Another member of this generation, Stuart Hall, who passed away only weeks before Laclau, once described the practice of theorising as a way of 'wrestling with the angels'. For this generation, to wrestle with the angels of theory and to wrestle with the beasts of politics was one and the same thing.

This double-sided totality, I assume, explains Laclau's choice of the cover photograph for the critical reader. For Laclau, the university was not simply a place to engage in occasional political fights. The university was an entirely political arena, and, at the same time, it was a refuge entirely devoted to scholarship. Therefore, the baroque façade of his *alma mater* must have appeared to him as a symbol of the scholarly as much as a symbol of political militancy. He felt no need to demonstrate his own involvement in violent political struggles by putting his bombed editorial office on the cover. It was his old university that, for Laclau, symbolised the identity of the scholarly and the militant. To unite the opposites and forge a politico-intellectual identity, while accepting their respective specificity and opposite nature, should be the – perhaps paradoxical – aim of thinking as reflective intervention. The virtue of obstinate rigour can serve as a common denominator and ethical bracket around the scholarly and the militant. It will prevent us from capitulating to wishful thinking, ideological dogmatism or a naïve moralism. And it will keep our thinking focused on the ever-changing effects of negativity, the multifarious forms of antagonism encountered in political and social reality.

Notes

Introduction

1. See Torfing (1999); Marttila (2015); Deutsche (1998); Bowman (2007); Roskamm (2017); Marchart (2018); for an overview see Critchley and Marchart (2004) as well as Marchart (2017).
2. For a first attempt see Marchart (2007a, 2013a).
3. Obviously, in our attempt to elucidate the antagonistic nature of the social world, we do not wish to embark on a mystical quest for the ineffable in the style of a negative theology; nor do we plan to investigate – as some object ontologists and speculative realists might do – into the grounds of physical matter in a vain attempt at speculatively exhuming natural philosophy as an academic discipline (it would be bizarre to claim to have insight, in a Faustian fashion, into the inner secrets of the natural universe). Political ontology is all about *social* being, and there is nothing ineffable about the social. Thinking is of an order entirely different from mystical or cosmological speculation (no matter whether the latter speculation is dressed up as 'materialist' or not).

Chapter 1

1. For the ontological turn in political theory see White (2000); Strathausen (2009); Paipais (2016); Mihai et al. (2017). For an overview on the much discussed ontological turn in anthropology see Holbraad and Pedersen (2017). Social ontology in the analytic tradition will not be our concern in this book, even though important philosophical positions have evolved in this tradition (Searle 2010); for a discussion of social ontologies in the tradition of sociological thought see Marchart (2013a).

2. Needless to say, today's political ontologies, in their attempt to answer this basic question, vary greatly in aim and outlook. Stephen K. White, who was one of the first to observe the ontological turn in political thought, enlists, next to Connolly, George Kateb, Charles Taylor and Judith Butler among those who cultivate an interest in ontopolitical interpretation. Yet, the number of theorists is significantly larger. Today we are confronted with ontologies of 'lack' (Žižek 1999; Stavrakakis 2007), of 'the void' (Badiou 2007; Prozorov 2014), or, alternatively, of 'becoming' (Bennett 2010; Connolly 2011), of 'abundance' (Tønder and Thomassen 2005), of 'the multitude' (Negri 2002), of 'com-pearance' or 'being-with' (Nancy 2000), of 'potentiality' (Agamben 1999, 2015) or historical 'actuality' (Vattimo 2011). Whereas, for instance, ontological questioning has led Antonio Negri to the never-ending workings of 'the multitude' as the constitutive force of social being (Negri 2002), for Slavoj Žižek it is the subject that constitutes 'the absent centre of political ontology' (Žižek 1999). Intellectual inspirations are no less variable. While Negri's ontology of the multitude, for instance, is informed by Spinoza, Marx and Deleuze, Žižek relies on Hegel and Lacan.

3. Historically, the term 'ontology', designating the science of being in general, appears for the first time at the beginning of the seventeenth century and is eventually granted the status of a *metaphysica generalis* in German 'school philosophy' by Christian Wolff, thereby assuming the role of a *prima philosophia* vis-à-vis the other metaphysical disciplines of the time, such as cosmology, psychology and theology. Simultaneously, in a process that started with Descartes (a more complex case, as we will see) and culminated in the work of Berkeley, Kant and their heirs, ontology as a discipline was increasingly displaced by modern epistemology. Foucault's reference to the Kant of 'What Is Enlightenment?' complicates the picture by detecting an internal counter-tendency at work in at least some epistemologists.

4. Taylor follows Heidegger in putting most of the blame on Descartes who had initiated the landslide 'epistemological turn' that let the Hydra out of her cage. The Heideggerianism of what I will call the left-Heideggerian branch of post-foundational political thought is most obvious in the case of Jean-Luc Nancy's social ontology of 'being-with' or in Gianni Vattimo's defence of a 'weak ontology' in the tradition of Heideggerian fundamental ontology (Nancy 2000; Vattimo 2003). Heideggerian inclinations are also present, although

less obvious, where theorists – such as Roberto Esposito (2013; see also Bosteels 2011) – have recourse to Michel Foucault's idea of historical ontology.

5. Therein lies what I would consider the true significance of Foucault's famous notion of an 'ontology of ourselves'. When thinking politically, as we will see in Part III, we implicate *ourselves* in the matter of our thought, since the process of self-implication, to the extent to which it is political, is a collective and, to some degree, organised process.

6. Connolly makes a similar point against the epistemological *doxa* of the social sciences: 'There is a particular presumption – let us call it the primacy of epistemology – that unites most American social scientists, shielding them from this debate. To give primacy to epistemology is to think either that you have access to criteria of knowledge that leave the realm of ontology behind or that your epistemology provides neutral test procedures through which to pose and resolve every ontological question. [. . .] The primacy of epistemology turns out itself, of course, to embody a contestable social ontology. The empiricist version, for instance, treats human beings as subjects or agents of knowledge; it treats things as independent objects susceptible to representation; it treats language as primarily a medium of representation, or, at least, a medium in which the designative dimension of concepts can be disconnected rigorously from the contexts of rhetoric/action/evaluation in which they originate' (Connolly 1995: 5–6).

7. Consequently, *thinking*, to the extent to which it is implicated in the field of political ontology, passes through these instances. Thinking is a self-affirmative enactment of conflict, power, subordination, oppression, exclusion, decision, resistance, opposition, confrontation, association or consensus-building. I will tackle this, perhaps, counter-intuitive notion of thinking in Part III.

8. If Heidegger's claim was that metaphysical thought has always differentiated between beings and being, yet this difference has never come into view *as difference*, then similarly, we have to say that in contemporary political thought there is frequent use made of the political difference but until recently it was rarely asked what we have to make of this difference *as difference*. Thinkers such as Badiou, Rancière, Mouffe, Laclau, Nancy or Esposito may make diverse, if not opposing, use of it (sometimes shifting the normative emphasis from the political to politics), but they all consider the

difference to be of importance. In other words, they felt an ontopolitical need to introduce it.

9. And if it does, they may also ask, *what follows* from the political difference? Not much, I agree, as long as we abstain from developing a clearer picture of what we mean by politics and the political. But let us put on the record, if only in passing, that no *particular* political effect can be deduced from the political difference – which otherwise would serve as a determining Ground (which was precluded *ex hypothesi*). For this reason, the term 'leftist ontology' (Strathausen 2009), it has to be said, is a misnomer. As such, ontology, the science of being-qua-being, is neither leftist nor rightist – unless we are prepared to nonsensically ascribe to social being a particular political orientation. This is why a generic term such as 'political ontology' (or, in our case, 'ontology of the political') is preferable.

10. To give a simplistic example: the term 'sister' has no intrinsic substance and only assumes meaning within a system of differences, that is, in relation to terms such as 'brother', 'father' and 'mother'.

11. 'Hauntological' in the sense of the spectral presence of a ground which remains absent, or as Derrida put it: 'To haunt does not mean to be present, and it is necessary to introduce haunting into the very construction of a concept. Of every concept, beginning with the concepts of being and time. This is what we would be calling here a hauntology' (Derrida 1994: 161).

12. For a reading of Laclau that goes the opposite way by disengaging ontological negativity from the political see Hansen (2014).

13. This (onto-)logic – which underlies discourse theory in the Essex School tradition – was most systematically explained and expanded into an explanatory approach for the social sciences by Jason Glynos and David Howarth with their 'logics approach' (Glynos and Howarth 2007). Laclau defended his own use of the term 'logic' in an exchange with Butler and Žižek (see Laclau 2000b: 283–4).

14. In the latter sense, Laclau indeed tends to speak about 'social antagonisms' (in the plural) rather than *antagonism* in the singular. The tension between Laclau's two ontologies can be clearly perceived in his last book. In a review, John Kraniauskas has rightly highlighted that, apart from the chapter on 'Articulation and the Limits of Metaphor', in which Laclau presents his 'rhetorised' political ontology, there is another essay which counts among the volume's most important contributions. It is this last major text of Laclau's,

entitled 'Antagonism, Subjectivity and Politics', with which he delivers a renewed theory of antagonism. He does so, as Kraniauskas observes, 'through a brief reflection on Heidegger's notion of "ontological difference", seeking – so as to fold it back into his version of hegemony – to think through how the gap between Being and beings may be bridged as an anti-foundational foundation' (Kraniauskas 2014: 30). This constitutes 'a new departure for Laclau', as Kraniauskas underlines, even though it 'remains only slightly developed as a feature of a possible political ontology' (30). The crux is that Laclau did not have time to develop his intuitions any further.

15. For instance, assimilating, as Laclau regularly does, the ontological with the universal and the ontic with the particular, means to remain within the ambit of a metaphysical form/content distinction, as will be demonstrated in the subsequent chapter.

16. He, in fact, did so explicitly: 'In other words, the distortion – partial fixation – is the only means of representing that which is constitutively non-representable. This – in words of Marchart – is the location of the distinction between "anti-foundationalism" and "post-foundationalism". "Anti-foundationalism" would be the pure and simple absence of a ground, which could only be expressed through a proliferation of ontic identities. "Post-foundationalism" means something different: the ground does not disappear, but is penetrated by a dimension of absence or contingency that renders impossible any reduction of the ontological to the ontic' (*RFS* 119–20).

17. As, for instance, Pierre Bourdieu has shown, a great deal of effort is required by the better-off to defend their stock of cultural capital against aspiring factions. There is nothing innocent about cultural taste: taste is a weapon that helps to keep symbolic distance, to defend one's own position in society.

18. Or to demonstrate, in the case of conservative protest, that change is not necessary – which also amounts to a demonstration of contingency.

Chapter 2

1. Something points in this last direction, for, in concluding, Swinton adds a very last sentence to Marx's oracle: 'At first it seemed as though I had heard the echo of despair; but, peradventure, it was

the law of life.' With this comment, struggle is retrospectively biologised. It would have never occurred to Marx himself to declare struggle to be the 'law of life'. Class struggle, for Marx, is the law of all social being before it is pacified into harmonious communism. As one knows from the *Communist Manifesto*, the history of hitherto existing societies is the history of class struggles. This does not leave room for interpreting class struggle along the lines of natural philosophy or Social Darwinism.

2. Which is something entirely different from disregarding the economy, it must be said. Quite the contrary, a meaningful empirical economic analysis – for instance, in the tradition of the French 'regulation school' – can only begin once economic determinism is discarded and 'political economy' is seen as the discipline of studying, precisely, the political forces that shape the economy.

3. The latter problem of 'bellicism' will be addressed in the subsequent chapter.

4. Certainly, with Hegel's idea of contradiction, negativity – the main 'ingredient' of Laclau's later notion of antagonism – had to be granted a central role; yet in Hegel, as I will discuss presently, negativity was domesticated and subjected to his pan-logism, which led Laclau, in a still Althusserian vein, to resolutely disband Hegel.

5. This also means, as we will see, that from a post-foundational perspective the whole notion of a negative ground of the social, to which Laclau's later theory of antagonism gravitates, becomes inconceivable.

6. See as one of the passages where struggle is equivocated with antagonism Laclau (2014: 123).

7. This belief was copy-pasted in today's version of technological progressivism, the philosophically meagre, but largely popular school of 'accelerationism'. Of course, the idea that technological progress instigates social progress is as wrong today as it was in the nineteenth century.

8. As 'classes', the identity of the agents of struggle is determined by their position within the process of production.

9. Of course, Kant himself did not hold on to the radical consequences of his own theory of antinomies, but sought to rationally and morally dissolve them.

10. The same can be said about Jacques Lacan's psychoanalytic notion of a subject-of-lack that results from Lacan's combination of Freudianism with Kojèvian dialectics and the Sartrean *manque-à-être*.

11. It will also provide us with a vocabulary that will help to translate Laclau's concern with signification and discourse, still very much located in the linguistic turn, into the language of social ontology.

12. Not in the narrow sense of the political system, to be sure, but in an integral sense of 'hegemonic efforts' which involve and spread over all areas of the social. Political ontology, hence, aims at explaining the political logic behind the construction of all social beings. The 'political', here, refers to what, on a different occasion, I have called 'integral politics' (see Marchart 2013b: 195) – in analogy to what Gramsci calls the 'integral State' as the sum total of political society (the State in the conventional sense) and civil society. Integral politics can be understood as the sum total of political action, including, as we will see, the most minimal forms of politics, wherever in the social topography such action occurs.

13. As William Connolly observed, 'what is figured from one perspective as a *lack* of fullness can also be figured as the *abundance* over identity that keeps desire moving' (Connolly 1995: 55). A similar point was made by Laclau: 'I do not see "lack" and "excess" as two opposite categories, so that asserting the priority of one would necessarily exclude the other, but as being two necessary moments of a unique ontological condition. It is because there is lack, conceived as deficient being, that excess becomes possible. An immanent fullness, without any internal rents, would make both lack and excess redundant' (Laclau 2005c: 256).

Chapter 3

1. It should not be ignored, though, that in the Marxist tradition bellicism is also at work wherever the Marxist conception of class struggle is misconceived in terms of 'class war'.

2. In this respect he stands in a lineage leading back, not to Marx, but to Max Weber, the other great polemologist in social thought (see Marchart 2013a: 231–62).

3. We have to bypass the complex question of Foucault's secret Heideggerianism. Generally speaking, the difference between Heidegger's and Foucault's ontologies, according to Hubert Dreyfus, lies in the fact that, for Heidegger, humans stand in a receptive, some would say passive, relation to being's self-disclosure, while for Foucault,

'the background practices reveal, as they do for Nietzsche, a constantly shifting struggle' with which one has to actively engage (Dreyfus 2003: 50). While this description is quite accurate, Dreyfus appears to downplay the key role the ontological notions of struggle and *polemos* play for Heidegger (for an overview see Fried 2000).

4. This dissolution of genealogy, in its polemological variant, is the effect of a certain degree of self-criticism on Foucault's part, even as it is certainly true that Foucault had always formulated his polemology in hypothetical terms.

5. Rather, he insists, 'there will have been nothing at the origin but the fault, a fault that is nothing but the de-fault of origin or the origin as de-fault [*le défaut d'origine ou l'origine comme défaut*]. There will have been no appearance except through disappearance. Everything will have taken place at the same time, in the same step' (Stiegler 1998: 188). What else is this, we may ask, if not a reformulation of the Heideggerian notion of 'ground': a ground, that is, which at the very same time is constituted as an abyss and only constitutes itself in its grounding *and* ungrounding as the very play between ground and abyss.

6. In the history of metaphysics, this scandal of technicity will then be interpreted in terms of a 'fall into technics' (Stiegler 1998: 96), followed by the search for or recollection of an original 'im-mediacy' (108), a harmonious state untainted by technicity – a state of nature, in Rousseau for instance, in which man, as an entirely self-sufficient being, would do without prostheses, while 'technics is what leads us down the road to decay in depriving us of our originary power' (115). Yet our condition is one 'in which nothing is any longer immediately at hand, where everything is found mediated and instrumentalized, technicized, unbalanced' (133).

7. Some passages in Stiegler's account foster this impression. When it is claimed, for instance, that the 'art of the political' is 'directly ensuing from the technical' (Stiegler 1998: 188), he seems to argue for a derivative and subordinated role for politics, or even the political. And when it is held that '*techne* [as writing] gives rise to the *polis*' (205), the *techne* of politics may be considered secondary with respect to the *techne* of writing. Of course, a very intimate relation is retained between politics and *techne*, but ontological priority is granted to technics, to the detriment of politics: before the Epimethean fault, the mortals, as he puts it, 'do not yet possess the

art of the political, called for by their de-fault of origin, and arising from their technicity' (192–3).

8. Stiegler cannot explain convincingly the logic by which a given 'we', a political collectivity, is constructed. His reference to Simondon's concept of individuation, which always involves both the individual and the collective, does not do the trick. Without a notion of *antagonism* we cannot fully explain how a 'we' is delineated (and subverted) vis-à-vis other 'we's. It can thus be suspected that there is no concept of politics in Simondon either (for a discussion of this question see Toscano 2004).

9. If this is the case, will it not disprove our claim that a concept of antagonism – as the single name for the twofold experience of conflict and contingency – could only be elaborated in modernity? There is no contradiction here, as long as it is taken into account that, if we are to really speak of quasi-*transcendental* definitions, experiences of conflict and contingency cannot be limited to modern societies alone. Social being *as such* is contingent (society could always be ordered differently, or even – the threat of Hobbesian civil war – not ordered at all). And it is, at the same time, always pervaded by conflicts. Society, and not only modern society, therefore rests on the ground and abyss of antagonism. Modern society is, however, different from other societies in that *all* (not only some) social facts are experienced as being alterable by way of conflict.

10. Apart from the obvious difference that for the Greeks *stasis* occurred in moments of exception, while, from an ontological point of view, antagonism lies at the ground of all social being at all times.

Chapter 4

1. This remainder, which we call antagonism, is what Heidegger would have described as 'most thought-provoking' (1968: 17). To be clear, what is thought-provoking is not empty 'Being' at its most ineffable, as Heidegger himself was tempted to portray it. There is nothing mystical to antagonism as the ontological 'ab-ground' of all social beings. Antagonism can easily be inferred from the fact that we *can* change the world by negating the given – an experience which, at the very same time, makes us encounter, in occasionally brutal ways, the very *limits* of constructability. To claim that an ultimate ground is not obtainable is another way of saying that the social can be

reconstructed in principle; but it also recalls that constructions will eventually crumble, for all our provisional foundations have to be built on a receding abyss.

2. As soon as the radical character of antagonism is acknowledged, many household concepts of social theory – such as ideas about 'public space' – will have to be reconceived from the ground up (see Marchart 2018).

3. This process implied that relativity and subjectivity, as rooted in the life-world, were also devaluated in the course of objectivism increasingly gaining hegemony. Husserl claims that the history of modern philosophy is marked by a constitutive tension between the two conflicting currents of objectivism and transcendentalism. By transcendentalism Husserl understands a process of returning to the last source and ground of all cognition: pre-scientific *subjectivity*. Priority should not be granted to the being of the world, but to subjectivity as the instance which, in all scientific and pre-scientific modes, gives meaning to the world (*Weltgeltung*). A non-objectivist, i.e., transcendentalist approach to the world would then have to take the inward road towards a subject who unfolds herself onto the world. Such approach can be traced back historically to the instituting moment of Descartes who not only invented modern objectivist rationalism (as it presents itself in the dualism of *res cogitans* and *res extensa*), but also modern transcendentalism with his idea of the *ego cogito* as the *fundamentum inconcussum* of all cognition. This *ego cogito*, actually and more primordially an *ego dubito* ('I doubt therefore I am'), turns out to be a distant forerunner of the phenomenological *epoche* and Husserl's project of a transcendental 'egology'. For this reason, Husserlian phenomenology does not entirely succeed in abandoning the foundationalist terrain of modern metaphysics. Despite his critique of objectivist foundationalism, Husserl does not manage to deconstruct the other side of the foundationalist double-current: subjectivism. Of course, our line of reasoning has moved away from Husserl's critique of objectivism in so far as it is not any longer concerned with rehabilitating the instance of transcendental subjectivity as opposed to objectivist scientism. From a discourse theoretical perspective, what disappears together with the idea of social objectivity is the possibility of an egological alternative to objectivism as it was defended by Husserl and his pupils in social phenomenology, such as Alfred Schütz.

4. It should be added, however, that it is not every logical alternative that is excluded in the moment of original institution; it is the set of historically available and actually articulated alternatives: 'rejected alternatives do not mean everything that is *logically* possible, but those alternatives which were *in fact* attempted, which thus represented antagonistic alternatives' (*NR* 34).

5. This at the same time implies that every 'original' institution will necessarily be somewhat less than original, as it will occur within a context of already sedimented practices. Just as the moment of the last instance, for Louis Althusser, never arrives, for Laclau nothing can be traced back to a primordial 'original institution'. Every first institution has already begun as a secondary institution, or, to put it in Husserl's terminology: every 'absolute original institution' (*absolute Urstiftung*) presents itself to us as a 'relative original institution' (*relative Urstiftung*) (Husserl 1993: 421). This implies that the so-called original institution will never serve as a firm ground of the social, it can never be reached as such, and is only present in its effects: the sedimented layers of the social.

6. Within the field of the discursive – the order of differences – there will never be a return of exactly the same differential position, since every *iteration*, as Derrida puts it, will be characterised by aberrations and displacements of the very element iterated.

7. At the end of the day it is, of course, impossible to fully spatialise time: in such a case the social would be ossified into a self-enclosed totality; everything would be reduced to pure repetition, all social practices would be fully institutionalised, leaving no room for variation or innovation. The dimension of temporality would have disappeared. If it is impossible to overcome temporality completely, if the event cannot be fully spatialised, the plausibility of the idea of fully established social structures or institutions starts to vanish. With these considerations we return full circle to Husserl's critique of objectivism. An entirely *objectivised* social space would simply amount to a space governed by repetitive practices only; as Laclau puts it: 'If society had an ultimate objectivity, then social practices, even the most innovative ones, would essentially be repetitive: they would only be the explication or reiteration of something that was there from the beginning' (*NR* 183–4).

8. See Massey (1992); Howarth (1993); Reid (1994); Miles (1997); Marchart (2014). See also Glasze (2007, 2009); Glasze and Mattissek (2009); Stavrakakis (2008); Roskamm (2017).

9. This seems to be exactly what follows for spatial theory from an ontology of antagonism: a given spatial topography does not manage to fully constitute itself as *space* because it is traversed by its antagonistic limits and therefore will always be dislocated. Thus, temporality will be a necessary outcome of any process of building a particular social topography – simply because the very construction of such topography relies on the construction of a limit which can only be drawn in a more or less antagonistic fashion as it relies on an outside of pure negativity.

10. How did this impression come about? Laclau himself was not entirely clear on the topic, which might partly account for the misunderstanding. Take the following passage. Social relations, in Laclau's words, 'are constituted by the very distinction between the social and the political'. And he continues by saying that '[t]he distinction between the social and the political is thus ontologically constitutive of social relations' (*NR 35*; as to the difference between politics, the political and police see also Dikeç 2005, 2007; and more critically with respect to Laclau and Mouffe's notion of the political Featherstone 2008). As a matter of fact, the term 'distinction' is a misnomer given the Heideggerian underpinnings of his theory. It is obvious that Laclau wants to stress that there can be no complete overlapping between the social and the political. However, in terms of the ontological difference the grounding question does not aim at the *distinction* between the ontic and the ontological (which would be the classical metaphysical way of framing the ontological difference) but at their difference *as difference*. So while it is correct to claim that on the one hand there can clearly be no total overlapping between the social and the political, on the other hand, there is constant intertwining. Some of the misunderstandings of earlier debates between critical geography and discourse theory, I suppose, had to do with the fact that these philosophical underpinnings of discourse theory have not been recognised.

11. In this respect, our ontology of the political, i.e. of antagonism, has little to do with what is often called 'social ontologies' (think of Bruno Latour's *actant-rhizome ontology* or the 'ontological turn' in anthropology). If anything, it is an ontology of the social *conceived as political*.

12. Nor will the moment of the political be a singularly rare event (as in the case of revolutions), but it will happen constantly in different degrees. As we are never entirely oblivious to the antagonistic nature

of our life-world, space is always to some degree already dislocated (temporalised). Space is constantly 'on the move', every topography is constantly done and undone, as Massey rightly claims.

13. Of course, let this be said from the outset, Nancy's reading of Hegel is not a faithful interpretation, but rather a kind of *wishful misreading*. It gives us a Hegelianism that is utterly cleared of Hegel's panlogism. This Hegelianism on the one hand takes a philological route that is far too simple, but on the other hand, it at least creates an image of what a micrological theory of radical negativity might look like today.

14. Philosophical phenomenology has addressed politics and the political with more intensity. Compare, for example, Marc Richir's large-scale attempt, in particular the concluding part on the 'abyss of political foundation' (Richir 1991: 437–81).

15. Even though antagonism, in the mode of a virtuous circle, is produced 'ontically' by way of political practice, as defined in Chapter 8 as the negation of the given.

16. Again, in this insistence on an a-subjective force of antagonism, the post-foundational ontology of the political follows Heidegger's rejection of epistemology. After all, such ontology is not looking for an epistemological or even cognitivistic interpretation of negativity. It is not looking for the endless rehearsal of classical epistemological questions, neither does it want to pass the issues on to brain research (as if it were possible to locate a region of the brain that is responsible for antagonistic negation). Negativity is not the way in which our brain perceives the world, it is the way in which the society constructs and destructs *itself*. We are therefore not playing a language game of epistemology or, more currently, cognition science, but of ontology.

17. Hence, for example, the feeling of outrage and the affect of outrage are miles apart.

18. How else could we explain the strange phenomenon that despite the electronic media of communication, we still occupy physical spaces? That even political systems can collapse, only because a few bodies assembled on a public space or stormed a government building? If the media of communication play a role in such places, then they do so not least because they can pass on the affects of the bodies at the location to those bodies that are at their TV or computer screens. They make it possible for the enthusiasm of the protesters to infect quite physically an audience that is spatially removed. However, an assembly on location remains indispensable.

Chapter 5

1. It thereby refers the reader back to Laclau's theory of New Social Movements developed together with Chantal Mouffe in *Hegemony and Socialist Strategy*. Even as at first sight, the connection between Laclau's work on populist movements and Laclau and Mouffe's discussion of New Social Movements may not be obvious, Latin-American populism always had more to do with what in the 1970s and 1980s came to be called New Social Movements – defined by their strong reliance on cultural factors in the process of political identity-building (Melucci 1989; Touraine 1981) – than with the traditional party politics of exclusively class-based movements.

2. This concept is considered the key term, not only in post-foundational discourse theory, but also in Cultural Studies where it has a history that reaches back to the late 1970s (see Slack 1996). It should be added that, despite some earlier reservations, in the later work of Stuart Hall (1997) the concept of the cultural tends to become co-extensive with the concept of the discursive in Laclau's sense, which is not that surprising since the cultural has often been defined, in the Birmingham tradition, as that dimension of the social where social meaning is produced, reproduced, altered and challenged.

3. It is understandable, given the background of Cultural Studies' emancipation from orthodox versions of Marxist determinism, that exactly the contingent nature of cultural identities was emphasised by one of the main proponents of British Cultural Studies.

4. There is nothing particularly post-structuralist to this insight (which is one of the reasons why it is preferable to use the broader qualifier post-foundational). Already in Antonio Gramsci's initial formulation of hegemony theory, Gramsci is aware of this fact – without being a post-structuralist, obviously. When he speaks about hegemony as the construction of what he calls a 'political will' or 'common or collective will', Gramsci does not take this political will – which is absolutely indispensable for any hegemonic project – to be the *source* of a hegemonic effort; rather, the political will is precisely what has to be constructed, it is the desired outcome of the articulation of a hegemonic project.

5. Despite Cultural Studies' self-understanding as a political project and despite an eminently political research focus on culture, Cultural Studies has not yet managed to develop a fully convincing theory of political protest. In fact, apart from a handful of studies (compare Hall 1988; Hall et al. 1978; Grossberg 1992) which have assumed

quasi-canonical status in the field, it would be hard to register any significant wider engagement with macro-political questions – that is, with questions concerning political mobilisation and the construction of hegemonic formations on a larger scale. There have been some exceptions to the rule which, however, have not yet managed to establish a wider dialogue between Cultural Studies and political science (see particularly Street 1997; Finlayson and Martin 1997; Dean 2000; Bowman 2007).

6. It goes without saying that populism here is understood in the political sense of Laclau, not in the critical sense given to 'cultural populism' by McGuigan (1992).

7. Interestingly, the denigration of populism went hand in hand with a forgetting of one of the founding moments for the history of Cultural Studies: Peronism. It is not without justification that the Latin-Americanist Jon Beasley-Murray (1998: 191) speaks about 'the secret (unheralded, unofficial) history of cultural studies', which 'necessarily passes through the figures of Juan and Evita Perón and the thirty-year political movement they inaugurated' (193). In his symptomatological reading, which, as I see it, supports our previous argument as to the secret disavowal of populism in much of Cultural Studies, he argues that 'the cultural studies tradition has been elaborated around a populist anxiety that is at times repressed, at times more or less expressed but hardly theorised: that cultural studies' development and expansion has coincided with – and is both symptom and reaction to – an era of populism in Britain and the United States' (197). And, as he continues, '[m]apping the secret history of cultural studies via this detour through Laclau, Latin America, and Peronism does more than add merely a more nuanced and less parochially Anglophone element to the founding fictions of cultural studies; it also restores to cultural studies its full political investment in social theory and questions of strategy and organization' (199).

8. One can suspect that their negligence regarding the difference between politics and the political – which is of categorical and not only gradual nature – has to do with their allegiance to a certain objectivism that is hard to eradicate in the social sciences.

9. From the perspective of a theory of social protest, a potentially fruitful further differentiation issues from Laclau's distinction – analogous to the concepts of request and demand respectively – between democratic demand and popular demand. While the former tends towards a logic of difference, the latter mainly functions according

to a logic of equivalence. Hence, '[t]he first can be accommodated within an expanding hegemonic formation; the second presents a challenge to the hegemonic formation as such' (*PR* 82). Along the same lines it becomes possible for the study of protest movements to differentiate between forms of tendentially 'democratic protest' and those of tendentially 'popular protest' where the former exhibit a low degree of antagonisation due to the defence of merely corporate or sectorial interests, while the latter aim at a much wider alliance of struggles directed against, for instance, the 'power bloc' as such. It should be noted that there is no value claim involved here: 'democratic' simply means, in Laclau's terminology, *differentially* articulated (while 'popular' means equivalentially articulated) and has nothing to do with democracy as a political regime.

10. The same must be said with respect to the classical subcultural studies approach and a certain reluctance or inability to theorise the *counter*-cultural function of protest formations. As long as subcultures are supposed to remain on the level of 'symbolic resistance' or 'resistance through rituals', they will remain within the sphere of micro-politics. Only when these rituals enter a chain of equivalence do they become *politicised*. Hence, to restrict the analysis to matters of 'style' and 'aesthetics' rather than political mobilisation will necessarily lead to a depoliticised account of subcultures.

Chapter 6

1. The more dislocated a given society, the more jumping-off points for political protest. In this respect, protests appear to emerge everywhere – which is the reason why we are living in 'protest societies' or 'social movement societies' as some sociologists claim (see Meyer and Tarrow 1998; Rucht and Neidhart 2002).
2. We have argued in Chapter 4 that what is usually called micro-politics has nothing to do with politics, but tends to describe those reverberations of the political that make the social tremble.
3. Let me stress once again that I am not denying that the echo of the political (of the political institutions of the social) pervades even all the way into our hospitals' maternity wards. The social is the echo chamber of the political, but it is not in itself politics.
4. The whole quote, which is crucial, reads as follows: 'The Desire for Recognition which provokes the Fight is the desire for a desire – that is, for something that does not *exist* really (since Desire is

the "manifest" presence of the *absence* of a reality): to want to be "recognized" is to want to be accepted as a positive "value" – that is, precisely speaking, to cause oneself to be "desired." To want to risk one's *life*, which is the *whole* reality of a living being, in favor of something that does not *exist* and cannot exist as inert or merely living real *things* exist – this, then, is indeed to *negate* the given which one is oneself, this is to be *free* or *independent* of it. Now, to negate oneself, in this full sense, and nevertheless to preserve oneself in existence, is indeed to *create* oneself as new and therefore to exist as created by oneself – that is, as free or autonomous' (Kojève 1980: 225–6).

5. Lacan criticises Hegel (and whenever he says Hegel he means Kojève) for not integrating the Symbolic into the framework of the dialectics of recognition, thus remaining within the impasse of the Imaginary. While Lacan also uses the Kojèvian dialectics as a model for the dialectics of the Imaginary (where the other is written with a small o), Lacan's capitalisation of the Kojèvian Imaginary other into the Other (of the Symbolic) can be seen as a way out of that impasse.

6. This concurs with our thesis that minimal politics aims to maximise politics.

7. It is apparent that this game is exposed to the danger of circularity, except that it is not a danger but a necessary implication of the model of political difference (Marchart 2007a): Politics and the political can only emerge from each other, yet there remains that minimal difference of non-concurrence that precludes coming full circle and blocks every deductive thought. Hence the inevitability of political judgement as the virtue that is absolutely necessary to achieve plausible articulation on both sides of the difference.

8. And vice versa: every – initially – successful grounding causes a new degrounding, as, in Laclau's words, older sediments of the social are dislocated by new institutions and in turn set off alternative efforts at institution.

Chapter 7

1. I went so far as proposing that *all* social being, to the extent to which it is constantly grounded and ungrounded by an outside instance of radical negativity, is nothing other than the political in a different mode, i.e. in the aggregate state of social sedimentation.

2. In contrast to epistemology, to remind us of what was said in Chapter 1, ontological claims are not launched from the position of presumably detached, outer-worldly mind. They are *enacted* within a social world defined, in its entirety, by *the political*. In this enlarged sense of the political, rather than politics, a practice of ontological questioning is always already imbued with a 'weak' political force. It is inscribed, and inscribes itself, into social relations which, in the last instance, are grounded in the political moment of institution.

3. This move from inhabiting to enacting is congruent with a left-Heideggerian ontology of the political: inhabiting, as understood here, is but the political version of what Heidegger, in an entirely unpolitical way, called 'dwelling'.

4. This is not to say that being can or should be named in *any* way. The name of being will always be debated and any particular proposal will encounter resistance.

5. For clarification it should be remarked that within the Laclauian framework any positive difference within a system of differences can be considered 'conceptual'. This implies that concepts are not necessarily ideational items, but descriptive features – or, in yet another paradigm, systemic *functions* – are also conceptual to the extent to which they operate within a system of differences (as far as, for instance, the societal function of the political system can be differentiated from the respective functions of the economic system, the educational system, etc.).

6. To void confusion with mystical vacuity, it should be stressed that the empty signifier is not a 'pure' signifier or 'signifier without signified' (as Heidegger sometimes seems to forget, ontological being is never untainted by the ontic). The latter notion, for Laclau, would be self-defeating, since a signifier without *any* signified could only produce noise and the process of signification would break down completely. Consequently, the empty signifier is not located *outside* the realm of signification, but 'is a place, within the system of signification which is constitutively irrepresentable; in that sense it remains empty, but this is an emptiness which I can signify, because we are dealing with a void *within* signification' (*PR* 105). Put differently, there will always be a remainder of signifieds, there will be traces of a particular content, and hence the empty signifier will always only be *tendentially* empty: the longer the chain of equivalence, the 'emptier' the signifier that serves as a nodal point for this chain.

And the longer the chain of equivalences, the more we move from the conceptual order to the *nominal* order. See also Laclau's own engagement with the mystical tradition in his article 'On the Names of God' (*RFS* 37–51; see also *RFS* 26–30).

7. A perhaps surprising consequence of this political theory of naming could be that, in the strict sense, a *personal* name might *not* be regarded as a name from the perspective of political ontology. There are exceptional cases, though, when, as in revolutionary times, children are given the names of heroes of the revolution. In cases like these, the name is inscribed into a revolutionary chain of equivalence *against* the Ancien Régime and therefore functions to signify unity against an outside threat. In most cases, however, personal names belong to the sedimented realm of differences, where they are indeed semantically overdetermined (they are associated with a particular culture, region, language, gender or social class), i.e. they *do* signify, but their originally political meaning is largely forgotten and becomes only reactivated in moments of conflict, ethnic war for instance, when personal names are experienced as markers of group affiliation.

8. Admittedly, a name of this scope will go beyond the horizon of most rival political ontologies and will be difficult to accommodate within the conceptual order of a scientific discipline. It may even sound, from the strictly 'scientific' perspective, like utter nonsense – which should not surprise us, given that emptying a signifier of its signifieds can only result in nonsense. Meaning production is interrupted. What we are looking for, however, is a form of regulated 'nonsense' that results from a reflective intervention into the conceptual field, whereby a certain degree of conceptual content is retained, as will be explained presently. While antagonism is an empty signifier to some degree, it is also a concept to some degree.

9. It goes without saying that Laclau, of course, does not abandon the conceptual order of theory. The point of the matter is that, apart from his theoretical work, which to a significant degree – simply by being theoretical – remains within the conceptual order, Laclau's theory of naming, when applied to his own theoretical intervention, allows us to exactly determine the moment of antagonism (of equivalence) in his own work. It consists in the reflective intervention of moving populism to the centre of political theory. Laclau is, first and foremost, the thinker of populism.

10. A more careful reading of epistemologists along the lines of Heidegger's engagement with Kant would show, however, that it is impossible to completely bypass ontological questions.

11. As a reflective intervention that will transform philosophy into a practice of 'thinking' that is both 'more' than philosophy and 'less' than philosophy, political ontology may well assume the status of a *prima philosophia* vis-à-vis other philosophical sub-disciplines (see Marchart 2007a: 162–9; 2013a: 245–88).

12. Since the dualism between ego and world remains ultimately unbridgeable, this goal can only be attained, of course, via the bridging vertical connection to 'God', the foundation of the foundation, so to speak – confirming Heidegger's notion that every metaphysics is onto-theology.

13. See the political diagram of powers in the Netherlands during Spinoza's time in Balibar (2008a: 22); on Balibar's own differentiation between *la* and *le politique* at the hands of Spinozism see Balibar (1993).

14. The only systematic attempt to this effect that I am aware of was made by the French Suárez specialist Jean-Paul Coujou (2006). Unfortunately, there is no scope for a detailed discussion of this effort here.

15. Any historically more specific delineation of ontology would thwart the ahistorical Heideggerian division of occidental history into a small number of great eras. On the Heideggerian Left, Reiner Schürmann's otherwise magnificent study of the history of Western philosophy *Broken Hegemonies* (2003) has the one fault that it follows Heidegger in the division of history into great eras – Schürmann established the Greek, the Latin and the modern eras. In contrast to Heidegger, Schürmann at least provides a historico-political index to his theory of stages. The eras each have an attendant hegemonic fantasm – in Laclau's theory of hegemony, one would speak of an *imaginary horizon* – which allows a given culture 'to say what is', i.e. to classify the world and divide power: 'A fantasm is hegemonic when an entire culture relies on it as if it provided that in the name of which one speaks and acts' (Schürmann 2003: 7). The history of such fantasms is thus, he argues, the history of ultimate points of reference or standards (Laclau would probably speak of empty signifiers here), which have no proper being beyond their relational function of reference and are therefore literally 'nothing': *non-res*. In the history of philosophy,

these points of reference are principles and foundations which do not appear in the realm of all being and yet – or because of this – have an ultimate authority. It has traditionally been the task of philosophy to secure the delivery of such sovereign signifiers. With great precision, Schürmann traces the self-deconstruction of the hegemonic fantasms he found in the history of philosophy and in doing so confirms that hegemonic formations are never monolithic systems of suppression, but that all hegemonies have indeed for ever been 'broken', that is to say, *in the process of breaking apart*. This insight is characteristic for a post-foundational understanding of politics. Yet, Schürmann keeps his sights firmly set on the *longue durée* and only three grand paradigms. Even if we accept that metaphysical points of reference can certainly be of a long-lived nature, we must ask for the origins of their durability. An explanation that is exclusively immanent in philosophy – 'inner plausibility', for instance – would obviously not suffice. This reason could more likely lie within the scope of what Negri described as the 'implicit political dispositif' of a given ontology. It lingers in a political project that is able to implicitly formulate an ontology in the field of philosophy and guarantee its connectivity with the conditions of the hegemonic situation, i.e. the social struggles, of its time. One might assume that this political dispositive of an ontology continues to exist as long as it is an inseparable part of the hegemonic formations of a given society – or provides a symptomatic marker of its crisis. We will return to Schürmann in the next chapter.

Chapter 8

1. In fact, reversing the order of priority is absolutely congruent with the reversible nature of the political difference. It was claimed throughout our study that politics should be seen as an attempt at instantiating the political (which, *eo ipso*, remains absent). The political, far from serving as a stable ground, re-emerges from its aggregate state of social routines only by way of politics as the practice of activating dormant antagonisms. The social, in turn, is also made of a particular kind of practices, but these are iterative practices by which a given set of differences is kept in place, while, to stick to Laclauian terminology, political action involves the articulation of differences into a chain of equivalence.

2. Schürmann points out that such a reversal goes against the grain of the metaphysical tradition of Western foundationalism and, therefore, is 'more than a simple inversion of the relationship between being and acting; it is the subversion of that classical relation, its overturn (*vertere*) from the base (*sub-*)' (Schürmann 1990: 7).

3. It should be noted that Schürmann is not alone in pointing out the practical nature of being. A 'praxeological' turn has always been an option in the tradition of left Heideggerianism and was prominently defended, for instance, by philosophers associated with the Yugoslavian Praxis Group, most prominently by Gajo Petrović.

4. A certain aloofness characteristic of Heidegger's notion of 'being' thereby reflects in his notions of acting and thinking.

5. This is the reason why I have insisted on the notion of 'differentialised *negativity*' rather than simply equating negativity with theoretical tropes of difference as is the tendency in Diana Coole's otherwise impressive study on 'Negativity and Politics' (Coole 2000).

6. To the banal juxtaposition of materialism and idealism, i.e. to a 'struggle' of two trends allegedly present throughout the history of philosophy, one must object that neither is materialism *per se* progressive, nor is idealism *per se* bourgeois in the sense of 'reactionary'. Their political spin depends on their given hegemonic articulation with political positions outside of the field of philosophy (which are also, of course, represented within the field of philosophy).

7. Political action, in other words, is a deeply metaphysical enterprise based on the foundationalist working assumption that the social can be provided with a stable ground by a political subject – for otherwise there would be no action to start with. Only *democratic* politics may at the same time encourage us to accept the ultimately groundless nature of the social.

8. To specify: I negate because (a) my being is negated, and (b) my pre-political requests emerging from that dislocation remain frustrated.

9. Here we can see the difference with regard to a strategy of populist mobilisation. In the latter case, 'the power bloc' may also be portrayed as a homogeneous entity, yet in many cases it will have a determinable content such as the governing party, the ruling elite, etc. The moment when populists start portraying the power bloc in terms of an all-powerful entity, their discourse moves from the political terrain to the phantasmatic (to conspiracy theories, for instance, such as a world-wide Jewish network).

Conclusion

1. If examples are needed: antagonism is experienced, in its aggregate state of relations of subordination, in moments when women, migrants or workers may encounter institutional 'glass ceilings' or get the impression of 'being stuck' socially. In moments like these, the social world appears to us, not as a smooth and plain space, but as an uneven and slippery terrain full of traps and institutionalised obstacles. But, as soon as these sedimented relations of subordination become reactivated by an emergent antagonism, the pre-political experience of subordination will be transformed into a politicised experience of oppression. A process of politicisation begins where negativity is being experienced *as such* – unmediated, as it were, by social institutions and routines.

Bibliography

Abensour, Miguel (2011), *Democracy Against the State: Marx and the Machiavellian Moment*, Cambridge: Polity Press.

Adorno, Theodor W. (1975), *Negative Dialektik, Gesammelte Schriften*, vol. 6, Frankfurt am Main: Suhrkamp.

Agamben, Giorgio (1999), *Potentialities: Collected Essays in Philosophy*, Stanford: Stanford University Press.

Agamben, Giorgio (2015), *Stasis: Civil War as a Political Paradigm*, Stanford: Stanford University Press.

Agamben, Giorgio (2016), *The Use of Bodies: Homo Sacer IV, 2*, trans. Adam Kotsko, Stanford: Stanford University Press.

Althusser, Louis (1976), *Essays in Self-Criticism*, London: New Left Books.

Althusser, Louis (2017), *Philosophy for Non-Philosophers*, London and New York: Bloomsbury.

Arndt, Andreas (2009), 'Widerstreit und Widerspruch. Gegensatzbeziehungen in frühromantischen Diskursen', *Romanticism: International Yearbook of German Idealism 6/2008*, Berlin and New York: de Gruyter, pp. 102–22.

Badiou, Alain (2000), 'Of Life as a Name of Being, or, Deleuze's Vitalist Ontology', *Pli* 10, pp. 191–9.

Badiou, Alain (2007), *Being and Event*, London: Continuum.

Badiou, Alain (2010), *The Communist Hypothesis*, London and New York: Verso.

Baldassari, Marco and Diego Melegari (eds) (2012), *Populismo e democrazia radicale. In dialogo con Ernesto Laclau*, Verona: ombre corte.

Balibar, Étienne (1993), 'Le Politique, La Politique: De Rousseau à Marx, de Marx à Spinoza', *Studia Spinozana* 9, pp. 203–15.

Balibar, Étienne (2008a), *Spinoza and Politics*, London and New York: Verso.

Balibar, Étienne (2008b), 'Historical Dilemmas of Democracy and Their Contemporary Relevance for Citizenship', *Rethinking Marxism* 20(4), pp. 522–38.

Barthes, Roland (1990), *The Fashion System*, Berkeley, Los Angeles and London: University of California Press.

Beasley-Murray, Jon (1998), 'Peronism and the Secret History of Cultural Studies: Populism and the Substitution of Culture for State', *Cultural Critique* 39 (Spring), pp. 189–217.

Bennett, Jane (2010), *Vibrant Matter: A Political Ecology of Things*, Durham, NC: Duke University Press.

Bosteels, Bruno (2011), *The Actuality of Communism*, London and New York: Verso.

Bowman, Paul (2007), *Post-Marxism Versus Cultural Studies: Theory, Politics and Intervention*, Edinburgh: Edinburgh University Press.

Braver, Lee (2012), *Groundless Grounds: A Study of Wittgenstein and Heidegger*, Cambridge, MA and London: MIT Press.

Buck-Morss, Susan (2013), 'A Communist Ethics', in Slavoj Žižek (ed.), *The Idea of Communism 2*, London and New York: Verso, pp. 57–76.

Butler, Judith (1992), 'Contingent Foundations: Feminism and the Question of "Postmodernism"', in Judith Butler and Joan W. Scott (eds), *Feminists Theorize the Political*, New York and London: Routledge, pp. 3–21.

Butler, Judith (1997), *The Psychic Life of Power: Theories in Subjection*, Stanford: Stanford University Press.

Butler, Judith (2015), *Notes Toward a Performative Theory of Assembly*, Cambridge, MA and London: Harvard University Press.

Certeau, Michel de (1988), *The Practice of Everyday Life*, Berkeley and Los Angeles: University of California Press.

Chevallier, Philippe (2004), *Michel Foucault: Le pouvoir et la bataille*, Nantes: Pleins Feux.

Connolly, William (1995), *The Ethos of Pluralization*, Minneapolis and London: University of Minnesota Press.

Connolly, William (2011), *A World of Becoming*, Durham, NC: Duke University Press.

Coole, Diana (2000), *Negativity and Politics: Dionysus and Dialectics from Kant to Poststructuralism*, London and New York: Routledge.

Coujou, Jean-Paul (2006), *Philosophie politique et ontologie: Remarques sur la fonction de l'ontologie dans la constitution de la pensée politique*, vol. 1, Paris: L'Harmattan.

Critchley, Simon and Oliver Marchart (eds) (2004), *Laclau: A Critical Reader*, London and New York: Routledge.

Dallmayr, F. R. (1988), 'Hegemony and Democracy: On Laclau and Mouffe', *Strategies* 30 (Fall), pp. 29–49.

Daly, Glyn (2008), 'Ology Schmology: A Post-Structuralist Approach', *Politics* 28(1), pp. 57–60.

Dean, Jodi (ed.) (2000), *Cultural Studies and Political Theory*, Ithaca, NY and London: Cornell University Press.

Dean, Jodi (2012), *The Communist Horizon*, London and New York: Verso.

Deleuze, Gilles (1986), *Nietzsche and Philosophy*, London and New York: Continuum.

Deleuze, Gilles (1992), *The Fold: Leibniz and the Baroque*, Minnesota: University of Minnesota Press.

Deleuze, Gilles (1997), *Essays Critical and Clinical*, Minnesota: University of Minnesota Press.

Deleuze, Gilles and Félix Guattari (1986), *Kafka: Toward a Minor Literature*, Minneapolis and London: University of Minnesota Press.

Della Volpe, Galvano (1956), *Logica come scienza positive*, 2nd edn, Messina and Florence: D'Anna.

Derrida, Jacques (1988), *Limited Inc.*, Evanston, IL: Northwestern University Press.

Derrida, Jacques (1994), *Specters of Marx: The State of the Debt, the Work of Mourning, and the New International*, New York and London: Routledge.

Derrida, Jacques (2005), *On Touching – Jean-Luc Nancy*, Stanford: Stanford University Press.

Deutsche, Penelope (1998), *Evictions: Art and Spatial Politics*, Cambridge, MA and London: MIT Press.

Dikeç, Mustafa (2005), 'Space, Politics, and the Political', *Environment and Planning D: Society and Space* 23(2), pp. 171–88.

Dikeç, Mustafa (2007), *Badlands of the Republic: Space, Politics and Urban Policy*, London: Blackwell.

Dreyfus, Hubert L. (2003), '"Being and Power" Revisited', in Alan Milchmann and Alan Rosenberg (eds), *Foucault and Heidegger: Critical Encounters*, Minneapolis and London: University of Minnesota Press, pp. 30–54.

Esposito, Roberto (2013), 'Immunization and Violence', in Roberto Esposito, *Terms of the Political: Community, Immunity, Biopolitics*, trans. Rhiannon Noel Welch, New York: Fordham University Press, pp. 57–66.

Featherstone, David (2008), *Resistance, Space and Political Identities: The Making of Counter-Global Networks*, London: Blackwell.

Ferrara, Alessandro (2008), *The Force of the Example: Explorations in the Paradigm of Judgment*, New York: Columbia University Press.

Finlayson, Alan and James Martin (1997), 'Political Studies and Cultural Studies', *Politics* 17(3), pp. 183–9.

Fiske, John (1991), *Understanding Popular Culture*, London and New York: Routledge.

Fontana, Alessandro and Mauro Bertani (2003), 'Situating the Lectures', in Michel Foucault, *'Society Must Be Defended': Lectures at the Collège de France 1975–76*, New York: Picador, pp. 273–93.

Foucault, Michel (1977), *Discipline and Punish: The Birth of the Prison*, New York: Vintage Books.

Foucault, Michel (1980), *Power/Knowledge: Selected Interviews and Other Writings 1972–1977*, New York: Pantheon Books.

Foucault, Michel (2003), *'Society Must Be Defended': Lectures at the Collège de France 1975–76*, New York: Picador.

Foucault, Michel (2011), *The Government of Self and Others: Lectures at the Collège de France 1982–1983*, Houndmills: Palgrave Macmillan.

Freud, Sigmund (1999), 'Jenseits des Lustprinzips', in Sigmund Freud, *Gesammelte Werke*, vol. XIII, Frankfurt am Main: Fischer, pp. 1–70.

Fried, Gregory (2000), *Heidegger's Polemos: From Being to Politics*, New Haven, CT and London: Yale University Press.

Gehlen, Arnold [1940] (2016), *Der Mensch. Seine Natur und seine Stellung in der Welt*, Frankfurt am Main: Klostermann.

Gill, Stephen (2000), 'Towards a Postmodern Prince? The Battle in Seattle as a Moment in the New Politics of Globalisation', *Millennium: Journal of International Studies* 29(1), pp. 131–40.

Glasze, Georg (2007), 'The Discursive Constitution of a World Spanning Region and the Role of Empty Signifiers: The Case of Francophonia', *Geopolitics* 12(4), pp. 656–79.

Glasze, Georg (2009), 'Der Raumbegriff bei Laclau – auf dem Weg zu einem politischen Konzept von Räumen', in Georg Glasze and Annika Mattissek (eds), *Handbuch Diskurs und Raum. Theorien und Methoden für die Humangeographie sowie die sozial- und kulturwissenschaftliche Raumforschung*, Bielefeld: Transcript, pp. 213–18.

Glasze, Georg and Annika Mattissek (2009), 'Die Hegemonie- und Diskurstheorie von Laclau und Mouffe', in Georg Glasze and Annika Mattissek (eds), *Handbuch Diskurs und Raum. Theorien und Methoden für die Humangeographie sowie die sozial- und kulturwissenschaftliche Raumforschung*, Bielefeld: Transcript, pp. 153–81.

Glynos, Jason and David Howarth (2007), *Logics of Critical Explanation in Social and Political Theory*, London and New York: Routledge.

Goetz, Benoît (2002), *La Dislocation: Architecture et philosophie*, Paris: Éditions de la Passion.

Goldmann, Lucien (2013), *The Hidden God: A Study of Tragic Vision in the* Pensées *of Pascal and the Tragedies of Racine*, London and New York: Routledge.

Gramsci, Antonio (1971), *Selections from the Prison Notebooks*, ed. Quintin Hoare and Geoffrey Nowell Smith, New York: International Publishers.

Grossberg, Lawrence (1992), *We Gotta Get Out of This Place: Popular Conservatism and Postmodern Culture*, New York and London: Routledge.

Guattari, Félix and Suely Rolnik (2007), *Micropolitiques*, Paris: Les Empêcheurs de penser en rond/Le Seuil.

Hall, Stuart (1988), *The Hard Road to Renewal: Thatcherism and the Crisis of the Left*, London and New York: Verso.

Hall, Stuart (1996a), 'An Interview with Stuart Hall', in David Morley and Kuan-Hsing Chen (eds), *Stuart Hall: Critical Dialogues in Cultural Studies*, London and New York: Routledge, pp. 131–50.

Hall, Stuart (1996b), 'Cultural Studies and Its Theoretical Legacies', in David Morley and Kuan-Hsing Chen (eds), *Stuart Hall: Critical Dialogues in Cultural Studies*, London and New York: Routledge, pp. 262–75.

Hall, Stuart (1997), 'The Centrality of Culture: Notes on the Cultural Revolutions of Our Time', in Kenneth Thompson (ed.), *Media and Cultural Regulation*, London, Thousand Oaks and New Delhi: Sage, pp. 207–38.

Hall, Stuart, Charles Critcher, Tony Jefferson, John Clarke and Brian Roberts (1978), *Policing the Crisis*, London: Macmillan.

Hall, Stuart and Tony Jefferson (eds) (1975), *Resistance Through Rituals: Youth Subcultures in Post-War Britain*, Birmingham: The Centre for Contemporary Cultural Studies.

Hansen, Allan Dreyer (2014), 'Laclau and Mouffe and the Ontology of Radical Negativity', *Distinktion: Scandinavian Journal of Social Theory* 15(3), pp. 283–95.

Harney, Stefano and Fred Moten (2013), *The Undercommons: Fugitive Planning & Black Study*, New York: Minor Compositions.

Hebdige, Dick (1987), *Subculture: The Meaning of Style*, London and New York: Routledge.

Hegel, G. W. F. [1807] (1999), *Phänomenologie des Geistes, Hauptwerke in sechs Bänden*, vol. 2, Hamburg: Meiner.

Hegel, G. W. F. [1813] (1999), *Wissenschaft der Logik, Hauptwerke in sechs Bänden*, vol. 3, Hamburg: Meiner.

Heidegger, Martin (1953), *Being and Time*, Albany, NY: State University of New York Press.

Heidegger, Martin (1957), *Identität und Differenz*, Stuttgart: Neske.

Heidegger, Martin (1961), *Nietzsche*, vol. 1, Stuttgart: Neske.

Heidegger, Martin (1968), *What Is Called Thinking?*, trans. Fred. D. Wieck and J. Glenn Gray, New York, Evanston, IL and London: Harper & Row.

Heidegger, Martin (1994), *Beiträge zur Philosophie (Vom Ereignis), Gesamtausgabe*, vol. 65, Frankfurt am Main: Vittorio Klostermann.

Heidegger, Martin (1998), *Basic Concepts*, trans. Gary E. Aylesworth, Bloomington and Indianapolis: Indiana University Press.

Heidegger, Martin (1999), 'Letter on "Humanism"', in Martin Heidegger, *Pathmarks*, ed. William McNeill, Cambridge: Cambridge University Press, pp. 239–76.

Heidegger, Martin (2009), *Hegel, Gesamtausgabe*, Abteilung III, vol. 68, Frankfurt am Main: Klostermann.

Holbraad, Martin and Morten Axel Pedersen (2017), *The Ontological Turn: An Anthropological Exposition*, Cambridge: Cambridge University Press.

Howarth, David (1993), 'Reflections on the Politics of Space and Time', *Angelaki* 1(1), pp. 43–55.

Howarth, David (ed.) (2015), *Ernesto Laclau: Post-Marxism, Populism and Critique*, London and New York: Routledge.

Howarth, David, Aletta Norval and Yannis Stavrakakis (eds) (2000), *Discourse Theory and Political Analysis: Identities, Hegemonies and Social Change*, Manchester: Manchester University Press.

Howarth, David and Jacob Torfing (eds) (2005), *Discourse Theory in European Politics: Identity, Policy and Governance*, Basingstoke: Palgrave Macmillan.

Husserl, Edmund (1962), *Die Krisis der europäischen Wissenschaften und die transzendentale Phänomenologie, Husserliana*, vol. VI, The Hague: Martinus Nijhoff.

Husserl, Edmund (1993), *Die Krisis der europäischen Wissenschaften und die transzendentale Phänomenologie*, Ergänzungsband: *Texte aus dem Nachlaß 1934–1937, Husserliana*, vol. XXIX, The Hague: Kluwer.

Israel, Jonathan (2002), *Radical Enlightenment: Philosophy and the Making of Modernity 1650–1750*, Oxford: Oxford University Press.

Janicaud, Dominique (2001), *Heidegger en France*, 2 vols, Paris: Bibliothèque Albin Michel.

Kant, Immanuel [1781] (1983), *Kritik der reinen Vernunft*, in Immanuel Kant, *Werke*, vols 3 and 4, 1st part, Darmstadt: Wissenschaftliche Buchgesellschaft.

Kaprow, Allan (2003), *Essays on the Blurring of Art and Life*, Berkeley, Los Angeles and London: University of California Press.

Kojève, Alexandre (1980), *Introduction to the Reading of Hegel*, Ithaca, NY and London: Cornell University Press.

Kompridis, Niklas (2011), *Critique and Disclosure: Critical Theory Between Past and Future*, Cambridge, MA: MIT Press.

Koselleck, Reinhart (1972), 'Einleitung', in Otto Brunner, Werner Conze and Reinhart Koselleck (eds), *Geschichtliche Grundbegriffe*, vol. 1, Stuttgart: Klett, pp. xiii–xxvii.

Kraniauskas, John (2014), 'Rhetorics of Populism. Ernesto Laclau, 1935–2014', *Radical Philosophy* 186 (July/August), pp. 29–36.

Kripke, Saul (1980), *Naming and Necessity*, Cambridge, MA: Cambridge University Press.

Laclau, Ernesto (1977), *Politics and Ideology in Marxist Theory: Capitalism, Fascism, Populism*, London: New Left Books.

Laclau, Ernesto (1990), *New Reflections on the Revolution of Our Time*, London: Verso.

Laclau, Ernesto (1993), 'Discourse', in Robert E. Goodin and Philip Pettit (eds), *A Companion to Contemporary Political Philosophy*, Oxford: Basil Blackwell, pp. 431–7.

Laclau, Ernesto (1994), 'Introduction', in Ernesto Laclau (ed.), *The Making of Political Identities*, London and New York: Verso, pp. 1–8.

Laclau, Ernesto (1996a), *Emancipation(s)*, London: Verso.

Laclau, Ernesto (1996b), 'Deconstruction, Pragmatism, Hegemony', in Chantal Mouffe (ed.), *Deconstruction and Pragmatism*, London and New York: Routledge, pp. 47–67.

Laclau, Ernesto (1999), 'Hegemony and the Future of Democracy: Ernesto Laclau's Political Philosophy', in Lynn Worsham and Gary A. Olson (eds), *Race, Rhetoric, and the Postcolonial*, Albany, NY: State University of New York Press, pp. 129–62.

Laclau, Ernesto (2000a), 'Identity and Hegemony: The Role of Universality in the Constitution of Political Logics', in Judith Butler, Ernesto Laclau and Slavoj Žižek, *Contingency, Hegemony, Universality:*

Contemporary Dialogues on the Left, London and New York: Verso, pp. 44–89.

Laclau, Ernesto (2000b), 'Constructing Universality', in Judith Butler, Ernesto Laclau and Slavoj Žižek, *Contingency, Hegemony, Universality: Contemporary Dialogues on the Left*, London and New York: Verso, pp. 281–307.

Laclau, Ernesto (2003), 'Democracy Between Autonomy and Heteronomy', in Okwui Enwezor, Carlos Basualdo, Ute Meta Bauer, Susanne Ghez, Sarat Maharaj, Mark Nash and Octavio Zaya (eds), *Democracy Unrealized*, Ostfildern: Hatje Cantz, pp. 377–86.

Laclau, Ernesto (2004), 'Glimpsing the Future', in Simon Critchley and Oliver Marchart (eds), *Laclau: A Critical Reader*, London and New York: Routledge, pp. 279–328.

Laclau, Ernesto (2005a), *On Populist Reason*, London: Verso.

Laclau, Ernesto (2005b), 'Populism: What's in a Name?', in Francisco Panizza (ed.), *Populism and the Mirror of Democracy*, London and New York: Verso, pp. 32–49.

Laclau, Ernesto (2005c), 'The Future of Radical Democracy', in Lars Tønder and Lasse Thomassen (eds), *Radical Democracy: Politics Between Abundance and Lack*, Manchester: Manchester University Press, pp. 256–62.

Laclau, Ernesto (2014), *The Rhetorical Foundations of Society*, London: Verso.

Laclau, Ernesto and Chantal Mouffe (1985), *Hegemony and Socialist Strategy: Towards a Radical Democratic Politics*, London: Verso.

Laclau, Ernesto and Lilian Zac (1994), 'Minding the Gap. The Subject of Politics', in Ernesto Laclau (ed.), *The Making of Political Identities*, London and New York: Verso, pp. 11–39.

Lacoue-Labarthe, Philippe and Jean-Luc Nancy (eds) (1983), *Le retrait du politique*, Paris: Galilée.

Lefort, Claude (1986), *The Political Forms of Modern Society: Bureaucracy, Democracy, Totalitarianism*, Cambridge, MA: MIT Press.

Lefort, Claude (1988), *Democracy and Political Theory*, Minneapolis: University of Minnesota Press.

Lefort, Claude (2000), *Writing: The Political Test*, Durham, NC and London: Duke University Press.

Lefort, Claude (2008a), 'Le désordre nouveau', in Edgar Morin, Claude Lefort and Cornelius Castoriadis, *Mai 68: La Brèche* suivi de *Vingt ans après*, Paris: Fayard, pp. 43–82.

Lefort, Claude (2008b), 'Relecture', in Edgar Morin, Claude Lefort and Cornelius Castoriadis, *Mai 68: La Brèche* suivi de *Vingt ans après*, Paris: Fayard, pp. 269–86.

Lefort, Claude (2012), *Machiavelli in the Making*, Evanston, IL: Northwestern University Press.

Loraux, Nicole (2006), *The Divided City: On Memory and Forgetting in Ancient Athens*, New York: Zone Books.

Lordon, Frédéric (2013), *La societé des affects: Pour un structuralisme des passions*, Paris: Éditions du Seuil.

Lordon, Frédéric (2016), *Les affects de la politique*, Paris: Éditions du Seuil.

Luke, Timothy W. (1996), 'Identity, Meaning and Globalization: Detraditionalization in Postmodern Space-Time Compression', in Paul Heelas, Scott Lash and Paul Morris (eds), *Detraditionalization*, Oxford: Blackwell, pp. 109–33.

McGuigan, Jim (1992), *Cultural Populism*, London and New York: Routledge.

McNay, Lois (2014), *The Misguided Search for the Political: Social Weightlessness in Radical Democratic Theory*, Cambridge: Polity Press.

Macpherson, C. B. (1962), *The Political Theory of Possessive Individualism: Hobbes to Locke*, Oxford: Clarendon Press.

McRobbie, Angela (1994), *Postmodernism and Cultural Studies*, London and New York: Routledge.

Mann, Patricia S. (1994), *Micro-Politics: Agency in a Post-Feminist Era*, Minneapolis and London: University of Minnesota Press.

Marchart, Oliver (1999a), 'Einleitung: Undarstellbarkeit und "ontologische Differenz"', in Oliver Marchart (ed.), *Das Undarstellbare der Politik. Zur Hegemonietheorie Ernesto Laclaus*, Vienna: Turia+Kant, pp. 7–20.

Marchart, Oliver (1999b), 'Das unbewußte Politische. Zum *psychoanalytic turn* in der politischen Theorie: Jameson, Butler, Laclau, Žižek', in Jürgen Trinks (ed.), *Bewußtsein und Unbewußtes*, Vienna: Turia+Kant, pp. 196–234.

Marchart, Oliver (2002), 'On Drawing a Line. Politics and the Significatory Logic of Inclusion/Exclusion', in Urs Stäheli (ed.), *Inclusion/Exclusion and Socio-Cultural Identities*, special issue of *Soziale Systeme* 8(1), pp. 69–87.

Marchart, Oliver (2003a), 'The Other Side of Order: Towards a Political Theory of Terror and Dislocation', *Parallax* 9(1), pp. 97–113.

Marchart, Oliver (2003b), 'Bridging the Micro-Macro Gap: Is There Such a Thing as Post-Subcultural Politics?', in David Muggleton and Rupert Weinzierl (eds), *The Post-Subcultures Reader*, New York and Oxford: Berg, pp. 83–97.

Marchart, Oliver (2004), 'Politics and the Ontological Difference: On the "Strictly Philosophical" in Ernesto Laclau's Work', in Simon

Critchley and Oliver Marchart (eds), *Laclau: A Critical Reader*, London and New York: Routledge, pp. 54–72.

Marchart, Oliver (2005), 'The Absence at the Heart of Presence: Radical Democracy and the "Ontology of Lack"', in Lars Tønder and Lasse Thomassen (eds), *Radical Democracy: Politics Between Abundance and Lack*, Manchester: Manchester University Press, pp. 17–31.

Marchart, Oliver (2007a), *Post-Foundational Political Thought: Political Difference in Nancy, Lefort, Badiou and Laclau*, Edinburgh: Edinburgh University Press.

Marchart, Oliver (2007b), 'Acting and the Act: On Slavoj Žižek's Political Ontology', in Paul Bowman and Richard Stamp (eds), *The Truth of Žižek*, London: Continuum, pp. 99–116.

Marchart, Oliver (2010), *Die politische Differenz. Zum Denken des Politischen bei Nancy, Lefort, Badiou, Laclau und Agamben*, Berlin: Suhrkamp.

Marchart, Oliver (2013a), *Das unmögliche Objekt. Eine postfundamentalistische Theorie der Gesellschaft*, Berlin: Suhrkamp.

Marchart, Oliver (2013b), *Die Prekarisierungsgesellschaft. Prekäre Proteste. Politik und Ökonomie im Zeichen der Prekarisierung*, Bielefeld: Transcript.

Marchart, Oliver (2014), 'Institution and Dislocation: Philosophical Roots of Laclau's Discourse Theory of Space and Antagonism', *Distinktion: Scandinavian Journal of Social Theory* 15(3), pp. 271–83.

Marchart, Oliver (ed.) (2017), *Ordnungen des Politischen. Einsätze und Wirkungen der Hegemonietheorie Ernesto Laclaus*, Wiesbaden: Springer.

Marchart, Oliver (2018), *Conflictual Aesthetics: Artistic Activism and the Public Sphere*, Berlin: Sternberg Press.

Marchart, Oliver (forthcoming), *Post-Foundational Theories of Democracy: Reclaiming Freedom, Equality, Solidarity*, Edinburgh: Edinburgh University Press.

Marttila, Tomas (2015), *Post-Foundational Discourse Analysis: From Political Difference to Empirical Research*, Basingstoke: Palgrave Macmillan.

Marx, Karl (1961), 'Zur Kritik der politischen Ökonomie, Vorwort', in *Marx-Engels-Werke* (MEW), vol. 13, Berlin: Dietz, pp. 7–11.

Marx, Karl [1880] (1985), 'John Swinton. Account of an Interview with Karl Marx', in *Marx-Engels-Gesamtausgabe* (MEGA), Abteilung I, vol. 25, Berlin: Berlin-Brandenburgische Akademie der Wissenschaften, p. 443.

Massey, Doreen (1992), 'Politics and Space/Time', *New Left Review* 196, pp. 65–84.

Massey, Doreen (1999), 'Spaces of Politics', in Doreen Massey, John Allen and Phil Sarre (eds), *Human Geography Today*, Polity: Cambridge, pp. 279–94.

Massey, Doreen (2005), *For Space*, Los Angeles: Sage.

Massumi, Brian (2015), *The Politics of Affect*, Cambridge: Polity Press.

Meiksins Wood, Ellen (2012), *Liberty and Property: A Social History of Western Political Thought from Renaissance to Enlightenment*, London and New York: Verso.

Melucci, Alberto (1989), *Nomads of the Present: Social Movements and Individual Needs in Contemporary Society*, Philadelphia: Temple University Press.

Meyer, David S. and Sidney Tarrow (eds) (1998), *The Social Movement Society: Contentious Politics for a New Century*, Lanham, MD: Rowman & Littlefield.

Mihai, Mihaela, Lois McNay, Oliver Marchart, Aletta Norval, Vassilios Paipais, Sergei Prozorov and Mathias Thaler (2017), 'Democracy, Critique and the Ontological Turn', *Contemporary Political Theory* 16(4), pp. 501–31.

Miles, Malcolm (1997), *Art, Space and the City: Public Art and Urban Futures*, London: Routledge.

Mouffe, Chantal (2000), *The Democratic Paradox*, London and New York: Verso.

Mouffe, Chantal (2013), *Agonistics: Thinking the World Politically*, London and New York: Verso.

Nancy, Jean-Luc (2000), *Being Singular Plural*, Stanford: Stanford University Press.

Nancy, Jean-Luc (2002), *Hegel: The Restlessness of the Negative*, Minneapolis and London: University of Minnesota Press.

Nash, Kate (2010), *Contemporary Political Sociology*, Oxford: Blackwell.

Negri, Antonio (1991), *The Savage Anomaly: The Power of Spinoza's Metaphysics and Politics*, Minneapolis: University of Minnesota Press.

Negri, Antonio (2002), 'Pour une définition ontologique de la multitude', *Multitudes* 9 (May–June), pp. 36–48.

Negri, Antonio (2004), *Subversive Spinoza: (Un)Contemporary Variations*, Manchester: Manchester University Press.

Negri, Antonio (2007), *Political Descartes: Reason, Ideology and the Bourgeois Project*, London and New York: Verso.

Nietzsche, Friedrich (1999), *Also sprach Zarathustra, Kritische Studienausgabe*, vol. 4, ed. Giorgi Colli and Mazzino Montinari, Berlin and New York: Walter de Gruyter.

Norval, Aletta (1996), *Deconstructing Apartheid Discourse*, London and New York: Verso.

Paipais, Vassilios (2016), *Political Ontology and International Political Thought: Voiding a Pluralist World*, Basingstoke: Palgrave Macmillan.

Prozorov, Sergei (2014), *Ontology and World Politics: Void Universalism I*, London and New York: Routledge.

Rancière, Jacques (1999), *Disagreement: Politics and Philosophy*, Minneapolis and London: University of Minnesota Press.

Reid, Michael (1994), 'The Aims of Radicalism: A Reply to David Howarth', *Angelaki* 3(1), pp. 181–4.

Richir, Marc (1991), *Du Sublime en politique*, Paris: Éditions Payot.

Ricœur, Paul (1965), 'The Political Paradox', in Paul Ricœur, *History and Truth*, Evanston, IL: Northwestern University Press, pp. 247–70.

Roskamm, Nikolai (2017), *Die unbesetzte Stadt. Postfundamentalistisches Denken und das urbanistische Feld*, Basel: Birkhäuser.

Roth, Michael S. (1988), *Knowing and History: Appropriations of Hegel in Twentieth-Century France*, Ithaca, NY and London: Cornell University Press.

Rucht, Dieter and Friedhelm Neidhart (2002), 'Towards a "Movement Society"? On the Possibilities of Institutionalizing Social Movements', *Social Movement Studies* 1(1), pp. 7–30.

Sardinha, Diogo (2010), 'Motus, Meute, Meuterei: Formen wüster Bewegung', *Paragrana* 19(1), pp. 122–39.

Sartre, Jean-Paul (1956), *Being and Nothingness*, London: Philosophical Library.

Schmitt, Carl (1963), *Der Begriff des Politischen*, Berlin: Duncker & Humblot.

Schürmann, Reiner (1990), *Heidegger on Being and Acting: From Principles to Anarchy*, Bloomington: Indiana University Press.

Schürmann, Reiner (2003), *Broken Hegemonies*, Bloomington: Indiana University Press.

Searle, John R. (2010), *Making the Social World: The Structure of Human Civilization*, Oxford: Oxford University Press.

Slack, Jennifer Daryl (1996), 'The Theory and Method of Articulation in Cultural Studies', in David Morley and Kuan-Hsing Chen (eds), *Stuart Hall: Critical Dialogues in Cultural Studies*, London and New York: Routledge, pp. 112–30.

Smith, Anna-Marie (1994), *New Right Discourse on Race and Sexuality*, Cambridge: Cambridge University Press.

Stavrakakis, Yannis (1999), *Lacan and the Political*, London and New York: Routledge.

Stavrakakis, Yannis (2004), 'Antinomies of Formalism: Laclau's Theory of Populism and the Lessons from Religious Populism in Greece', *Journal of Political Ideologies* 9(3) (October), pp. 253–67.

Stavrakakis, Yannis (2007), *The Lacanian Left*, Edinburgh: Edinburgh University Press.

Stavrakakis, Yannis (2008), 'Antinomies of Space: From the Representation of Politics to a Topology of the Political', in BAVO (ed.), *Urban Politics Now: Re-imagining Democracy in the Neoliberal City*, Rotterdam: NAi Publishers, pp. 143–61.

Stavrakakis, Yannis (2014), '"The Return of the People": Populism and Anti-Populism in the Shadow of the European Crisis', *Constellations* 21(4), pp. 505–17.

Stiegler, Bernard (1998), *Technics and Time 1: The Fault of Epimetheus*, Stanford: Stanford University Press.

Stiegler, Bernard (2003), 'Technics of Decision: An Interview', *Angelaki* 8(2), pp. 151–68.

Stiegler, Bernard (2004), *De la misère symbolique 1: L'époque hyperindustrielle*, Paris: Galilée.

Stiegler, Bernard (2010), *Taking Care of Youth and the Generations*, Stanford: Stanford University Press.

Strathausen, Carsten (ed.) (2009), *A Leftist Ontology: Beyond Relativism and Identity Politics*, Minneapolis and London: University of Minnesota Press.

Street, John (1997), *Politics and Popular Culture*, Cambridge: Polity Press.

Tassin, Étienne (2003), *Un monde commun: Pour une cosmo-politique des conflits*, Paris: Seuil.

Taylor, Charles (1995), *Philosophical Arguments*, Cambridge, MA and London: Harvard University Press.

The Invisible Committee (2009), *The Coming Insurrection*, Los Angeles: Semiotext(e).

Tønder, Lars and Lasse Thomassen (eds) (2005), *Radical Democracy: Politics Between Abundance and Lack*, Manchester: Manchester University Press.

Torfing, Jacob (1999), *New Theories of Discourse: Laclau, Mouffe and Žižek*, Oxford: Blackwell.

Toscano, Alberto (2004), 'La disparation. Politique et sujet chez Simondon', *Multitudes* 18 (Autumn), pp. 73–82.

Touraine, Alain (1981), *The Voice and the Eye: An Analysis of Social Movements*, Cambridge: Cambridge University Press.

Townshend, Jules (2003), 'Discourse Theory and Political Analysis: A New Paradigm from the Essex School?', *The British Journal of Politics and International Relations* 5(1), pp. 129–42.

Vattimo, Gianni (2003), *Nihilism & Emancipation: Ethics, Politics, Law*, New York: Columbia University Press.

Vattimo, Gianni (2011), *A Farewell to Truth*, New York: Columbia University Press.

Vattimo, Gianni and Santiago Zabala (2011), *Hermeneutic Communism: From Heidegger to Marx*, New York: Columbia University Press.

Wagner-Pacifici, Robin (2000), *Theorizing the Standoff: Contingency in Action*, Cambridge: Cambridge University Press.

White, Stephen K. (2000), *Sustaining Affirmation: The Strengths of Weak Ontology in Political Theory*, Princeton, NJ and Oxford: Princeton University Press.

Wolin, Richard (2001), *Heidegger's Children: Hannah Arendt, Karl Löwith, Hans Jonas, and Herbert Marcuse*, Princeton, NJ and Oxford: Princeton University Press.

Wood, Neil (1983), *The Politics of Locke's Philosophy: A Social Study of 'An Essay Concerning Human Understanding'*, Berkeley: University of California Press.

Žižek, Slavoj (1989), *The Sublime Object of Ideology*, London and New York: Verso.

Žižek, Slavoj (1990), 'Beyond Discourse-Analysis', in Ernesto Laclau, *New Reflections on the Revolution of Our Time*, London: Verso, pp. 249–60.

Žižek, Slavoj (1999), *The Ticklish Subject: The Absent Centre of Political Ontology*, London: Verso.

Žižek, Slavoj (2002), 'Introduction: Between the Two Revolutions', in Slavoj Žižek (ed.), *Revolution at the Gates*, London and New York: Verso, pp. 3–12.

Index